What others... MW01519626

"Dr. William Senyard has provided a thorough biblical theology of forgiving others. In *Cupology 101*: A Biblical Theology of Forgiveness, Dr. Senyard asks you to think about whether you've been hurt or victimized and feel like someone has emptied your cup. By providing a theology of forgiveness from both the Hebrew Scriptures and the New Testament, he helps you realize that God can and does refill our cups. There are many books on Christian forgiveness, but Dr. Senyard provides a theological approach that is thorough and healing."
  —Everett L. Worthington, Jr., author of *Forgiving and Reconciling* and *Moving Forward: Six Steps to Forgiving Yourself and Breaking Free from the Past.*

"It has been my experience that forgiveness is one of the least taught themes in Christianity. Yet the great irony is that it is a central feature of Jesus' teachings—let alone the rest of the Bible—and it affects every person alive. *Cupology 101* is a timely and unique book that really has it all: real-life examples and engaging stories, thoughtful discussion questions, mastery of the subject material, a gentle and pastoral spirit, and sound biblical teaching. Regardless of whether you think of yourself as a cup that is half-empty or half-full, you will learn much about yourself, others, and God as you read through this restorative work. And may your cup be filled as you do so."
  —Derek Cooper, PhD, author of *Thomas Merton: A Guided Tour of the Life and Thought of a Puritan Pastor* and *Hazardous: Committing to the Cost of Following Jesus.*

"Before reading this book I saw Christian forgiveness mostly as a yardstick to measure failed faith. Another ideal like "pray without ceasing." Just an aspirational goal only attainable in part. Forgiveness seemed more guilt inducing and phony than redeeming. I wanted justice more than I wanted to forgive. I thought them doctrinally mutual exclusive. You got one by giving up the other. I was crushingly wrong. Unnecessarily wrong. You'll see. I believe that Christian forgiveness is so broadly and harmfully misunderstood that I have great hope that this book can change the world."
  —Eric Protzman, *Young Life*

"With the intellect of a scholar and the heart of a pastor, Dr. Bill Senyard offers a biblical and practical approach to forgiveness in his unique book, *Cupology 101*. His incisive questions and compelling illustrations will engage you from page 1. Is your emotional and spiritual cup empty as a result of an offense? Then read this book!"
  —Michael J. Klassen, pastor, book coach, and author of *Strange Fire, Holy Fire*

"This book brings clarity to the unfathomable. How can I forgive those who have taken so much from me? Deep in these pages, you will discover truth—the offensive, scandalous liberating truth!
    —Shari Johansson LPC

Cupology 101:

A Biblical Theology of Forgiveness

by Dr. Bill Senyard

ISBN-13: 978-1479384976

ISBN-10: 1479384976

Unless otherwise noted, Scripture quotations are from the *New International Version* (NIV), ©1994 International Bible Society.

Cover art and design by Anne Thompson (ebooksannie.com)

Acknowledgements

I would like to thank my family and friends for their support in this project. I would like to especially acknowledge my wife Eunice, my children Aubrey (and her talented husband Jeff Buster), John and Allison, my Biblical Theological Seminary doctoral advisor, Dr. Bryan Maier, the doctoral program director, Dr. Derek Cooper for their support, encouragement and advice on this six-year project. I would also thank my friend and mentor David Sanford for believing in my abilities as an author.

I would also like to acknowledge Eric Protzman, Howie and Lanay James, and Dwight Gilliland for their incessant encouragement and hours of reading to move this book along.

I also thank the congregation of my church, Lookout Mountain Community Church (Golden, CO) for their support and willing participation in the *Forgiveness Labyrinth*.

Also check out this second book in the
Can't Forgive Series by Dr. Bill Senyard

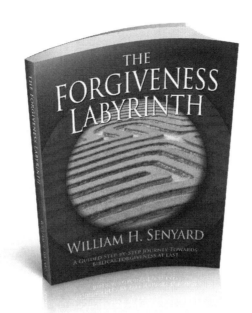

The Forgiveness Labyrinth

Have you found it impossible to forgive a certain crime that was committed against you? Maybe the reason that you have not been able to forgive is that your heart needs justice first.

Good news! God never forgives any crime until there has been real objective justice. Why would He expect you to be more magnanimous than Him? Victim, you can't do it.

The Labyrinth is carefully designed to bring biblical justice to bear upon your deep hurt. You might be surprised how an experience of justice from God changes everything. You have not been able to forgive because you have not had your day in court yet. Just bring to the Forgiveness Labyrinth one crime that you have not been able to forgive.

What others are saying about The Forgiveness Labyrinth

"Dr. William Senyard has provided a practical intervention to help people forgive. In his book, *The Forgiveness Labyrinth*, he uses the traditional Christian contemplative method of a labyrinth. He directs you goes station by station through the physical labyrinth. The approach is both personal and experiential, and many people will be blessed by it. I recommend it. It will enhance your experience of forgiving."

—Everett L. Worthington, Jr., author of *Forgiving and Reconciling*

"*The Forgiveness Labyrinth* allows readers to experience first-hand the critical link between justice and forgiveness, and then carefully shows them how to forgive otherwise unforgivable wrongs. Share this book with everyone you know. It's *that* profound and life-changing."

—David Sanford, author of *If God Disappears*

"*The Forgiveness Labyrinth* by Bill Senyard is a thoroughly biblical yet also highly interactive and life-giving resource for the church today. This is the best resource I ever read on this topic, and I highly recommend it."

—Derek Cooper, author of *Hazardous: Committing to the Cost of Following Jesus.*

"With the intellect of a scholar and the heart of a pastor, Dr. Bill Senyard offers a biblical and practical approach to forgiveness in his unique book, *Cupology 101*. His incisive questions and compelling illustrations will engage you from page 1. Is your emotional and spiritual cup empty as a result of an offense? Then read this book!"

—Michael J. Klassen, pastor, book coach, and author of *Strange Fire, Holy Fire*

The Forgiveness Labyrinth available online
at www.drbillministries.com, Amazon, Kindle and Nook.

Also check out the ongoing dialogue on
www.facebook.com/cantforgive.com.

Contents

Preface

Real forgiveness is a tough, tough process, but it is
absolutely necessary for your mental health. Before
we can forgive, we must put the offender on trial
so a judgment can be rendered. It is only when
a guilty verdict is brought in…that
the work of real forgiveness can begin.
M. Scott Peck

Welcome to Cupology 101!

If you have been victimized by abuse, rape, dishonor, betrayal,
indifference, greed, anger, self-centeredness, welcome. Let me ask a
question.

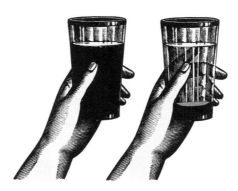

Illustration 1

Which cup (see above) do you identify with more? The full cup on the left, or the emptied one on the right? Pretty over-simplistic, I know. But the point is that in all of the years that I have pastorally counseled those who have been victimized, there is one huge similarity. To one degree or another, they feel like empty cups.

Follow me for a moment. You have been deeply hurt. Someone has taken something from you, done something to you against your will, without your permission. Your life has been changed—for the worse. Perhaps the crime committed against you happened years ago—and you have tried everything to be set free from the oppressive memory, the tightness in your chest, the sadness, the anger, the disorientation, the desire for vengeance, the depression, the inner cries of unfairness—but nothing has brought anything more than temporary relief.

Maybe you confronted the person who hurt you, tried to reason with them? Maybe you went further and took them to trial? Or to mediators? To the elders, pastors or priests of your church? Maybe you have gone to counselors, seminars, read one or more of the myriad of books out there today? Forgiveness must be a trillion dollar industry.

Maybe you have just tried to suck it up and move on—but are noticing that you are more irritable, silent, impatient, critical than you were? Maybe friends have noticed that you get angry quicker? Or more depressed? Every situation is unique and complicated.

Lots of questions? Has the one who hurt you shown remorse? Admitted their indifference, their abuse? Have they said to you how sorry they are? Or have they defended their actions, their words? Have they blamed others, or worse blamed you? Perhaps it was a "drive-by shooting"—and they are going about their life not even knowing that they hurt you? Perhaps the judicial system further betrayed you and let the guilty off scot-free?

Here's the point. No matter what the crime was, the result is that you have been left diminished, disempowered, depreciated, drained, minimized, reduced—your cup has been emptied to some degree. To build on the metaphor, someone *without your permission* drank of your substance, value, worth, identity and dignity. No matter what you have done to restore the level to pre-crime status nothing really worked. Does this ring true?

Primary Crimes

rape	infliction of emotional distress
murder	withholding love
hatred	lies
betrayal	deception
robbery	hurt
abuse	disrespect
gossip	disobeying
slander	embarrassment
criticism	treating indifferently
adultery	judgment
breach of contract	bigotry
abandonment	prejudice
negligence	other
loss of consortium	

Figure 1- List of Primary Crimes

So let's begin at the beginning. Let us begin with the core initial question: "What happened to you?" In Figure 1, I offer you a number of primary crime descriptors. There are more. This list is extensive but far from complete. Primary crimes are what happened to you. These are the descriptors that end up in police reports and at trials. These are the answers to the question, "What happened to you?" I was robbed, raped, slandered, betrayed, etc.

Secondary Crimes

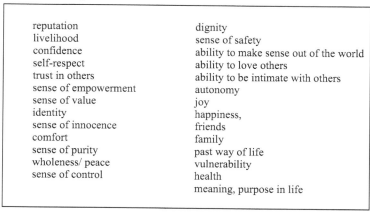

reputation	dignity
livelihood	sense of safety
confidence	ability to make sense out of the world
self-respect	ability to love others
trust in others	ability to be intimate with others
sense of empowerment	autonomy
sense of value	joy
identity	happiness,
sense of innocence	friends
comfort	family
sense of purity	past way of life
wholeness/ peace	vulnerability
sense of control	health
	meaning, purpose in life

Figure 2- List of Secondary Crimes

But have you ever thought that what happened to you went further than the *primary* crimes? You also were subjected to *secondary* crimes. Figure 2 lists some of the things that are important to you feeling good about yourself, and in one fell swoop, one or likely more of these were ripped away from you. Someone took your sense of wholeness, safety, your health, your ability to trust others, your sense of control of your environment, your purity, etc. These are destructive *secondary* crimes. What your deepest soul really wants is to have what was taken put back.

It is the *secondary* crimes that are so hard to admit, to identify and to grab hold of. But they are the necessary consequences of violations that happened deep in your soul, the long lasting nagging fears and diminishments.

Someone has violated your inner boundaries and consumed your core substance. They not only *did* something to you, they *took* something of unspeakable value from you. The level in your cup has been lowered. And nothing that you have done to date has slaked the desperate thirst that remains.

If you have been victimized somehow, is this making some sense regarding how you feel right now?

But what if I can't think of a crime committed against me?

Sometimes as I speak on this topic, someone asks this very good question. I will admit, as I speak or write about this subject, I do have in mind the person who can *easily* come up with a hurt that they have not dealt with successfully.

If you are reading this book and just can't connect with murder or rape survivors, I urge you to keep on reading. We have all been treated indifferently sometime along our journey. We have all had someone withhold something that was rightfully ours. We have all been treated unfairly. These things seem comparatively small to us—insignificant, really. But God does not see those crimes as small—not at all. I would remind you that you are an image-bearer of God and if a Christian, you are a full card-carrying son or daughter of His. If someone treats you lightly, the penalty is still *death* in God's court. Please keep on reading.

Cupology 101

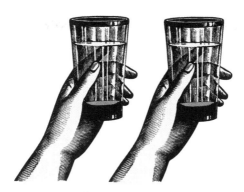

Illustration 2

It might make things clearer if I put things in Cupology terms. In lectures before audiences, I usually begin by holding up two mostly empty cups. The point is to illustrate a largely misunderstood driving motivational power behind most of our relationships.

The mostly-emptied cup on the left needs the mostly-emptied cup on the right to have any hope of ever getting fuller—or so it thinks.

I am not implying evil intentions. People need to be filled. We want value, worth, appreciation, identity, and gravitas. We gravitate to people who tend to fill our cup with compliments, appreciation, and at-a-boys (or at-a-girls). We tend to avoid people who rob us of our stuff through criticism, belittling and judgment.

How does this relate to forgiveness? When that crime was committed against you, something was *taken* from you. Your cup level was diminished without your permission. Part of you is desperate to have your original level restored. Perhaps an allegory could be helpful. Welcome to Cupworld.

Cupworld

Imagine a world— Cupworld—where everybody is a cup containing some liquid. The cups vary in size, shape, texture and volume—but in essence they are all cups—they have a rim at the top, they have sides and a bottom and are freestanding in some fashion. The life-purpose of all cups is to be carriers of liquid. It is this inner-stuff that represents who they are, their identity, worth, value and name.

Imagine one cup, average height and diameter, average liquid capacity. It looks strangely like one of those old clear jars that enterprising Grandmas used to fill with jelly and jams. As you inspect this cup—let's call him "Mason," you notice that he is a little over half-full by your estimation.

It is important to mention now that the cups in Cupworld have an innate yearning to be full cups. It is how they are made. They long to be filled to the brim. It is part of essential cupness. Cups are not made to be half-filled, or even ¾ full. They are engineered to be able to handle cup-fullness. So the cup—Mason—is not whole to some degree.

We don't know where Mason came from. Yesterday he may have been ¼ full and so now he is enjoying the internal feeling of joy and satisfaction that comes from being more full than he was. But on the other hand, Mason may have lost his fullness. We can only speculate.

It is sometimes true in Cupworld that some cups have long denied their cup-fullness—their hunger to be full—they have buried it deep in their cuphearts.

Maybe they have been told by other cups in authority that they are not good cups, or that they will never succeed because of some flaw—maybe they have been shamed by their parent cups and feel small. Who knows, cups rarely show their emotions on the surface.

But here is what we know. Since Mason is a cup, he—to some degree—longs to be *more* full—even if that longing is repressed and deeply buried. Mason has a nagging inner murmur of discontent—a longing to pick up some liquid from somewhere. Cups need to find another external source of liquid in order to become full.

Where do cups typically look for inner-stuff? They normally try to find inner-stuff in their jobs, relationships, amusements, education, money, entertainment, drugs, stimulants, sex, sexuality, etc. Cupworld offers cups plentiful sights and sounds packaged to fill cups just a little perhaps. Fullness hits are nice feelings—a bit addictive if the truth were known—to emptied cups.

So as we watch, another cup enters our view. This cup looks like one of those man-size coffee mugs that you find in airport gift shops—big, textured, thick dark blue sides, "Welcome to Chicago" artistically written in a banner across its front. From our vantage point we can't see how much liquid is in this cup, but we watch in dismay at what happens next.

Chicago bumps into Mason. He tips him over and steals some of his precious liquid. Mason can't seem to resist the rape of liquid. In an instant, Mason's cupness has been violated. He has been reduced—in the length of time it takes to swallow two big gulps—to ¼ full.

A crime has been committed. A great injustice. So what happens next? Mason could run (or whatever cups do) after Chicago and take the liquid back. Cup-vengeance is not a pretty sight typically. Or he can make a judicial complaint against Chicago in the Cup-courts—but everyone knows that it takes a lot of liquid to go to court. Lawyer cups are very thirsty— bottomless some say.

In the end, Chicago could be arrested, tried and found guilty for the violation—even banished from Cupworld for the crime against Mason. The most likely scenario is for Chicago to be sentenced to the Punishment Cup-Cabinet where he cannot commit a similar crime on the streets of Cupworld for the time that he is incarcerated. But in general, the judicial system is not designed to get the liquid back to Mason. Mason remains diminished.

So, diminished Mason could justify getting liquid from someone else. This is often what emptied cups do—often even without thinking. It's not right of course, but life is not fair in Cupworld, he tells himself. It is cup-eat-cup out there. So he decides to bump up against someone else, or go to his cup-spouse and drink up some of her liquid—subtly of course. "Hasn't he contributed enough of his hard earned liquid for years," he thinks to himself?

Or Mason could just swallow the loss, give up his right to the liquid, turn the rim 70 times seven times. There is a legend of a cup long ago who endured severe cracks—lost all of his liquid without resisting the perpetrators. He is reported to have said at the end, "Don't try to get your liquid back—just forgive them!" But there is something in Mason that wonders if the adherents of the great Cracked Cup got the story quite right. Something about that doesn't seem right and fair and would seem to lead to anarchy where the Chicagos of Cupworld could go unchecked. Cupanarchy.

If Mason was answering the question, "What was done to you?" he might write (in Cupworld, cups can write, of course), "I was robbed of critical liquid substance from my cup by the bully cup Chicago." But in answer to the next appropriate question, "What was taken from you?", Mason might write,

> "I lost a large portion of my identity and sense of cupness—wholeness, my former sense of fulfillment, sense of accomplishment, sense of safety—in Cupworld. I lost a portion of my reputation—I am now publicly seen as a weak target for the Chicagos of Cupworld. I now feel shame, I feel a sense of failure and perhaps even a lack of hope in a good future. I want my ¼ cup back!"

If the loss was large enough, deep enough and extensive enough, Mason could come to believe that there is no justice in Cupworld. He could resolve that life is what it is and move forward diminished with diminishing hope that there will ever be any restoration. There are no hero cups in Cupworld.

Cupology Case Study #1- Anatomy of an Affair

Let me stay for a moment with Cupology 101 but shift to the real world.

Consider a husband who found out that his wife was having an affair. They had been separated for a month or two, for a lot of surface reasons, none clear to the husband. The husband had wondered if the reason for the sudden separation was someone else, but honestly thought that everything was fine.

Sure there was stress, and arguments. Who doesn't have arguments? But the wife wasn't the type to have an affair. She was a good woman— she would never do that to him and to the kids. And so when he asked if she was having an affair early on in the separation, she denied it and was offended that he would ask. Relieved, he even felt bad asking the question, somehow allowing mistrust to enter into his heart.

But now, he knows, after months of denial, not only was she an adulterer but a flat out liar.

So what was the crime against the husband? From the list of primary crimes, we can begin with "adultery," "betrayal," "breech of trust" and "lying." These primary crimes overlap of course, but they make a substantial case against the wife.

From Cupology perspective, by the time of the affair, the husband is probably more or less an empty vessel. He probably had gained very little substance from his wife recently. They may have been married a while, but likely that sense of 'Wow!' had long been diminished. Sexual intimacy could be decent—maybe even good, but not like it was.

Since cups must seek filling, he has adapted to search for filling outside the home—career, sports, buddies, hobbies, etc. Let's just say for illustration purposes that this husband finds "filling" in the accolades from people who work for him, his appreciative customers and suppliers. If the truth were known, this filling is very slight, in fact, a mere mist—but it feels good to him nonetheless. He naturally drifts to spending more and more of his emotional energy and time at work.

When the husband comes home, he has learned not to expect much filling. There were the draining day-to-day pressures and stresses of raising children, paying bills, honey-do lists, etc.—criticism and complaints from his wife—you get the idea. His wife had for the most part stopped being a source of filling. She too was not "evil" per se. Her cup is pretty empty as well.[1] She was not satisfied by the filling that she got from him, from sex, or the few compliments that he gave on special occasions. She used to complain that she felt empty—only to confused looks from the husband.

Then along came another man: a predator. He appeared—though looks are so deceiving—more full than the husband. The predator strategically showed interest in slinging precious substance her way—at least at the beginning. The attention, the honor, the pursuit felt good to the wife—and admittedly exciting and even dangerous. Though from a cup measurement, the affair was only a mere rush of mist, she would say that it caused her to feel more alive—more attractive—more like a woman. Her head told her that the affair was foolish, wrong and harmful to those that she loved. But in the end, "We need to be filled," she told herself.

The predator—if the truth were known—was rather empty too. However, he was more than willing to initially invest minimal precious substance of his own if it meant the hope of an affair. Don't mistake this. Predators intrinsically desire to *be* filled—not to be fillers.

By the way, in my observation, there are people who are indeed pathological predators. Typically, they are largely empty persons who have learned to appear full. They would say that they are addicted to the hit they achieve from robbing the substance of others. Then they move on, and on, and on. They are immensely skilled at identifying and manipulating other empty people. They use "hope of filling" as their bait.

Then there are the perennial targets, emptied people who regularly get sucked into affairs—those who, all too readily, let themselves get diminished—but have great difficulty dealing with the truth that they were fooled, rubes, played, used for the pleasure of another. These individuals can live in denial for a long time, ripped with self-loathing at a deep level.

And so the dangerous game begins. Affairs are exciting things to emptied people. There is the rush of nerves and energy, that sense of danger, that sense of excitement. For emptied people who feel less and less of anything, they can be wildly appealing—even if there are dangers and likely very costly consequences. Emptied people often can only think short-term. For now, the possibility of feeling whole is all they can imagine.

No doubt, if the truth were known, they are using each other. Both are empty, nothing of real substance to give. The lie of hope is powerful and ever-present, very real. Post-affair, if you measure the change in the experiential *wholeness* of participants, there is no distinguishable difference

---

[1] It has been my experience that it almost always takes two to tango. I am sure that the wife could also be a Plaintiff in her own separate trial against the husband for crimes he has committed against her. That is how these things work of course in real life. But, for the purpose of simplicity, we will narrow our investigation to the crimes committed by her against him.

to speak of. They are *still* empty. Likely they are now immersed in destructive shame and guilt. They are even more miserable.

So the wife was lured into an affair with the hopes that she would at last be full. It will not satisfy. It cannot satisfy. In the end, she may be sucked even lower due to the skills of the predator, in addition to the shame of failure. In her denial, she may continue to blame her husband. Why? Blaming herself is too painful.

If unhealed, she might with even more desperation plunge into other affairs—or find other ways to desperately get her cup filled.

So back to the husband's case. The *primary* crimes against him? Adultery, betrayal, breech of trust, and lying would lead the list. But what was taken? What were the *secondary* crimes? I would likely begin with:

Sense of value
The husband might have valued his marriage (as dysfunctional as it was) and had hopes of a future life with his family. The plans and dreams had now been shattered.

Loss of his reputation
The husband likely thought that he was a "good" husband who was skilled at satisfying his wife, emotionally, physically, financially and sexually. But now, he wonders. He is clearly a failure at being a good husband. His reputation as a husband and father is now suspect.

Loss of being in control of his life
He no doubt thought that he could manage his life, family and career. But now he has become aware that he was out of control. He had been living unaware with someone who—unbeknownst to him—despised him. What is wrong with him? Is he missing some sensitivity that would detect it when people around him become betrayers?

Loss of hope
He had hope in the marriage and future. Now? Where is hope? They had shared friends and neighbors. It is unknown who will be friends now. Perhaps one of them has betrayed him. "Have others?," he wonders.

The husband now feels like a failed man, unable to satisfy his wife romantically, unable to detect that an affair is taking place, and somehow blamable for the whole mess. Even if she has a drastic change of heart, his wife cannot begin to repay what she has stolen from him. No amount of repentance, apologies, groveling, promises of good behavior will replace what was taken.

Hope for Emptied Cups

Such are the relational physics of emptied cups. It would seem that life would be a never-ending series of violent draining and partial filling of substance from emptied cups to emptied cups. But the good news is that there is another huge source of real experiential filling for emptied cups.

> "Come, all you who are thirsty, come to the waters; and you who have no money, come, buy and eat! Come, buy wine and milk without money and without cost. Why spend money on what is not bread, and your labor on what does not satisfy?" (Isa 55:1-2)

Husbands and wives, listen. There is an external source of deep worth and value, identity and even joy. In light of this, it is abject foolishness to target other fractured cups.

Come all of you emptied cups to the vast place with plenty of substance—an open and welcoming place for all who are in need—and to come as you are. Once there, you can by faith just drink and drink and drink. It is astounding news. It sounds too simplistic, too childish. Exactly. But honestly, what else has worked for you? God has the stuff, and desire, to restore what was taken from you.

At this point, I beg you to just be open to hear this good news. It is very biblical, even though I admit it will sound a bit too good to believe at first.

In this book, I hope to lay out the Biblical path of such a re-filling for emptied cups. Chapters 1-4 will frame the problem of forgiveness in familiar, modern terms and contexts—including an overview of the modern secular and Christian socio-psychological models of forgiveness. Chapters 5-7 offer a biblical theology of horizontal forgiveness from the Old Testament—in Chapters 8-10, a New Testament perspective. As far as I am aware, there has been no other biblical theological study completed strictly on the topic of horizontal forgiveness until now.

One other thing. From this point on, I will rarely speak of you as the "victim."[2] Rather, I will speak of you as the "Plaintiff." What is the

---

[2] I understand that today, the descriptor *"victim"* can carry two very different meanings. There is the technical meaning where *victim* simply refers to a person who had been victimized somehow. They have been an object of diminishment. This is the sense that I use the term in this book. As far as I am aware, there is no better word to describe a person who has been subjected to victimization. The other use of the term is to describe someone whose very identity has become a *victim*. They do not see themselves as a valued person anymore, they see themselves as merely an object to be mistreated. The goal of this book is to point both categories of *"victims"* to a path that offers redemptive healing and honor— neither that comes from within them, nor can be achieved by self-esteem exercises, but rather that miraculously comes from God.

difference? I define the Plaintiff as a person who has been subjected to diminishment, but is pursuing resolution. I am not in anyway encouraging you to deny the crime at all. In fact, just the opposite is true. Your healing depends upon a severe honesty regarding the crime and its cost to you. But, at the core, what defines you is that you are not relegating yourself to your current victim status. You are moving forward.

Welcome to Cupology 101, Plaintiff.

Reflection Questions for Individuals or Groups

1) The author imagines that all of us—to some degree—are empty cups looking to be filled. Does that ring true to you? In your own words, what does this "emptiness" feel like?

2) Where have you gone to be filled? Has it worked for you? Why or why not?

3) Now think of the crime that was committed against you. What was taken from you? Consider the list of secondary crimes.

4) What strategies have you personally employed to relieve that sense of loss and diminishment—in effect to fill the hole left by the loss.

5) Consider some of the many verses in the Bible that use "filling" as a metaphor for God's hope for empty humanity. Read Isa 55:1, Jer 2:13, Eph 3:14-19. Respond to this statement: "God desires to fill emptied cups."

PART ONE

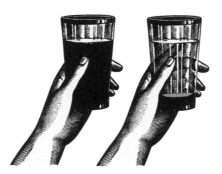

Core Questions for Cracked Cups

1

First Core Question from Cracked Cups

> If Whales Could Think On Certain Happy Days"
> "Surely the Maker of Whales made me for a purpose."
> [Thinks a whale enjoying its "being at
> oneness with the universe"]
> Just then the harpoon slammed into his side
> Tearing a hole in it as wide as the sky.
> Irving Layton

It's the nature of your fractured heart. When you are abused, diminished, robbed, betrayed or beat-up unfairly in anyway, three questions cry out from your lacerated inner being:

- Where is justice for you?

- Where is the happy ending?

- Who are you now in the aftermath of your loss?

One question may be more prevalent than the others. The questions may feel to you like a mere trickle or a raging torrent, but they are there nonetheless. When your cup is violated and diminished, your soul cries out—needing some answers. Until these questions are resolved you remain a Plaintiff. We will look at each in some detail. This chapter considers Question #1, *Where is Justice for you?*

Core Question #1- Where is Justice?

Here's the point. When something bad happens—not little crimes like someone not paying you back the $5 they owe you—rather some tragic violation of trust, some abuse, some betrayal, some robbery—your cup is diminished. If it is a small diminishment then you probably can deal with it through normal coping mechanisms. It is about small violations that it is said, "Time heals all wounds!" This book is about those wounds that time does not have the power to heal.

Maybe the crime committed against you involved someone close to you. The normal expectation of the heart is that you should expect honor from those close to you. Maybe the crime was public. Or premeditated? Maybe the violation was an accident that was obviously foreseeable—and therefore preventable. Maybe your pain has been exacerbated due to the absence of any apology or attempt at restitution. Or maybe you have been offered no freedom or platform to voice pain and anger to an objective, listening, compassionate fair authority figure.

Every situation is unique, every temperament is unique, every crime is complex, everyone copes differently, but this can always be said: Your heart has recorded the event and its consequence and weighed a debt. The scales of your heart are tipped and unbalanced. It is not only that someone did something *to* you; they also took something *from* you. You are emptier than you were before the crime.

At the very core of your soul is a balance scale that strictly measures fairness. It is universal. One of the first sentences that our children form is "But, that's not fair!" So when someone comes along and negatively tips your scale, intrinsically you *need* to restore the balance.

Perhaps it is fair to consider this question relative to a time scale. At first, immediately after the violation, you may have high expectations that you will get judicial satisfaction for the crime. You might initially expect that your offender will get busted and found guilty—punished for the crime against you. You probably expect full vindication and just assume that you will soon feel whole: the scale balanced.

But for many who are reading this book, the justice processes have let you down, further betraying you. Now, as more time has passed, you no longer believe that you will experience real life-giving justice, no respite, no fairness, no trial, no punishment—the guilty may be let off scot-free. Maybe, just maybe you are wondering aloud if there is any justice for you at all. I talk to many Plaintiffs who have totally given up on any experience of justice. "Life's not fair! There is no justice this side of heaven." This is tragic.

The *Aaaaah! Factor?*

I watch a significant amount of "law TV"—*Law and Order, The Firm, CSI*—all the usual suspects. No matter what the show, it seems there is always one point where I can't look away, even if I want to. You know the scene. The Plaintiff has been called back into court because the jury has completed its deliberations.

The jury enters. The foreperson passes a folded piece of paper to the judge. The judge reads the paper without emotion, giving no clue as to what will happen next. He passes the paper back.

> "Foreperson, with regard to the case against the Defendant, what have you decided?," asks the judge.

> "We, the jury, find the Defendant..." begins the foreperson.

At this point, the rotation of the planet slows. The tension in the room—even through the television—is palpable. The shoulders and the neck muscles of the Plaintiff tighten. How can he or she go on if the Defendant is let off?

> "We the jury, find the Defendant....guilty!" the foreperson says at last.

Once the words leave the foreperson's lips, you can hear the collective sigh from people on both sides of the glass: it's the *"Aaaaah!" factor*. At that moment, there is a true visceral lifting of a burden—an "Aaaaah" heard far and wide. Justice has been done.

Of course, sometimes the opposite happens. When the verdict was read in the O. J. Simpson trial, many people felt devastated, unraveled, shocked. For many that day, there was no "Aaaaah!" but instead, a corporate sense of anger, frustration and confusion. The burden was not lifted. In fact, it became heavier. Remember what you felt at the end of the Casey Anthony trial?

Plaintiff, with regard to the crime(s) committed against you, have you experienced the *"Aaaaah!" factor*? Or are you resigned to the possibility that there might not be justice forthcoming for you? The prophet Isaiah proclaims that without such a sense of present justice, you die a little.

"The way of peace they do not know; there is no justice in their paths. They have turned them into crooked roads; no one who walks in them will know peace." (Isa 59:8 NIV)

The Injustice Gap

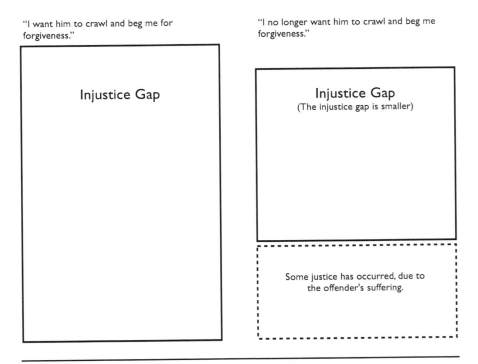

Figure 3- Two injustice gaps (adapted from Worthington 2009)

Christian socio-psychologist and leading forgiveness expert, E. Worthington and colleagues have labeled the lack of perceived *Aaaaah!*

Factor as the "*Injustice Gap.*"[3] They suggest that there is an inner calculator in the gut of Plaintiffs that subjectively calculates whether the outcomes surrounding a transgression are fair or not.

The larger the perceived injustice gap, the more negative emotions are generated and forgiveness is much harder to achieve.

In the figure above (from Worthington, 2006) such an injustice gap is graphically portrayed.[4] A Plaintiff with the perceived injustice gap on the left—needless to say—will have little empathy for their offender, no desire to forgive them. Instead, they want justice, vindication, even revenge. "I want him to crawl and beg me for forgiveness."

On the other hand, for the Plaintiff represented by the smaller injustice gap on the right, there is a sense that to some degree justice has been served so they need less vindication or vengeance. "I no longer want him to crawl and beg me for forgiveness."

The larger the injustice gap, the more they need and want more justice says Worthington.

"The bigger the gap, the more angry, bitter and resentful we feel. If the gap persists, it can lead to lurking, vengeful motivation that seeks an object to project the guilt onto and direct the anger toward."[5]

Until the gap is reduced, it "yawns and spews out the venom of unforgiving emotions and vengeful motivations" and [the Plaintiff] feels righteously indignant. *"How could the offender be so callous, so unfeeling, so insensitive, so wrong?"*[6] There was no *Aaaah! Factor.*

What reduces the gap? Maybe you have experienced some justice, perhaps a trial, perhaps someone that you trust believed your story. Maybe the person who offended you is remorseful, has offered an apology, has offered to pay restitution? Maybe the perpetrator has also suffered pain as well. Maybe you have done something or said something that brought them some payback pain?

Or there is another indirect way that you can reduce the gap on your own—often done in cases where the perpetrator is absent. When justice does not seem to be forthcoming, you can *choose* to just reduce your

---

[3] E. Worthington, Jr., A Just Forgiveness: Responsible Healing Without Excusing Injustice. (Downers Grove, Il: InterVarsity Press, 2009); J. Exline, et al., "Forgiveness and Justice: A Research Agenda for Social and Personality Psychology," Personality and Social Psychology Review, 7(4), (2003): 337-348 and Witvliet, C., et al., "Unresolved Injustice: Christian Religious Commitment, Forgiveness, Revenge, and Cardiovascular Responding," Journal of Psychology and Christianity, 27(2), (2008):110-119.
[4] Worthington, *Just Forgiveness*, 29.
[5] E. Worthington, Forgiveness and Reconciliation: Theory and Application. (New York: Routledge, 2006), 62.
[6] Worthington, *Just Forgiveness*, 63.

expectations of justice. You can *choose* to work against your heart's natural bent for fairness and forcibly struggle to lower your heart's demands for justice. It sounds like—and feels like—a self-inflicted violation. It is. But we do this all the time.

Through the help of well-meaning counseling, you could just *choose* to give up your rights to justice and fairness and make a bold, super-human commitment to forgive. You could, once again with some professional help, reframe the crime and criminal by considering motives, contexts, etc.[7]

But Is It Enough?

This is the real question. Plaintiff, you have probably been down this path. So here is my question. Have all of the gap-reduction efforts really been enough for you? Or do you still feel diminished?

As I write this chapter, the NCAA has invoked historically harsh sanctions against Penn State University in the light of the ten years of gross dehumanizing child abuse perpetrated by Assistant Coach Jerry Sandusky and the apparent cover-up (conspiracy) from leading university officials, showing reportedly a total disregard for those whom Sandusky victimized. So the Twitter questions? *Was that enough?* Sandusky's actions were arrogant, totally self-focused, indifferent to others, vile and destructive. So he has received life in prison, and the University gets harsh sanctions. *Plaintiffs, is that enough?*

---

[7] Apologies, perceived offender remorse and concrete forms of restitution seem to reduce perceived *injustice gap* and facilitate forgiveness. In one study, there was a strong correlation noted between the presence of a strong apology and fair restitution and an experience of decreased grudges, desire for revenge, avoidance motivations, anger, and/or fear. Those who even imagined such a believable apology and fair restitution also experienced measurable physical benefits such as a lower heart rate and lower muscular tension at the corrugator (brow muscle) and *orbicularis oculi* (near the eye) facial muscles. It appears that the perceived *injustice gap* is reduced in the presence of a strong apology and fair restitution. The researcher concludes that the experience of credible justice increased the offended party's motivation to forgive (Exline et al., *Forgiveness and Justice*). Injustice gap reducers can also come unilaterally from the offended party: 1) social acts such as revenge, pursuing retributive justice (through the court system), seeking restitution by socially approved means or otherwise, 2) spiritual acts such as trusting God to rightly judge the offender, and 3) psychological acts such as denial, projecting unforgiveness onto another person, cognitively reframing a transgression in a way that excuses, justifies or denies the injustice, accepting the transgression, or emotionally forgiving (Worthington, *A Just Forgiveness*). Likewise, if the offended party observes something bad happening to the perpetrator and interprets the event as just punishment by God, their experiential injustice gap may be reduced. For small gaps, the offended party can merely forget, or the passing of time can ameliorate the negative emotions. One interesting study suggests that even the present experience of a believed *delayed* justice (i.e., justice to be eventually received in the afterlife) might effectively reduce the injustice gap and facilitate present forgiveness (Exline et al., *Forgiveness and Justice*).

It is a very strange and inadequate question—a bit insensitive isn't it? I think that the question is roughly the equivalence of "Was justice served?" But again, the answer depends on who you ask. Probably representatives of the judicial system would mean "Was the punishment to the Defendants severe enough, measured to the crime, and appropriate according to the law?"

I would guess that the survivors and the families of the survivors might have other answers. Was it enough? The harsh sanctions may have reduced the injustice gap some—maybe? But tragically, not a great deal.

Was it enough? Didn't they expect more? What was really done to restore their lost identity, value, dignity? Honestly, what the Plaintiffs really, really may want is to have the hands of the clock turned back to a time before the rapes. So that they can have a re-do. So that they can live out normal lives just like everybody else, without the deep cup-reduction that they must shoulder.

So was it enough? Yes and No!

Yes. Our judicial system "is-what-it-is" and does exactly what it is designed to do. It is designed to do *Retributive Justice*. Its prime driving concern is to determine the appropriate punishment after considering all of the evidence, case law, context, etc. Does the guilty Defendant (or University) get one year or life behind bars.

Now, *Retributive Justice* might arguably reduce the injustice gap for the surviving Plaintiffs and Plaintiff's family—but honestly, no one would say that it was anywhere near enough. So was justice served? In a narrow retributive sense, perhaps so. But there are others aspects or types of justice at the disposal of a just society: distributive, restorative and procedural.

Distributive Justice

Distributive Justice refers to the desire of all of the participants in a dispute that the ultimate resolution is fair and equitable.[8] So Plaintiff, when your soul cries out "That's just not fair," it has unknowingly entered the realm of *Distributive Justice*. What result, what resolution would be fair to *all* involved? This is a good thing. *Retributive Justice* is not concerned with fair outcomes, only what the law prescribes to be the appropriate punishment

---

[8] Walker notes that while individuals are inclined to view positive outcomes as more satisfactory than negative outcomes, the satisfaction that a judgment or award engenders depends also on beliefs about what the individual receiving the judgment deserves. Even positive awards may be considered unfair if it is believed that the individual deserves more or less in view of his contribution to the transaction from which the dispute arose (Walker, L., A. Lind, and J. Thibaut, "The Relation Between Procedural and Distributive Justice," Virginia Law Review, 65(8) (1979): 1402.

to the Defendant. It is largely blindfolded to the needs of the offended party.

Restorative Justice

Restorative Justice involves the active participation of the Plaintiff, offender *and* the community. *Restorative Justice* attempts to find equitable and just solutions that likely include remorse, repentance, a plan of restitution from the offender (where appropriate), and forgiveness from the Plaintiff. The Plaintiff, offender and the affected community are all active in discussions regarding what "justice" is to entail.[9]

Howard Zehr in his landmark book, *Changing Lenses*, compares *Restorative* and *Retributive* justices (see figure below). Where *Retributive Justice* asks "What laws have been broken?," and "What do they deserve?" *Restorative Justice* asks "Who has been hurt?," "What are their needs?" and "Whose obligations are these?"

Retributive Justice	Restorative Justice
Crime is a violation of law and the state.	Crime is a violation of people and relationships.
Violations create guilt.	Violations create obligations.
Justice requires the state to determine blame and impose pain	Justice involves victims and offenders putting things right.
Central focus: Offenders getting what they deserve	Central focus: Victim's needs and offender's responsibility to repair harm

Figure 4- Contrast of Retributive and Restorative Justice from Changing Lenses

Has Sandusky accepted the obligation to restore the Plaintiffs to wholeness? Absolutely not. He was subjected to *Retributive Justice* alone. So his punishment is life in prison—but unfortunately he is totally off the hook for any restorative obligations.

---

[9] Worthington, *A Just Forgiveness.*

Procedural Justice

Procedural Justice arguably may be the *most* important of all the types of justice. *Procedural Justice* refers to the
> "fairness of the methods, mechanisms, and processes used to determine outcomes as opposed to the fairness of the outcomes themselves."[10]

According to the research, Plaintiffs care as much about *how* their disputes are resolved (procedural) as they do about the actual outcomes they receive. Experts in *Procedural Justice*[11] speak about three important aspects of effective Plaintiff-honoring judicial process.

First, it has been shown that Plaintiffs need the opportunity to personally present their case in whatever way they feel serves them best. Plaintiffs who have been given such "voice" feel much more positive about the outcome of such a trial even if it goes against them.

Second, Plaintiffs report being honored if they sense that that have been given a fair hearing before an unbiased decision maker who makes their verdict based upon logically probative evidence.[12]

Third, for *Procedural Justice* to be powerful and effective, the process must

---

[10] Miller, D. T. "Disrespect and the Experience of Injustice," Annual Review of Psychology, 52, (2001): 528. Folger & Greenberg (*Procedural Justice*, 43) concur. Procedural justice is "the perceived fairness of the procedures used in making decisions...the 'means' whereby various 'ends' are attained." See also Folger, F., and J. Greenberg. "Procedural Justice: An Interpretive Analysis of Personnel Systems." *Research in Personnel and Human Resources Management*, 3, (1985):141-183.

[11] Blader, S., & T. Tyler, "A Four-Component Model of Procedural Justice: Defining the Meaning of a 'Fair' Process," Personality and Social Psychology Bulletin (2003): 29(6), 747-758;and Miller, *Disrespect*.

[12] Fair procedural due process requires a neutral and trustworthy judge. Warren says that "the notion of a 'neutral' magistrate, an impartial decision maker, a judicial officer free of bias, interest, or improper motive, and committed to equality under the law, are central to the concepts of judicial independence and the rule of the law." (Warren, *Public Trust*, 14). Trustworthiness is a function of the litigant's perception of the judge's character and motives—whether the judge seems to truly care about the litigant and appears to be seeking to do right by them (R. Warren, "Public Trust and Procedural Justice." *Court Review*. (2000): 12-16).

treat Plaintiffs as persons to whom honor and dignity is due.[13]

Isn't this good news, Plaintiff? Wouldn't you deeply appreciate a trial or judicial proceeding where you are intentionally treated as a person of honor? "The experience of a fair procedure tells [the Plaintiff] important things about their social relationships and their self-identity."[14]

It is the fairness of court *processes*, not necessarily the fairness of court *outcomes* or decisions that is most important. In the minds of both of the litigants, the importance of a favorable outcome is consistently outweighed by the impact of an unfair process.

> "A prevailing litigant might look back upon a recent court experience and say, "Yes, I won the case, but I don't know if it was worth it. It cost me too much, the judge wouldn't let me speak, I didn't understand what the judge was talking about, I was treated like dirt. I hope I never have to go through that again." On the other hand, an unsuccessful litigant can leave the courtroom saying, "I lost my case but I had my day in court, I was treated fairly, I can move on."[15]

Complete justice requires a perception of a fair trial and a fair resolution. There must be perceived to be both a fair and equitable outcome (*Distributive Justice*) but also a belief on the part of the litigants that the techniques used to resolve the dispute are likewise fair and satisfying in and of themselves (*Procedural Justice*). Ultimate resolution is a function of the disputant's belief that both the procedure and the outcome are fair.[16]

"Was justice served?" "Was the punishment enough?" Now can we see just how unnecessarily narrow and harmful these questions can be. I have noticed that as I teach on this topic, tears often begin to well up in the eyes of many Plaintiffs. Where are the life-giving judicial processes that actually honor the Plaintiffs? Many modern forgiveness therapists tend to demonize

---

[13] This "right to respect" (Miller, *Disrespect*; J. A. Rawls, *A Theory of Justice* (Cambridge: Harvard University Press, 1971)—the right to be treated in a way that fosters positive self-regard—is one of the perceived entitlements that Plaintiffs are due by virtue of their humanity. Disrespectful treatment is a common determinant of both anger and aggression and would lead to more motivation for avoidance or retaliation. When Plaintiffs are denied the respect to which they believe they are entitled, they feel unjustly treated (Miller, *Disrespect*). The research concludes that it is the procedure itself that informs disputants whether he or she is a valued member of their group. This is very important to any subsequent reconciliation. Miller has done an extensive survey of multiple studies pertaining to the psychology of injustice and concludes that the victim's perceived fairness of the judicial procedure (procedural justice) is often *as* important to the victim and eventual resolution as the actual objectivity and fairness of the outcome itself (distributive justice).

[14] Howieson, J. (2002). "Perceptions of Procedural Justice and Legitimacy in Local Court Mediation." *Murdoch University Electronic Journal of Law. 9*(2) (2002), n. 31.

[15] Warren, *Public Trust*, 13.

[16] Walker, *Relation*.

all justice as solely retributive—and so overlook the many life-giving benefits of procedural, restorative and distributive justices.

Plaintiff, what you really, really want and need is a full-orbed justice that is fair to all involved, that intentionally treats you as a person of honor, dignity and value, and ultimately does more than just reduce an injustice gap. Rather, the process itself can actually restore you to some wholeness: personally, spiritually and relationally.

The current judicial system in the US is narrowly retributive. This is its design and role. This fact does not make it evil or good. But it is wildly naïve to expect anything more from the judicial system than what it is designed to accomplish. The US judicial system is not geared to make the Plaintiff whole or to balance their inner scales of fairness and right. It holds the sword of justice and can only determine what the appropriate punishment is to be laid upon the perpetrator. It is extremely narrow in its focus. I fear—that alone—it often further victimizes the Plaintiffs—dishonors them, disavows their victimization, and somehow, strips them of voice and procedure that is due them.

Unforgiveness (1992)

In Clint Eastwood's 1992 *Unforgiveness*, there is a striking picture of the diminishment that comes from lack of full-orbed justice. An offended cowhand in a fit of rage sliced up the face of a prostitute (Delilah Fitzgerald, played by Anna Levine). Skinny (Anthony James), the owner of the brothel calls in Sheriff Little Bill Daggett (Gene Hackman) to see justice served, but it turns out that justice is severely lacking in the old west.

The impromptu trial in the brothel is very brief. Sheriff Little Bill sends a deputy to get a whip. Alice (Frances Fisher), the Madam of the brothel stands in the place of the Plaintiff,

Alice:
   A whipping, that's all they get after all they done?

Little Bill:
   A whipping ain't no little thing Alice...

Skinny:
   Little Bill, a whipping ain't gonna settle this. This here's a lawful contract between me and Delilah Fitzgerald, the cut whore...I got a contract that represents an investment of capital.

LB:
>   Property?

Skinny:
>   *Damaged* property.   Like I was to hamstring one of their cattle ponies…Nobody is going to pay good money for a cut up whore.

In the end, Little Bill fined the two cowhands seven ponies to be given to Skinny.   No whipping, no jail.   Not even an apology to the scarred prostitute.

Alice:
>   You ain't even gonna whip them.   …For what they done, Skinny gets some ponies and that's it?…That ain't fair Little Bill, that ain't fair.

LB:
>   Hell Alice, its not like they was tramps or loafers, or bad men, you know, they was just hard working boys that was foolish.   If they were given over to wickedness in a regular way …

Alice:
>   Like whores?   …Maybe we ain't nothing but whores but by-god we ain't horses.

So Plaintiff, let me ask, from Delilah's (the scarred prostitute) perspective, was justice served?   Was the punishment enough?   Absolutely not.   Was there procedural justice in the trial?   Virtually none.   Was she given a voice?
>   "Delilah, can you tell the court what happened?   What was taken from you?   How does the violation make you feel?   What could the cowboy do that would begin to make you feel honored?"

None of these things were present at all.   The judge was not objective. Little Bill did not see her as a person to whom honor and dignity was due. Was the trial fair to all involved?   Was Delilah's restoration to wholeness considered at all?   None of the above.   This was *Retributive Justice* at its worst.

What were the personal consequences of Little Bill's tragic justice to Delilah?   There is a very telling scene when the two cowhands return with the prescribed justice payment for Skinny.   Delilah is *physically* there, her face still scarred.   But in another sense, she is not engaged in the narrative anymore. She is silent, largely looking down or away. While the other prostitutes show humanly appropriate anger and displeasure at the cowboys, Delilah is noticeably emotionless. She is clearly uncomfortable when one of the cowboys attempts to honor her with a gift of a special hand-picked pony. At first she moves toward him, perhaps a natural response to being affirmed a bit. But the other prostitutes reject such an act as extremely insufficient.

Alice:
A pony, She ain't got no face left and you gonna give her a goddamn mangy pony?

This is such a great picture, this is what happens often to Plaintiffs. She is now marginalized on the side, scarred and diminished. She is no longer a real 3-D character—just a shadow—a wraith—no real emotions. This happens when there is no fair and equitable full-orbed justice.

Delilah's already shallow cup was drained dry, first by the crime and second, by the justice system itself. Little Bill's cowboy *Retributive Justice* may have temporarily bought the peace, but it did not bring life and resolution. So the Plaintiffs did what Plaintiffs do.

The other prostitutes decided that since there was no justice forthcoming from the powers that be, they would take matters into their own hands. They gathered together all of their savings and hired Bill Munny (Clint Eastwood) an over-the-hill bounty hunter to give them justice at last by murdering the cowboys who cut Delilah. By the end of the movie, the consequences of bad justice resulted in great destruction and loss of many lives—and still no inner or outer healing for Delilah. She remained an empty cup.

Delilah is a good image of someone who has learned that there is no justice left for them. Due to the events in her life that have made her an object of indignities, perhaps she has come to believe that she doesn't deserve justice anymore. Her question has morphed into an identity statement, "There is no justice for me."

How about you Plaintiff?

Core Question #1- *"Where is Justice for you?"*

15

Reflection Questions for Individuals or Groups

1)   Remember an actual trial where you thought that the verdict was suspect—or even wrong. Describe in your own words what it felt like to not experience the *Aaaah! Factor*. What would be the long-term effect to a society with a corrupt judicial system that always gets justice wrong?

2)   In your own words, discuss the four types of justices. What are the positive and negative aspects of each? What has been your personal experience of each? Do you rank one as being more important than the other three? Why? Please discuss.

3)   Think of a specific crime that has been committed against you. Which of the four aspects of justice did you most experience subsequent to the crime? What might it have looked like—or felt like—to have experienced a full-orbed (i.e., four-fold) justice?

4)   The author suggests that *Procedural* justice may in some ways be the most important of the four justice types those who were victimized. Does that surprise you? Discuss.

2

Second Core Question from Cracked Cups

Question #2: Where is the Happy Ending?

The second question that erupts from the soul of empty cups is "Where is the happy ending?" Normally, all human beings would expect that their lives would turn out well. There is a natural positivism expressed by children. But then bad things happen. After a few unresolved unfair crises and injustices, the once positive attitude and expectations matures into cynical adult reality. What happened to the once-dreamed-of happy ending? For many Plaintiffs, it is long gone.

"*Life Sucks…And Then You Die*" is the title of the 1988 debut album of the thrash metal band *Cerebral Fix*. Listen to some of the cynical titles on the album: Life Sucks, Looniverse, Soap Opera, Product of Disgust, Power Struggle, Fear of Death, Existing, Not Living, Give me Life, and Zombie. Plaintiff, you get the sense right? Something happened to you that was outside the box and irrevocably changed your narrative for the worse.

Denis Leary concurs:

"Most people think life sucks, and then you die. Not me. I beg to differ. I think life sucks, then you get cancer, then your dog dies, your wife leaves you, the cancer goes into remission, you get a new dog, you get remarried, you owe ten million dollars in medical bills but you work hard for thirty-five years and you pay it back and then—one day—you have a massive stroke, your whole right side is paralyzed, you have to limp along the streets and speak out of the left side of your mouth and drool but you go into rehabilitation and regain the power to walk and the power to talk and then—one day—you step off a curb at Sixty-seventh Street, and BANG you get hit by a city bus and then you die. Maybe."

Plaintiffs, some of you may object to this descriptor of how you may feel right now. Maybe what happened to you was emotionally manageable? Maybe you can testify that you have been more or less able to put the loss in perspective this time? Still, the crime likely affected your worldview more than you would care to admit.

Imagine a victimization scale, with "1"(on the far left) being "I don't feel this way at all" and "10" (on the far right) being "Exactly how I feel all day everyday!" Plaintiff, you may rightly score yourself a "3" or an "8," but the point here is that the crime pushed you experientially toward the right on the scale. If you were a "1" and now are a "3," that is very significant. The crime violated your life. The lack of full-orbed justice has probably further robbed you of hope. To some degree, you no longer really expect a happy ending anymore.

"Heroes are for kids stories and fairy tales, not real life." If enough injustices are unresolved, you will stop counting on anyone but yourself. Why would you expect some miraculous intervention that would make things right—restore what was taken? Right? Don't expect a miracle, no hero, no Prince Charming, no Superman. The Crash Test Dummies', *Superman's Song* captures some of the sense of the despair,

"Superman never made any money
For saving the world from Solomon Grundy
And sometimes I despair the world will never see
Another man like him."

The Dark Knight and Justice

The Dark Knight (2008), the second of Christopher Nolan's Batman trilogy, has grossed over a billion in worldwide revenue, currently number

12 all-time gross revenue (inflation adjusted). The late Heath Ledger received the Academy for Best Supporting Actor posthumously.

I remember leaving the theater with a cacophony of powerful reactions. It took me some time to sort them out. In fact I had to watch the movie a few more times for it to become clearer to me.

The movie is ultimately an exposé on the absurdity of order. Plaintiffs get it. This absurdity is overwhelming in the aftermath of a devastating crime. We live our lives (here in the United States) generally thinking that we are safe, that there are rules in society that are inviolable. Civilized people just don't walk into movie theaters, or high schools and just shoot people. We don't expect our children kidnapped or molested by neighbors, priests or coaches. We don't expect corrupt judges or police. Right?

We *do* expect deaths and injuries in war zones. We expect different rules on the field of battle, but normally that is a long way away from our day-to-day lives. We live in a bubble that we consider safe—at least under control. Our understanding is that our lives should be fair and equitable—just.

The Dark Knight explores the unthinkable—that in fact there is *no* safe place. Not really. Order is only a thin veneer. There is an ever-present chaos that is stronger and more powerful than order. There is an instrument of disorder out there that can in a moment threaten ordered society with very little effort.

This chaos doesn't fight according to the rules. We don't know how to guard ourselves from it or defeat it. Comics like Batman are *not* morality tales about good and evil. They are about the fragility of order.

As the movie opens, Gotham city is not perfect by any means—but the corruption and crime at least play by acceptable societal rules. Batman says to Alfred that criminals are not complicated. They are predictable, they play by understood rules. They can be tracked down and arrested. Even most criminals are "civilized" to a degree.

But what happens when someone comes along and plays by no rules; whose sole goal is to disrupt the order of society? Gotham's Joker broke all the rules. In the first action scene he robs the mob's bank. No one robs from the robber. The Joker does. The troubled corrupt bank manager ironically asks the Joker, "Criminals used to believe in honor and respect—what do you believe in?"

Gotham's Prisoner Dilemma

"Tonight you will all be part of a social experiment," blasts the twisted strained voice of the Joker over both of the ferries loud speakers." The

Joker produced, directed and starred in a classic game theory "prisoner's dilemma" experiment using Gotham as the laboratory for his chaos.

The populations on each of two ferries had been isolated from the general population and each other and must choose between only two options. Ferry #1 was a random group of "innocent" commuters. Ferry #2 was a control group consisting of convicted criminals being transferred to prison. Each group was given a choice. They could choose to 1) trigger the bombs on the other boat, or 2) choose to not trigger the bombs on the other boat. If either chose to blow up the *other* ferry their *own* ferry would survive; but if they both chose the compassionate route, the Joker said that he would blow up both ferries. If they blow up the other ferry, they survive, but are exposed as cowards and criminals—uncivilized. If they don't they are destroyed. Technically the social experiment was scientifically "fair" since both populations had the exact same choice.

The goal of the social experiment? "Introduce a little chaos …upset the order a little and everything becomes chaos." The Joker believed that Gotham City's veneer of "civilization," orderliness, and rules was a sham and would fall to pieces with just a little push of anarchy. In this experiment, there was no "good" decision—it was brilliantly lose-lose. Each of the populations could choose to be cowardly murderers (agents of societal anarchy) or tragic corpses. No matter what the choice, anarchy would *still* be injected into the general population and Joker *would* win. The absurdity and fragility of Gotham's order exposed.

At first blush, it would appear that the Joker's ugly experiment was disrupted by Batman. But if we look closer, the Joker accomplished exactly what he had hoped. The boat with "innocent" citizens proved to be much more self-centered and uncompassionate (i.e., criminal) than the ferry of condemned convicts. Whew! The Joker still wins—easily. Way too easily.

By the end of The Dark Knight, every good character is either killed, crosses the former lines of ethics/rules (i.e., breaks the rules) or is flipped in the movie.

Harvey Dent, the "face of hope," becomes Two Face. Good, order, rules, civilization are too fragile. "Good" is exposed as "Not-As-Good" as we thought and hoped.

Do you get it? The Dark Knight is an exploration of the absolute power and destructive capacity of chaos and anarchy, and the surprising vulnerability of ordered and civilized society. It pricks at one of the greatest fears of the hearts of western society in an age of terrorism—that we are far more vulnerable than we dare to imagine—that our order is really only a house of cards—easily brought down.

For the Joker, it was "about sending a message." The message? There is no *real* order in Gotham. The heroic DA Harvey Dent gets the fragility of order. "You either die a hero or live long enough to become a villain." Like in the Wizard of Oz, you are not supposed to look behind the curtain. You won't like what you see.

That's the frightening point. This order of ours—our civilization and society is very, very fragile at best. It inevitably tends to disorder. We felt that after the Oklahoma City bombing, the Aurora Colorado theater massacre, and 9/11. Civilized people don't fly planes into buildings—but now we are aware of a presence of people who do not follow the rules.

It doesn't take much. The truth of the matter is that we cannot stop chaos happening in our lives. Chaos happens.

Admittedly sometimes good comes out of chaos. Sometimes in the aftermath of chaos, the affected citizenry scramble to find meaning, explanations, new rules, and a restoration of controllable balance.

There is often a temporary measurable influx of people into churches asking higher questions—hoping that there really is a God who is above chaos. Hoping for answers, for reasons. But the surge typically subsides once the fragile veneer of societal order appears to be restored—for now. At least until the next catastrophe.

True to its comic book origins, The Dark Knight does not have a fairy tale ending at all. Sure some order is restored, but it is at the cost of "truth." Per one character, "Sometimes the truth is not good enough." The story is fabricated for the press, so that the "face" of good and order (Two-Face Harvey Dent before the accident) is held up as incorruptible and unchangeable. Batman will take the blame for all of the murders and become a public enemy. What is the purpose behind the lies? So that the people of Gotham can have that temporary sense of being in a calm and safe harbor for a while longer.

Plaintiffs, you get it, right? In the aftermath of the crime committed against you, you had a glimpse of the real world behind the façade—and it was far different than the fairy tale veneer by which you have been living your life. You can no longer trust the world to be fair, to be safe, to exude meaning for all citizenry. The forces of chaos are vast. Your life-story was rocked without your permission. In fact, you were helpless to stop it. Now your narrative has dramatically changed—not for good, it would seem.

The Black Psalm

Plaintiffs, do you sometimes wake up to believe that life has no happy endings—at least not for you? Have you been tempted to believe that what happened to your story is irrevocable and unredeemable? What good can come out of such a mess? Maybe you concur with the gifted psalmists, the sons of Korah?

"My soul is full of trouble and my life draws near the grave... I am like a man without strength...You [God] have put me in the lowest pit, in the darkest depths. Your wrath lies heavily upon me; you have overwhelmed me with all your waves. *Selah.* You have taken from me my closest friends and have made me repulsive to them. I am confined and cannot escape; my eyes are dim with grief....I cry to you for help, O Lord...Why, O Lord, do you reject me and hide your face from me?...the darkness is my closest friend." (Ps 88:3-18)

For the sons of Korah, there was no happy ending on the horizon. They had expected God to intervene—but have come to the realization, humanly speaking, that He's part of the problem. He seems to be their oppressor, not their friend. Darkness is their closest friend. Whew, no apparent hope there.

Meaningless or Meaningful Suffering?

After so much unresolved suffering, it would all seem so meaningless. I like how Psychologist Robert Aziz frames the difference between meaningful and meaningless suffering:

"Meaningful suffering, simply stated, carries us forward. Consciousness and life arise out of it. Meaningful suffering is transformational and to the extent that it is transformational we can speak of it as being a suffering that is clean burning. Meaningless suffering, by contrast is dirty burning. With meaningless suffering, life is left to smolder away unproductively. Meaningless suffering neither heals nor transforms."[17]

After sitting for a long time in the harsh wake of crimes against you, do you see any possibility of any redemption of the events that have occurred? Has the meaninglessness rewritten your narrative? Is your remaining life just smoldering "away unproductively?"

Have you come to believe that while others may have happy endings, their conflict wonderfully resolved into a great meaningful narrative, this is not your lot? Is the appropriate soundtrack for your story is ultimately the blues, country & western, or rage rock?

Core Question #2- *Where is your happy ending?*

---

[17] http://www.robertaziz.com/publications/meaningful_suffering_versus_me.php

Reflection Questions for Individuals or Group

1)   Discuss the following quote about the importance of "happy endings."

> "Consolation requires that the right order of the world is restored; this means punishment of the evildoer, tantamount to the elimination of evil from the hero's world—and then nothing stands any longer in the way of the hero's living happily ever after."[18]

Do you agree? Why or why not? Have you experienced such a consolation?

2)   Think about your favorite book, TV show or movie. How important was it to you that the movie had "consolation?"

3)   Now consider a recent real-life crime, or related trial. As you consider the closure of the crime and trial, did "consolation" happen? Why or why not?

---

[18] B. Bettelheim, *The Uses of Enchantment: The Meaning and Importance of Fairy Tales.* (New York: Vintage Books, 1977), 144.

3

Third Core Question from Cracked Cups

Question #3: Who are you now in the aftermath of your loss?

Before the crime, you were a person with loads of potential and freedom. Sure you had fears, but they were manageable. You described yourself with such adjectives as engaged, caring, free, confident and fun-loving.

Plaintiff, have you come to believe that what happened to you and the aftermath has fundamentally changed your identity into a victim? Or to put it in Cupological terminology, do you now fear that you will never be a full cup again—this side of heaven? Now all you can do is cope and survive as a diminished cup?

For example, if you were raped, have you come to believe that you are inherently unclean—merely a soiled used object suited only for the pleasures of others.

Or perhaps you grew up under constant criticism. So now, have you come to believe that you really were never good enough for your parents? And so now have you decided that you must live the rest of your life making up for your innate failure and live your life for the approval of others?

When the crime first happened, you may have longed for restoration to pre-crime status. This was reasonable, right? You wanted everything put back the way it was pre-crime. You were more naïve back then and even began to think that such a restoration was humanly possible—at least that was the goal.

But after days and weeks and months of failed attempts to return to the past, have you come to the conclusion that this is all there is? You *are* a new creature now—but not a better one (contra 2Cor 5:17)? You are a diminished version of your former self?

Your head is resigned to the fact that there is no turning back the clock. What's done is done. It is what it is. As you consider the present and the future, the wonderful life that you had imagined before the event is beyond imagination. You can only sadly "gird your loins" and gut it out in the new difficult path forward. When you look at your reflection in those quiet reflective moments, you wonder if you are and will always be a diminished Plaintiff.

Eternal Sunshine of the Spotless Mind (2004)

In the 2004 movie, *Eternal Sunshine of the Spotless Mind,* Jim Carrey and Kate Winslet pay for a special new technology that supposedly wipes out specific painful memories from their brains. In the end they hope that they can reshape their lives as if their destructive relationship with so much pain never happened.

Wouldn't it be great if there were technology to virtually wipe out the bad thing that happened to you. All loss, all memory, all consequences? What if someone could turn back the clock to where it never happened? But, hey, this is Science Fiction. There is no such technology as Carrey and Winslet find out. You cannot go back. Who are you post-crime?

Cupology Case Study #2- The Competitive Daughter

Let me go back to Cupology 101 for a moment. To oversimplify complex relational realities, there are generally two types of cup failures:

- Low levels of liquid due to lack of recent filling

- Low levels of liquid caused by ongoing leaking from hairline cracks in the walls formed early on during the formative years of the cups.

A great deal has been written on the importance of a daughter's earliest relationship with her father during her formative years. It is argued that from dad, little girls gain their first reflection of themselves as a female. From dad's relationship to them, they develop a sense of acceptance or non-acceptance; they feel valued or discounted. How dad treats them is critical to their later relationships.[19] One counselor laments,

> "Every week wounded women come into my office suffering from a poor self-image, from the inability to form lasting relationships, or from a lack of confidence in their ability to work and function in the world. On the surface these women often appear quite successful—confident businesswomen, contented housewives, carefree students, swinging divorcees. But underneath the veneer of success or contentment is the injured self, the hidden despair, the feelings of loneliness and isolation, the fear of abandonment and rejection, the tears and the rage. For many of these women, the root of their injury stems from a damaged relationship with the father."[20]

For many of you, Plaintiffs, this phenomenon is all too real. As you remember your childhood—and in particular your relationship with your father—there seemed to be nothing you could do to elicit his praise. You tried just about everything to please him—to be a good daughter/son—to make him proud of you; but it would seem that nothing you did worked. Nothing you did motivated your father to pour precious life-giving liquid into your cup.

Typically, Plaintiff, if the truth were fully known, the breakdown of the relationship was never about you anyway. Maybe your father was uncomfortable with dealing with children, or with the opposite sex. Maybe he was self-absorbed, indifferent and narcissistic. Maybe he was shamed early on in his childhood and was a fractured cup himself. Maybe this is how he was treated by his own father? Who knows?

But for whatever reason, your dad did not fill your cup the way that it was designed to be filled by him specifically—and you were left with pinhole leaks in the walls of your cups.

Leaky Pipes

A few years back, my family and I lived in a beautiful suburb north of Philadelphia. We came home one day to discover that we had a real issue with the copper water pipes which crisscrossed underneath the dry wall of

---

[19] Per Jane R. Rosen-Grandon, fathers teach their daughters how to regard themselves, what kinds of relationships are healthy, what to look for in a partner, and what to expect of men in co-parenting relationships. See http://www.dr-jane.com/chapters/Jane125.htm.
[20] Linda Schierse, *The Wounded Woman: Healing the Father–Daughter Relationship*, (Boston:Shambhala Publications, 1982).

our basement ceiling. It turned out that the natural acidity of the water in the ridge that we lived on had slowly diminished the thickness of the walls of the copper piping throughout the house. It didn't lead to huge floods of water, but rather little annoying pinhole leaks that could happen anywhere, anytime. Most of us enter adult years with acid-etched cup walls prone to pinhole leaks.

Judy

So for little girls, the lack of a father's love and adoration can—and usually does—lead to very thin cup walls and multiple pinhole leaks that must be filled by others. They enter adulthood and adult relationships often unaware and unprepared. "Judy" is one such very thirsty and leaky soul.

"My father was the type who couldn't express love—only approval or disapproval. Once I got a B on a report card, and he said, "What's this?" I said, "Why don't you say anything about all the A's?" He said, "I expect that. I expect you to be perfect." The good news is that he trained me to be extremely capable, so I am very successful—I can take care of myself. The downside is that I'm a driven workaholic. I can't make a mistake, and I'm always walking on eggshells. One false move, and it's all undone. I feel as if I'm only as good as my last accomplishment."[21]

Author Victoria Secunda, in her book *Women and Their Fathers*, labels Judy a "Competitive Daughter." She had, for whatever reason, "failed" to earn her father's love. Competitive Daughters are perennially empty cups needing to be filled. Ironically, on the surface Competitive Daughters might appear as confident beautiful persons—successful in school and career—in a word "driven" to be seen as successful.

Competitive Daughters often are notably successful in dating. They typically are very comfortable with men in this setting. They might have as many guy friends as girl friends.

For Judy it was noticeable to many that though she dated a lot, she had a hard time finding Mr. Perfect—there was always some flaw that led her to break up. If the truth were known relational intimacy was very confusing to her. She would always blame the guy of course. At last she married a man who was—of course—a recognized leader in his field and at least on the surface had few flaws. It was critical to her that he pass the "Father test." She *needed* her dad's approval.

---

[21] A quote from 'Judy, Forty-Three' in Victoria Secunda, *Women and Their Fathers: The Sexual and Romantic Impact of the First Man in Your Life*, (New York: Dell, 1992), 287.

To change our Cupology metaphor a bit, Judy's inner-wiring was twisted—not by an *evil* parent—but nevertheless destructive. The flagging father-daughter relationship left her emotionally dysfunctional and *needing* to continually earn the respect of others—in particular men—but never ever satisfied with herself—never whole. She worked hard at her career—needing to be recognized, win prizes, awards, acclaim. For all who knew her, the key descriptor is "needing."

For many Competitive Daughters, prize winning comes at a high psychic price—they pay dearly for accomplishment. Some pay through loneliness. These are women who are unable to form intimate attachments, who are so much a part of the good-old-boy network that, emotionally they are in a sense good old boys themselves. Anything "feminine" is to be denigrated, including female friendship. Such isolation precludes the capacity for mutually loving, freely sexual romantic attachments. *They resolve never to need or to want results in the inability to receive love.*

Risking all for tangible success, risking nothing for the uncertainties of love and sexual abandon, many Competitive Daughters spend their entire lives trying to measure up, alone. And for some of them the price of their perfectionism is painfully apparent when they do form romantic relationships: The self-control of such women can become self-denial. These are the women who cannot take any form of criticism. To admit they cannot do everything well means that they can do nothing well and that they are essentially unlovable. Said one woman,

> "It's only recently that my husband can say something mildly critical and I don't put up my dukes, translating his comment as an indictment of my entire worth. I tried all of those years to please my father through achievement. I had no ground rules about what was loveable. So I've always felt that my husband didn't want me because I was loveable but because I was useful to him in some way. The other day he said, 'Why do you get so upset if I tell you, say, the coffee is a little bitter? Don't you understand that it's a superficial thing and has nothing to do with my love for you?' I screwed up my courage and said, "I guess I don't know what makes someone loveable." He gave me this elegant answer: "I love you for your humanness." I burst into tears. No one ever said that to me before."[22]

Who is she post-crime? Competitive Daughters most often leave their family of origins fractured and dreadfully empty cups. Their father for whatever reason did not serve them well.

Many Competitive Daughters in their thirties or forties are able to assess their losses, to stop attempting to be their own fathers, and to allow their

---

[22] Secunda, *Women*, 308.

neglected nurturing and feeling sides to blossom. Shifting emotional gears is not always easy for these women; the Competitive Daughter has the most trouble summoning the nerve to be human and to admit she needs help.[23]

For some of you Plaintiffs, the crime was so deep or has been so chronic that you no longer think that there is a possibility that your cup could be filled again. Your cup has been drunk beneath your "Red Line."

Cupology Case Study #3: The Red Line

Maybe a geographical analogy would be helpful in this case. Bible readers are very familiar, of course, with the Dead Sea in Israel. There is no aquatic life in the Dead Sea. All life has been snuffed out by poisonous toxins that ooze out of the rifts in the floor of that body of water.

Just upstream along the Jordan River is the Sea of Galilee (the Lake of Kinneret to locals). The Sea of Galilee teems with fish. It is an important aspect to the Israeli economy to keep Galilee alive. The problem is that the same toxins that make the Dead Sea dead also ooze from the bottom of the Sea of Galilee.

Scientists have concluded that the Sea of Galilee will remain vibrant and alive as long as the level of the water does not drop below the infamous "Red Line," officially 213 meters below sea level.

Why would this natural huge "cup" drop below the Red Line? Scientists suggest that there are two ever-present dangers that could lead to the level dipping below the Red Line. *First*, in the semi-arid desert ecosystem of Israel, there is always the possibility of an extended drought— i.e., a lack of liquid being regularly put into the natural cup from rain and from the Jordan River.

Second, there is the possibility that the water of the Galilee be mismanaged—too much being taken out for the population's needs such as drinking, production, irrigation, etc.—and the natural cup being drained down by outside forces.

It is a geographic Cupology Case Study. If the level drops even further, the so-called "Black Line"—at 215 meters below sea level, permanent environmental damage will be caused to Kinneret. The Sea of Galilee will become another Dead Sea.

In Cupology terminology, I wonder if each of our cups has an inherent Red and Black Line below which if our substance level drops, there is severe—humanly speaking—permanent damage: a Dead Sea. Below this level the cup has given up on justice in this lifetime. Below this level, the Plaintiff no longer has any hopes of good coming out of their lives. They

---

23 Secunda, *Women*, 308.

must just survive the best they can. Below this level, the person-who-was-victimized can easily go down the rabbit hole of taking on the core identity of a person-who-is-a-victim. These are two very different core identities.

So hopefully Plaintiff, some of this is resonating. Three critical questions have captured the attention of your heart:

- Where is justice for you?

- Where is the happy ending?

- Who are you now in the aftermath of your loss?

Forget forgiveness right now. You have these important issues that relate to who you are and how you see the world. Compared to these, forgiveness is a secondary issue at this point in your journey.

Emptied cups don't forgive—not really. You want justice, you want your cup refilled and you want a happy ending.

Modern Forgiveness Approaches

How do modern forgiveness counselors assist you in answering these three core questions? In preparation for my doctoral thesis, I thoroughly researched the fast growing body of studies on forgiveness and forgiveness interventions, a large portion of which are being done by openly Christian practitioners.

Modern socio-psychological forgiveness research, the source of the majority of books and seminars on the topic of forgiveness—both secular and Christian today—largely ignores the three huge elephant questions in the room (mentioned above). Rather, modern research has largely focused on means and methods to encourage Plaintiffs to feel empathy for the one who hurt them, and to subsequently forgive. The key question today seems to be "How do you feel toward the perpetrator?" This is indeed an important question. I strongly suggest that this question should not even be asked until there are solid answers to the first three questions discussed earlier.

The Modern Path of Forgiveness

Walker and Gorsuch (2004) examined sixteen modern models of interpersonal forgiveness and reconciliation and discerned five common underlying constructs (see below).

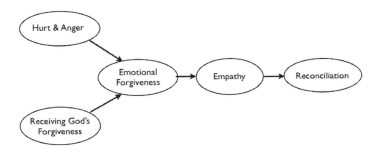

Figure 5- Path of Forgiveness and Reconciliation (adapted from Walker and Gorsuch 2004)

Hurt and Anger

The counselor leads the Plaintiff to identify and embrace the deep *hurt and anger* caused by the crime(s) committed against them. Then by means of cognitive therapeutic devices (education, visualization, reframing, meditation, journaling, etc.), the counselor will attempt to open the Plaintiff to new positive emotions toward the crime and criminal. These positive emotions displace some of the negative emotions, hopefully leading the Plaintiff to feel *less* desirous of revenge and separation, and *more* benevolent toward the offender.

Receiving God's Forgiveness

The process is largely initiated by the Plaintiff first choosing to give up their right of any justice for the crime—i.e., require no apology, no restitution, no vindication, or no punishment for the guilty. Plaintiffs must unilaterally choose between pursuing "justice" (e.g., retributive justice—the other aspects of justice are largely overlooked) or being emotionally set free. After all, the Christian Plaintiff is reminded that they too had committed great crimes against God and others and have *received vast forgiveness from God*. Certainly this changes things somewhat, right? Hopefully his or her feelings toward the crime and criminal starts to soften—to morph in a positive direction.

Choosing to Emotionally Forgive

As this *emotional forgiveness* displaces the powerful emotion of *unforgiveness*, the Plaintiff is more likely to feel new empathy for the perpetrator—quite a miracle—followed most naturally by a new openness to pursue forgiveness and reconciliation (where safe and appropriate of course).

It is fair to label modern Western forgiveness models as almost exclusively *victim-centric*—meaning that if forgiveness is to be achieved, the responsibility sits squarely upon the offended party's shoulders. You must choose to forgive the crime. Give up your right to justice, to an apology, to restitution. For the sake of being free and getting on with your post-crime life, you can and *must* choose to forgive. If you expect your perpetrator to change, or to initiate the process—you have put them in control—and you put yourself in subjection to their choices again. So, act like a free agent.

Empathy for the Perpetrator

That choice initiates the process—but it is long from complete. Typical modern forgiveness intervention models differ on means and methods, but the ultimate end game requires that you actually feel *empathy* toward the one who hurt you. Such *empathy* involves a fresh feeling of compassion toward the one who hurt you. This compassion stems from you at last beginning to see the events from the perpetrator's point of view, ideally creating a powerful positive emotional identification with them.[24]

So with the help and guidance of a skilled therapist the anger and hurt in your soul is displaced by positive emotions toward the one who hurt you.

Ideally at the end—for the forgiveness to be successful--you become less disposed to desire vengeance, or separation, and feel somewhat more benevolent toward the one that you hate right now.

So modern therapeutic forgiveness is

"a willingness [on the part of the Plaintiff] to abandon [their] right to resentment, negative judgment, and indifferent behavior toward one

---

[24] E. Worthington, *Forgiving and Reconciling: Bridges to Wholeness and Hope.* Downers Grove, Il: InterVarsity Press, 2003. It is clear that there is very little biblical evidence of the critical role of modern "empathy" as causal to forgiveness. This is not to say that we are not to be empathetic, or that people in the Old Testament were not empathetic. There just is very little evidence of directives to victims for the need to be empathetic toward their perpetrators. God never models for or instructs his people to "understand another person's perception of an interpersonal event as if one were that other person, rather than judging the other person's behavior from the perspective of one's own experience of that event" (Malcolm, W. & Greenberg, L. (2000). "Forgiveness as a Process of Change in Individual Psychotherapy," in *Forgiveness: Theory, Research and Practice,* edited by McCullough, M., K. Pergament, and C. E. Thoresen, 179-202. New York: Guilford, 2000, 179). *Raham* is perhaps the closest Hebrew word to the modern notion of empathy, but in other ways is very different. We will consider biblical *raham* from the perspective of the individual victim, the individual perpetrator and an individual who is arguably both.

who unjustly hurt [them], while fostering the undeserved qualities of compassion, generosity, and even love toward [the perpetrator]."[25]

Forgiveness involves "prosocial changes in one's motivations toward an offending relationship partner." [26] For the purposes of most socio-psychological practitioners today, forgiveness is simply defined as a process of reduction in the offended party's negative (viz., avoidance and revenge) motivations toward their offender, and an increase in the offended party's positive motivations toward their offender.[27]

Trim-18

One of the leading forgiveness empirical measurement devices that researchers use to determine success is the TRIM-18 (Transgression-Related Interpersonal Motivations). The TRIM-18 provides a before and after differential response to an offense along three dimensions: Avoidance, Revenge and Benevolence.[28]

- *First* there is the seven-item *Avoidance* scale that measures the offended party's motivation to avoid the offender (e.g., "I live as if he/she doesn't exist").

- *Second* there is the five-item *Revenge* subscale that measures the offended party's motivation to seek revenge (e.g., "I will make them pay").

25 Enright, R., and C. Coyle. "Researching the Process Model of Forgiveness Within Psychological Interventions," in *Dimensions of Forgiveness*, edited by In E. Worthington, 139-152. Philadelphia, Pa: Templeton Foundation Press, 1998; McCullough, M., W. Hoyt, and C. Rachal. "What We Know (and Need to Know) About Assessing Forgiveness Constructs," in *Forgiveness: Theory, Research and Practice*, edited by McCullough, M., K. Pergament, and C. E. Thoresen, 65-88. New York: Guilford, 2000, 8.

26 McCullough, M., C. Rachal, S. Sandage, E. Worthington, S. Brown, and T. Hight. (1998). "Interpersonal Forgiving in Close Relationships: II. Theoretical Elaboration and Measurement." *Journal of Personality and Social Psychology, 75*(6) (1998): 1586-1602; McCullough et al., *What We Know*, 8.

27 McCullough, M., E. Worthington, and K. Rachal. "Interpersonal Forgiving in Close Relationships," *Journal of Personality and Social Psychology, 73*(2) (1997): 321-336; McCullough et al., *Interpersonal*; M. McCullough, M., L. Root, and A. Cohen. "Writing about the Benefits of an Interpersonal Transgression Facilitates Forgiveness." *Journal of Consulting and Clinical Psychology, 74*(5) (2006): 887-897.

28 McCullough, et al., *Writing*.

- *Third* there is a six-item *Benevolence* subscale to measure benevolent motivation (e.g., "Even though his/her actions hurt me, I have goodwill for him/her").

All 18 items are rated on a 5-point Likert-type scale (1= *strongly disagree* to 5= *strongly agree*).

Forgiveness is then measured in decreases in the offended party's desire to avoid their offender or hurt them; and an increase in their feelings of benevolence toward them. The theory goes that if the offended party's begin to move forward according to these three measurable dimensions, they are indeed more willing to choose to forgive, to work toward feeling empathy for their offender, eventually emotionally forgiving them. Research in test cases has shown this to be a very viable approach.

Plaintiff, if you have recently been to counseling, I am sure that much of this is very familiar to you. There are variations and adaptations of course. Some therapists lean more toward *intra*personal (within the heart of the offended party) versus *inter*personal (moving toward working things out with the perpetrator). Some counselors focus on the importance of a *rational* decision to forgive—others focus on the importance of an *emotional* experience of forgiveness.

My guess is that if you are reading this book, this modern victim-centric, empathy driven (VCED) approach has not worked for you as much as you had hoped.

So let's say that you took full advantage of the best of the best of cognitive therapeutic forgiveness counseling, you may now feel a newfound empathy for the one who hurt you. You may even feel an emotional forgiveness toward them. How is this measured? You feel statistically more benevolent toward them, you feel statistically less likely to pursue revenge, and in fact, you are statistically less interested to avoid them. These are largely good and positive things. *But, you still have not experienced full-orbed justice.* Your inner scales of fairness are still out of whack. Your cup is still diminished and there is still no real happy ending to your story—not really. Do not despair, Plaintiff. The Bible has a great deal to say about you being set free and healed from crimes committed against you.

JRR Tolkien and Consolation for Emptied Cups

Here is the bottom line. If you *solely* pursue modern socio-psychological forgiveness, you may feel better about your situation, the victimization may feel diminished—you may be able to get on with your life and existence. But you are *not* whole. There is more for you.

Tolkien agrees. Tolkien, one of the greatest storytellers of the 20th century and author of the Lord of the Rings series, argues that there is something inherently sub-human about a tragic story that ends without justice and restoration. He observes that every good and lasting fairy tale has four distinct elements. The last, and perhaps most important of these elements, is "consolation."[29]

> "Consolation requires that the right order of the world is restored; this means punishment of the evildoer, tantamount to the elimination of evil from the hero's world—and then nothing stands any longer in the way of the hero's living happily ever after."[30]

Without such a consolation, the story is not really over. It leaves the reader feeling betrayed.

So in other words, the story is not really officially over until the bad guy gets exactly what's coming to them. By some means and mechanisms the bad guy is captured, judged, killed, put in jail, removed somehow. Evil is purged from the land. The armies of Mordor are finally defeated. The Ring to rule all rings destroyed. The Dark Lord Sauron is ignominiously destroyed.

The story is *also* not over until the Plaintiff gets restored to their former glory. Cinderella marries the handsome prince. Isildur's rightful heir Aragorn is crowned Elessar, King of Arnor and Gondor, and marries his longtime love, Arwen, daughter of Elrond. Middle Earth is restored to peace and tranquility, the threat of Mordor over. Now the story is done. Now the characters will at last be able to live happily ever after.

Tolkien also suggests that all lasting fairy tales have another wonderful attribute. In every great story there is a sudden joyous turn in the narrative where the story changes from being a tragedy and now moves toward the inevitable happy ending. This turn is not escapist or fugitive (or in modern terms repression or denial), rather it is a sudden and miraculous grace. This *eucatastrophe* (literally "a good catastrophe")

> "does not deny the existence of *dyscatastrophe*, of sorrow and failure: the possibility of these is necessary to the joy of deliverance; it denies...universal final defeat and in so far is *evangelium*, giving a fleeting glimpse of Joy, Joy beyond the walls of the world, poignant as grief. It is the mark of a good fairy-story, of the higher or more complete kind, that however wild its events, however fantastic or

---

[29]Tolkien helpfully offers the term "consolation" to define the state of being where justice is fully satisfied in the human soul. J. R. R. Tolkien, *Tree and Leaf, Smith of Wooton Major, the Homecoming of Beorhtnoth.* (London: Harper Collins Publishers, 2001), 68.

[30] B. Bettelheim, *The Uses of Enchantment: The Meaning and Importance of Fairy Tales.* (New York: Vintage Books, 1977), 144.

terrible the adventures, it can give to child or man that hears it, when the "turn" comes, a catch of the breath, a beat and lifting of the heart, near to (or indeed accompanied by) tears, as keen as that given by any form of literary art, and having a peculiar quality...It is not an easy thing to do; it depends on the whole story which is the setting of the turn, and yet it reflects a glory backwards."[31]

Plaintiff, imagine the possibility that you could experience such an unexpected awakening, a "turn" in your tale that takes your breath away, that lifts your beat-up heart, that reflects a glory backwards—that is a rewriting that redeems your earlier narrative—and gives it purpose and value. Listen carefully.

There is no mention of any required unilateral effort on your part—against your nature—to extend empathy to the undeserving perpetrator—or to forgive because you have been forgiven much.

Tolkien implies that interwoven into the fiber of every human being is an inherent and very clear need for injustices to be fully and objectively resolved *before* the Plaintiff can live happily ever after. It would be *dyscatastrophic* for one's tale to end without fair and complete judicial resolution; without a resolution beyond a just intrapersonal forgiveness forced from you. In other words, even if you come to the point after great effort to offer to the perpetrator the altruistic gift of forgiveness—you are still not free. Such *eucatastrophies* are in the wheelhouse of God alone.

For those who deny the presence of a God who regularly intervenes in lives and narratives, this might sound far-fetched. But for those of us with childlike faiths who really do know such a God, we have come to—or should have come to expect such an intervention.

Plaintiff, instead of working so hard on your own to "forgive" the crime (whatever that really looks like), it is far better to look forward to—by faith—a sudden joyous turn that extends to you an external consolation—a valid experience of an objective justice for that crime and an experience of a present, or a promise of future full restoration. In a word, "consolation." It is a capital "F" forgiveness that comes from a substantive and free heart. That is our goal in this book. Only such a capital "F" forgiveness can precede a real and honoring reconciliation.

For the most part, modern socio-psychological techniques—even overtly Christian ones—largely overlook the possibility—much less the necessity—of such an alien *eucatastrophic* intervention. Rather, they almost exclusively focus on the efforts of the beat-up Plaintiff alone to work out a self-designed and self-shaped decisional and emotional forgiveness.

---

[31] Tolkien, 69.

In the next chapter I want to expand on this assertion. Plaintiff, if you hear nothing else from this book, hear this! What you need is a miracle—a *eucatastrophic* miracle that changes the trajectory of your story from a tragedy to a happy ending. God can do this. There are answers to the three core questions, surprising answers.

Now I want to introduce you to the coffee lady.

Reflection Questions for Individuals or Groups

1) The author concludes that the offended party's need to forgive is a secondary concern as compared to the big three questions: "Where is justice for you?," "Where is the happy ending?," and "Who are you now in the aftermath of your loss?" Do you agree? Why or why not. Which one most resonates with you? Why?

2) Tolkien wrote of the necessity of an external surprising *eucatastrophic* intervention that alone can change the trajectory of a tragedy into a happy ending. Have you experienced such a *eucatastrophe* in your life? Please share it with the group. Can you think of biblical examples of God's *eucatastrophes*?

3) Modern forgiveness research measures forgiveness along three scales: 1) reduction in the offended party's desire to avoid the perpetrator, 2) reduction of offended party's desire to seek revenge and 3) the increase of a feeling of benevolence toward the perpetrator. Are these scales helpful? What are your thoughts? Are other scales missing? How is each related to forgiveness?

4) Compare and contrast the two models of forgiveness presented in the chapter,

> Model #1—forgiveness that requires the Plaintiff to first develop *empathy* for their perpetrator.

> Model #2—forgiveness that results from a pre-experience of *consolation.*

5) Can you find biblical examples of each of the two models? Which model describes best how God forgives sinners?

4

The Coffee Lady

I was very fortunate early in my ministry to have lived for over a decade in picturesque British Columbia. Early one morning, I decided to go out for a steaming hot thick cup of west coast java. It was so early that when I arrived at the beachfront coffee shop, it had not yet officially opened for the business day. The young, very attractive, coffee lady kindly let me in out of the breezy rain that regularly draped the White Rock coastline. I went to the back of the shop to study as I waited for the liquid black gold to brew.

Just as I sat down, another man burst in the door, stormed around the counter, and started yelling at the coffee lady; poking his finger into her chest. I got up and moved towards the coffee bar. He just as quickly left the shop—leaving her noticeably devastated.

I asked her if she wanted me to call the police. "No, no," she said, gathering her wits. "That's my live-in boyfriend. That's just his way." And then she calmly went back to making the coffee for the day. For me it was a surreal scene. Her calmness was unnerving to me. So I graciously inquired further about the event and the angry man. She felt comfortable enough to share significant details of her narrative. She confessed that she was raped by her father at 12, ran away from home at 13 in order to become part of a biker gang where she was passed from bike to bike. She had learned early on that her value was not based upon intrinsic worth but rather her utility to others. The abusive pinhead who was now her "boyfriend" was just the last in a long line of men who used her for their pleasure.

So here is the question. How would you counsel the coffee lady? Would you counsel her to strain against her better judgment to come up with some unreasonable empathy for her father—or for the long list of abusive men in her narrative? Would you counsel her to reframe how she sees her boyfriend so that she could forgive him?

If she were a Jesus-follower (by her own admission she was not) would you quote Jesus' words (out of context as I will show in a later chapter) that she must out of faithful obedience forgive each of her rapists seventy times seven times? Whether her father was sorry or not? Whether her former or current "boyfriends" truly repented or not? Certainly that can't be what Jesus had in mind when he said to all of those poor broken cups on the hillside by the Sea of Galilee,

> "But I tell you, do not resist an evil person. If someone strikes you on the right cheek, turn to him the other also." (Matt 5:39)

Certainly Jesus is not telling rape survivors who happened to be present to merely re-submit to more abusive treatment—is he? Of course not. That would be not only untenable, but horrifying.

Someone will likely argue that until the coffee lady forgives, she remains trapped by the past crimes; still enslaved by her oppressors. I would totally agree with you. Forgiveness is a great thing. I am pro-forgiveness. But the question on the table is "What is forgiveness?" How do Plaintiffs truly forgive? Perhaps there are multiple "forgivenesses." Maybe there are real and counterfeit ones. Remember counterfeits are only good to the extent that they really, really look like the real thing. But they are not the real thing. Plaintiff, do you really know what forgiveness is?

Here is the hard truth that must be considered as we proceed further— good and bad news for all true Plaintiffs. The coffee lady's cup had been so deeply violated for so many years that she had little to draw upon. Where would she even begin to find positive emotions toward her assailants?

She innately can't forgive! There, I said it. It isn't in her nature. Her "cup" has been so violated and drunk dry that she has nothing of substance left to magnanimously give anymore. She is a cracked empty vessel. I would argue that logically she shouldn't forgive until there has been an experience of consolation for her.

For the coffee lady to choose to forgive by sheer force of will, or to strain to find some emotional basis to forgive a crime apart from an experience of consolation—would be to go against the image of God in her. *Remember God never ever forgives until there has first been consolation.* Why would God require more of us?

Two Paths

Illustration 3

Jesus-follower, there are two broad philosophical approaches to a present experience of forgiveness for any and all crimes committed against you. Consider the two Cupology images above.

When a Plaintiff gives up their right of justice and unilaterally chooses to forgive the unrepentant Defendant, in Cupology terms it is as if he or she is pouring some of their precious remaining substance into the cup of the very person who robbed them in the first place. Since the forgiveness is unilateral, there is no pouring from the other cup—only a passive taking.

In the end, the Defendant (lower cup) is still not full, and the Plaintiff (upper cup) is painfully emptier.

In Cupology terminology, this is what modern forgiveness approaches largely encourage. Such a forgiveness does not fill the Defendant *or* the Plaintiff. It does not work.

How do counselors get emptied Plaintiff cups to buy in? It is packaged ultimately as the Plaintiff's biblical responsibility to unilaterally act out of faithful obedience that God would surely (hopefully) eventually bless. Perhaps with the help of a counselor, it is hoped that they would surprisingly develop empathy for the perpetrator that will motivate them to at last forgive, with or without any necessary participation of the perpetrator in any way. This first path could also include active prayers to God that He would be of *help* to you as you work hard to forgive.

This path is not inherently evil, in fact, there are many published cases where the participants *have* experienced significant measurable relief from pains and losses.

But to put it in Cupological terms, how could I ever ask you, or dare even invite you to choose to pour what little dignity that you have left into your perpetrator's cup—this time by your own choosing? How could I invite you to re-victimize yourself? This may be portrayed to you as Christ-like, as sacrificial—but it is actually a subtle re-victimization.

This book will present a second path—not at all antagonistic to the above and yet quite distinct. It is portrayed on the right side of Illustration 3, where the Plaintiff cup first runs to a free flowing abundant faucet to be filled up *before* they even think about dealing with the Defendant cup. *Full cups just do things differently.* What does this second path entail Plaintiff?

First you are invited to run to God as the Judge over all crimes and submit your case to His official timely jurisdiction. You are invited to enter your official day in court before God as the Plaintiff. Imagine that, *by faith,* you could experience an objective "right" trial for the crime(s) committed against you. Imagine you, *by faith,* sitting in front of the Judge's bench and being given the honor of voice, to tell Him what happened to you, what it felt like, what you want to happen next. There you sense no judgment, only compassion. He really hears you. Imagine hearing the Judge's verdict against the perpetrator—perfect un-emotional right justice. The *Aaaah! Factor.*

Second, Jesus-follower, by faith run to God as the source of your value, worth, and glory and have your cup experientially filled with the fullness of God (Eph 3:19) again, and again through His Spirit. Look again at the right-hand of the Illustration 2. In this case, the emptied Plaintiff cup is positioning itself underneath a faucet with an endless supply of liquid. That wholeness was purchased for you by Jesus some 2000 years ago. All theologians agree that such consolation, such peace, such restoration to wholeness from all crimes, will of course be yours in heaven. The theological term is "glorification."

"Kabod"

In the Old Testament, one of the main Hebrew words translated "glory" is *kabod*, literally it means "weight." A person of substance, value, social standing can be described as weighty.

So the point is this. Plaintiff, when you die and are raised to heaven, all of the weightiness that has been robbed from you, or you tragically gave away, will be restored. You will enter heaven "weighty."

Through the Holy Spirit in you—by faith—you can actually experience a foretaste of your future glorification—now! By faith, you have the right as a son or daughter of God (Gal 4:3-5, Eph 3:14-21) to access a remarkable life-changing foretaste of the consolation *now*.

This present powerful experience of the work of Christ available to you is largely unknown in Christian circles unfortunately. For the most part it is probably fair to observe that far too many Christians today function as *deists*. We know that we are saved (in the past). We accept that we will be made whole when we die and go to heaven (in the future), but the present benefits of being filled with His Spirit during this time in-between the two becomes a bit confusing.

One wonders after studying many modern pastors and theologians, if we no longer really think that Jesus' life, death and resurrection has any value to us right now. Do most of us functionally live our lives hardly expectant of any intervention by God on our behalf? But this is horrible theology. Let me briefly illustrate.

Paul's Single Prayer for the Ephesians

In the first century, just decades after Jesus' death and resurrection, the apostle Paul wrote provocatively to an endangered fledgling church in Ephesus. Of all of the things that he might have chosen to emphasize regarding their needs, he focuses on one. This small church in Ephesus, which will be the subject of great oppression and persecution (i.e., victimization) needed power—not a power from themselves but from God. Plaintiff, listen carefully.

> "I pray that out of his glorious riches he may strengthen you with power through his Spirit in your inner being, so that Christ may dwell in your hearts through faith. And I pray that you, being rooted and established in love, may have power, together with all the saints, to grasp how wide and long and high and deep is the love of Christ, and to know this love that surpasses knowledge—that you may be filled to the measure of all the fullness of God." (Eph 3:16-21)

This will be developed more in the Chapter on the Epistles. Isn't Paul speaking directly to you Plaintiff? The crime has robbed you of substantive power, identity, worth and value. Here Paul speaks of a spiritual power that is not *yours* per-se. No, it "resides"—that is, is accessible to you now by faith—in your inner being as a Christian. You can begin to actually feel strong again, honored—More than you can possibly imagine, much more than the perpetrator could ever begin to pay.

Next, Paul speaks to you of the capability of that external power to access the immensely vast love of Christ for you—a love that is as equally sacrificial and compassionate toward them as well as toward the believing perpetrator (in Christ).

Paul *never* tells Plaintiffs that they must, through helpful cognitive therapeutic exercises squeeze out some paltry empathy and emotional forgiveness for their perpetrator. Instead, Paul invites you to first run to God (the Holy Spirit in them) to access His power and His love for themselves *and* remarkably enough--the perpetrator.

Paul kindles our imaginations to see that it is from God, not the offender, and not brilliant interventions, and not even our own efforts, that we can access this wholeness from God.

Let me be very clear about this—and not be misunderstood. Restoration to literally pre-crime status is *never* promised in the Bible, but being made whole by the dynamic equivalence of the fullness of God himself *is* promised. In heaven, you will be perfectly and eternally filled to the fullness of God. But for now, by faith, you can begin to access a portion of that perfect fullness.

Paul sees the obvious connection between the death and resurrection of Jesus, the subsequent sending of the Spirit and the invitation to you who are Jesus-followers to come to God—by faith—to experience that wholeness. It is to the one already made whole by the fullness of God, who is to some degree experiencing the vast love of Christ for themselves and their perpetrator that Paul can say,

> "Be kind and compassionate to one another, forgiving each other, just as in Christ God forgave you." (Eph 4:32)

The stark wild implied truth of Paul's teaching is that you *cannot* forgive even the smallest of offense unless you have first helplessly and passively experienced the two-fold consolation of God: objective, full-orbed justice and the filling from the fullness of God (Eph 3:19). Here he is not specifically referring to the gifts of the Spirit per se.

To be filled with the Spirit is to tap into the vast fruit of the Spirit: love, joy, peace, patience, kindness, goodness, faith, gentleness and self-control (Gal 5:22-23). Only then can you truly feel the height and width, the length and depth of the love of Christ purchased for you now, as you are right now. This is a powerful awareness of your value to God, your new identity, and your worth. Surprisingly, this is far more substantial than what the perpetrator took from you.

The Coffee Lady

You can access such a powerful filling right now, through the faith given to you when you became a follower. Why haven't you? Could it be that you have not because you have asked not (James 4:2)?

You Foolish Galatians (Gal 3:1)

All I am suggesting is that there is another approach that is miraculously better than even the best of modern socio-psychological approaches. There is a forgiveness experience that is beyond your imagination. In Galatians 3, Paul blasts the Galatians for living their Christian lives as if God was not even there. Listen:

> "You foolish Galatians! Who has bewitched you? Before your very eyes Jesus Christ was clearly portrayed as crucified. I would like to learn just one thing from you: Did you receive the Spirit by observing the law, or by believing what you heard? Are you so foolish? After beginning with the Spirit, are you now trying to attain your goal by human effort? Have you suffered so much for nothing—if it really was for nothing? Does God give you his Spirit and work miracles among you because you observe the law, or because you believe what you heard?" (Gal 3:1-5)

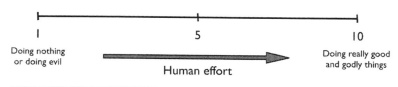

Figure 6- "Observing the Law" Spectrum (Galatians 3:1-5)

What is Paul referring to by the phrase "observing the law?" This is illustrated in Figure 6 above. The horizontal scale goes from 1-10. At the one end (left), the Christian does nothing, or acts ungodly. At the other end of the scale (right), the Christian commits to do good things—God-pleasing things: actions, words and thoughts that reflect godliness and righteousness.

According to this figure, if you do nothing to please God or disobey the law (on the left) then you should expect no blessings from God. On the other hand, if you are pious, and do all that you thought God requires of you (on the right), you have every reason to expect that your spiritual life would really take off.

Surprisingly, Paul curses this formula as another different gospel—which is not the gospel at all (Gal 1:6-9). If there were indeed no God, this spectrum is as good as it gets. It is after all the foundation of all pagan beliefs. If you scratch the back of the god, they will (sometimes) scratch yours.

But we live in the presence of a great and wonderful God, a God who delights in *eucatastrophes* for His children. Paul had told the Galatians about that God and His Son Jesus. They had experienced a stunning observable *eucatastrophe*, a miraculous redemption to salvation and sonship (Gal 3:1-5).

But, very shortly after Paul had left, Christian moralists (from James they said) arrived arguing that if the new Christians *really* wanted to please God, if they *really* wanted to be first class Christians, and earn God's blessings for their lives, they were to work harder to earn God's favor by the formula. Their logic might something like this:

> "Sure you are a Christian by Christ alone, but if you really want to move forward in Christ, if you want your spiritual life to really take off, you need to do such godly things as being circumcised, giving to charity, following the Jewish codified food laws, and the rest of the Law. Then your spiritual life will really take off."

Today we might interpretively translate the phrase,
> "...doing godly things so that God will take notice of you and give you what you deserve because of your disciplined good works."

Galatians, did God give you His Spirit because you did all of these religious good and godly things? No. He gave His Spirit to you unilaterally. You weren't doing any good things to tell you the truth, not according to God's perfect scale. And yet now, that you are a born-again believer, *now* you think that you can at last do godly things that earn you more than Jesus has already earned for you? Do you truly despise the cross that much?

Do you still think that if you do godly things that God will love you more than He loves you right now? Isn't all the love in the universe— which has already been earned for you by Christ—enough for you? It is absurd that you think that you can add to your Christ-record now by working harder. Rather, by faith, live out of the abundant treasure trove that the Spirit has for you right now.

In other words, you silly people, do you remember who God is? What happened that you became so arrogant so quickly? Or that you began to think so highly of your ability to do good works—that might impress Him. Seriously? If you want to live on that horizontal axis, then don't be disappointed when you don't get what you hoped for.

You see, for Paul, part of your rights and privileges as adopted children of God (Gal 4:4-6) is that you are no longer stuck on that horizontal scale. Before you were saved, you lived by implicit cause and effect rules. If you did nothing good, or in fact did evil deeds, then you expected to be punished by God.

On the other hand, if you took the opposite approach and religiously did good things, obeyed the law of God, then you expected that God would be pleased with your actions and bless you accordingly. Right?

But now, after your adoption, Paul argues, God's love and favor is no longer conditionally based upon your good works. Legally, God's love and favor toward you is solely conditional upon Christ's good work on your behalf. Get it?

God's favor *is* totally conditional to obedience and faithfulness—not your—but Jesus' on your behalf. Jesus perfectly completed all of those conditions and so now God (humanly speaking) must love you immensely. Now because of the faithfulness of Jesus, God loves you as much as He loves his own Son.

And so now there is another opposite of doing nothing or doing evil. The *other opposite* is to—by faith—expect miracles to happen among you. God has given you His Spirit. You can access the Spirit's fruit. If you really want to experience the spiritual life that you had at the beginning, repent of all of your conditional hard works and run to be filled with the Spirit again. Then miracles will happen again (see Figure 7 below). Do you see?

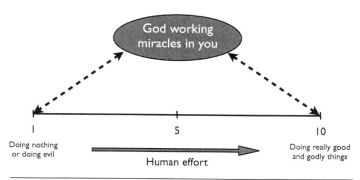

Figure 7- "Observing the Law" Spectrum (Galatians 3:1-5) Post-Cross

Paul provocatively imagines a second opposite to doing nothing or doing evil for Jesus-followers who have the indwelling Spirit of Christ. In fact, it is also an *opposite of doing good* works in order to earn God's favor as well.

The choices for you are no longer limited to doing nothing on the one side and working hard to do godly things on the other side.

Paul says the whole spectrum is—in a word—foolish. Not evil—stupid. At its heart though, it is a faithless denial of the presence of God's *eucatastrophic* Spirit in your inner-being. Paul urges the Galatians to remember that by faith they can experience God doing miraculous works in them.

You Foolish Plaintiff

So let me apply this notion to forgiveness. Jesus-follower Plaintiff, you have a choice. You can work really hard to be faithfully obedient to forgive the perpetrator seventy times seven times, turn the other cheek all in hopes that God will bless your heroic yet pitiful efforts, or you can first run to God in your hapless need and access His power. A miracle. What could such miraculous works look like? Feel like?

Do not misunderstand my point. Doing nothing, or doing evil, does not set you free. For you to be healed, for you to taste the freedom of God's forgiveness through you, you must choose to participate. Sanctification[32] is a participative sport. You are only to enter the forgiveness process humbled, helpless, and needing a rescuer. But your ultimate goal is no longer limited to your heroic efforts. Isn't this stunning good news? The goal is that a miracle would take place in your beat-up heart.

Imagine what that might feel like. It should feel like a miracle done on your behalf by the God who loves you far more than you have ever loved yourself. He hates the crime against you far more than you do—because He alone notes your perfect worth. He alone being the creator, can re-create what was taken from you. Isn't this good news?

But Wait, There's More!

But wait—at the risk of sounding like an infomercial—there is more! You may also begin to personally experience an alien new shocking compassion toward your perpetrator. I know, at this stage of the process this may cause you to want to run or throw up. I understand the reaction and beg your patience. At this stage just file that away.

I am not ordering you to feel compassion for someone who has hurt you so deeply. In fact, I would observe that it is humanly impossible on your own.

But God has the capacity and the desire to empower and motivate you to feel toward the perpetrator the way that He Himself does. He can give

---

[32] Per the Westminster Shorter Catechism of Faith, sanctification is the work of God's free grace, whereby we are renewed in the whole man, after the image of God, and are enabled more and more to die unto sin, and live unto righteousness. In Cupology terms, it is the process of having our emptied cups filled time and again with the fullness of God (Eph 3:19-21).

you His compassion for the perpetrator. "For it is God who works in you to will and to act according to his good purpose (Phil 2:13)." Plaintiff, imagine actually wanting to reconcile (of course where it is wise and safe) with the one who hurt you—with God's external vast "want to."

In the end, many of the socio-psychological techniques and models are very helpful and godly. But in the end, they fall short of the miraculous. Plaintiff, child of God, you have every right to—by faith—demand the miraculous.

So the coffee lady, and you Plaintiff, can't forgive—not really—until there is real consolation no matter how much reframing you can accomplish by sheer force of will. You can't really "pass on" forgiveness based upon your experience of forgiveness from others—not really. On the other hand, you can—through faith—powerfully and experientially access a miraculous consolation from God. It is so easy.

I have seen rape survivors access such consolation from God. I have witnessed an attempted murder survivor access such forgiveness toward his assailant—his own son. I have had a front row seat to see multiple survivors of affairs access forgiveness from God toward their offending spouses. These are stunning miracles of immense proportions beyond human capacity. In each case, the offended parties would agree that they were powerfully touched by the hand of God. In the end, the formerly tragic trajectory of their narrative was changed. They were vectored in a new direction—towards a previously unbelievable (Eph 3:20-21) happy ending.

Consolation: **The Biblical End Game?**

In the next few chapters I will unpack the Biblical understanding of the process of forgiveness. Would it surprise you to hear that there is a God who cares dearly for you? That He loves you far more than anyone else has ever loved you—far more than you have ever loved yourself? He sees your pain, what was taken from you. He alone has the capacity to restore what was taken. In fact, as you will see, He is committed to your wholeness. Isn't this stunning, almost unbelievable good news? He is also committed to your happy ending.

Do not give up on His intervention. Listen to what He has always had in mind for you. What you deeply, deeply want is the *consolation* that comes from His hand.

Doesn't this make sense? Isn't this hopeful? You no doubt have tried really hard to forgive your perpetrator many times and in many ways. You have read the myriad of books on forgiveness and have tried to give the altruistic gift of forgiveness to the perpetrator—but you cannot to date ignore the nagging cry of your soul that refuses to forgive until the scales of fairness are rebalanced and a legitimate restoration to reasonable wholeness has been experienced in some manner. Your deepest DNA demands *consolation*. God is the only author of such consolation. That is perfectly normal and perfectly human.

Good news. As a Christian you are not limited to human judicial processes and institutions. You are not limited by how well you succeed at your victim-centric, empathy-driven (VCED) therapy. You can now, by faith, *imperfectly* access *perfect* celestial forgiveness and begin to experience a much higher forgiveness—a foretaste of promised future *consolation*. Human justice, no matter how rational, sophisticated or objective, is flawed and often causes more injustices than it satisfies.

Hear this. There exists a perfect justice—an immense completed *consolation* that is available to you—as you are right now—through the faith given to you already when you were redeemed—which can actually provide a present experience of your future eternal peace, i.e., *shalom.*[33]

This "alien" justice[34] is perfectly accomplished in the two watershed judicial events: first, Jesus' perfect judicial work on the Cross and second, the future final judgment. By use of the terms alien, external and objective, it is meant that this *consolation* is not dependent upon either the offender or offended. This *consolation* is not dependent upon the world's justice system. This *consolation* is available, by faith to all Christian Plaintiffs and Christian Defendants for any offense—no matter how extensive, damaging or complex the offense may have been.

Apart from these two external judicial events, full justice—the consolation desired deep in your heart—and required in the heart of your offender, is impossible. On the other hand, with an appropriate grasp on these two events and the application by faith to day-to-day offenses, even the most helpless Christian Plaintiff—as you are—can presently experience a radical justice (though perhaps partial) that allows for radical empathetic and emotional forgiveness and ultimately radical restoration to intimate community.

Cupology 101 Case Study #4: Heaven

Imagine a huge vibrant sea, a sea of life giving substance, value, worth, identity, wholeness, and intimacy. This is the essence of the height and length, depth and width of the love of Christ that you have tasted at

---

[33] Shalom is a very broad Hebrew word that could refer to peace, fullness, wholeness, satisfaction, even reconciliation of community.
[34] My use of the word "alien" could be misunderstood. I am referring here to a justice that is external to us and to our efforts. It is innately God's but "alien" with regard to humanity.

moments here on earth. As you gaze out at the ocean, you notice that it is littered, just beneath the surface with myriad of cups, all different shapes, sizes, colors and textures—all broken to some degree. But now they are all full, in fact fully immersed in the life-giving ocean. They are filled inside and out with God's fullness. This is heaven.

In heaven, Jesus-follower Plaintiff, you will fully be embraced by His external consolation. You will be fully restored to wholeness and what the bad guy has taken will be put back in some dynamic equivalence. You will be made full with all the fullness of God (Eph 3:19-21).

Imagine with me for a moment. And when such a Healing Spirit comes upon you, you will be enthralled by the fact that at its foundation is stunning dynamic and powerful "justice." In that state, in that place, there will be no more tears, no more struggles, the former things will have passed away (Rev 21:4). Your aching soul will be silenced and will require no more from anyone, including the one who hurt you. Someone else will have paid you back what was owed.

In fact, God is the only one with pockets deep enough to pay you restitution. The one who hurt you could have done very little to restore what was taken. When the Spirit makes you whole, you are whole. Imagine what that will feel like.

All this book is saying is by faith, Jesus-follower, you can miraculously begin to access a very powerful experiential foretaste of that consolation now. Simple right? It changes everything.

That statement is penetrated by great fresh hope—a hope that is beyond any hope in your own efforts—no matter how brave and how "forgiving" you might have been to date. By faith, you can experience now a surprising life-changing foretaste of your future wholeness.

I have applied these truths pastorally to many persons and situations; from rape survivors to attempted murder survivors, to abused spouses, abused children, to those who have experienced deep betrayals. While every case is unique, every wound massive and complicated, the similarities are stunning.

Someone did something, took something away from, or put an unwanted burden upon you without permission—and to one degree or another you have not experienced consolation. No matter what you have done or not done, your violated self is screaming for a resolution of the scales in your soul. Until that occurs—you cannot rest—you cannot truly move on as a free person. One of the greatest aspects of the gospel of Jesus Christ is that you can by faith access a powerful foretaste of your future consolation now. A glorious *eucatastrophe* from God Himself.

This does not invalidate all of your efforts to-date necessarily. This does not take your perpetrator off the hook, at all. In fact, it is just the opposite

53

as will be explained. This does not invalidate the helpfulness of professional counselors and doctors for any specific situation.

Does This Imply That You Have Not Already Forgiven the One Who Hurt You?

It never fails that some people who hear me lecture ask—often very defensively, "Are you saying that I have not forgiven my rapist? I believe that I have, I worked very hard to forgive them. You seem to be invalidating all of my efforts." Absolutely not.

First You Make a Roux!

It is the eleventh commandment in my birth-state Louisiana. Other cultures of course make sauces out of cooked flour and oil (béchamel, velouté as well as many white sauces)—but in Louisiana we do not just make sauces—anyone can do that—no we make a roux. The roux is *the* foundation of the recipe. It is the heart and soul. There are other ingredients of course. But none as important. First you make a roux.

Mechanically, the cook takes equal parts of flour and oil and cooks them in a pan until the right color and smell is produced—all the while stirring like a madman. Scientifically what happens in the mix is that the hot oil breaks down the starch granulesin. The latter absorbs the liquids added later, creating a thick rich sauce. But it is more than a "sauce." It is a cult. Aileen McInnis captures the importance of the roux:

> "You don't eat roux by itself. Roux is a base that you add ingredients to and is used in all kinds of cooking, all around the world...Louisiana cooking uses mostly a darker roux for the nutty, kick-ass flavor that makes a gumbo really taste like a gumbo, or gives an etouffeé that distinctive earthy flavor. 'First you make a roux' has prefaced so many recipes in Louisiana cooking that it has become a cliché. 'How does a Cajun make love?' the joke goes. 'First he makes a roux.'"[35]

When I make gumbo, I begin with a 50/50 mixture of good flour and high quality corn oil in a cast iron skillet. I turn the heat to medium high and use a metal whisk to keep the mixture consistent and to avoid any burning. There is debate in Creole cooking circles where the actual boundary of being "burnt" lies. The process can take anywhere from 30 minutes to an hour and results in a dark chocolaty brown viscous mixture—almost swamp-water colored. But the aroma is intoxicating—a

---

[35] http://www.killerrubboard.com/magazine/magroux.html

rich toasty redolence drapes over the kitchen. There are—for the serious cooks—actual color charts available.

McInnis claims that the gold standard for roux comes from a Cajun-influenced community in Girdwood Alaska, whose Double Musky is almost black. The chef may have used butter instead of vegetable oil, or a wooden gravy whisk instead of a metal one. He may have chosen a lighter shade of rich brown versus my ideal of almost dark chocolate color—the lighter colors tend to thicken more. But beneath the later gumbo additions-- shrimp, crab, the Cajun "holy trinity" of onion, bell pepper and celery— must be the necessary integrative substructure of the roux. It is the difference between soup and gumbo.

The point is this. The real question is not whether you have truly forgiven before now or not. The goal is the freedom and restoration that comes from accessing real forgiveness. If you have experienced such a release, praise God.

What happened behind the scenes, deep in your inner being was undoubtedly similar to Cupology 101—though you may have been totally unaware. If you have forgiven with dignity, that implies that somehow God has intervened to refill your cup from what the perpetrator took. You didn't pursue it, you didn't specifically take the steps in this book. But still God filled your cup and now you feel whole again.

In roux-terms, you may have had gumbo or etouffeé in restaurants, without even knowing that the chef cared enough about his or her craft to put the important time in to stir like crazy for 30 minutes in order to bless you with a proper roux. You may not have done good research to determine if the restaurant had real roux—but nevertheless—"fat, dumb and happy" (as we say in the bayous) your lucky stomach was filled with the real stuff and you will never be the same. For such is the power of a legitimate roux.

If you have experienced such a filling and miraculous other-empowered consolation, then this book will be sweet music to your ears. This explains perhaps what you are feeling.

Plaintiff, it is not my plan to provide a single formulaic path to forgiveness—rather a Biblical trajectory that can lead you into the healing presence of God. The goal is not how-to-steps—rather the goal is to raise your hope that a real miracle can take place—a miracle that was promised to adopted sons and daughters of God through the work of Jesus' life, death and resurrection.

Back to the Coffee Lady

Now I am poignantly aware that all of this will sound largely strange to most Jesus-followers much less to those who are not. I have wondered how the coffee lady might respond to such outlandishly hopeful possibilities. She had been deeply conditioned by her extensive history of tragic dehumanizing abuse to the point where at some level—to some degree— she devalued and objectified herself.

She would not, or could not imagine an external being who might be favorable toward her, who could see her value as a glorious human being with great worth and substance, without her doing anything to earn His favor. She had no concept of a God who would dare to love her as she was right now. But to some degree we are all the coffee lady. All of us have been devalued by people in our context—our narrative. Paul reminds us that though saved, we still live in a present evil age (Gal 1:4). To some degree each of us—including we Jesus-followers, have come to devalue ourselves as well. Tragic.

So my hope in writing this book is to inject the possibility of such good news into the ongoing conversation—even if at first it might be mocked as too good to believe.

A Question for Non-Christians at This Point

A word to those who read the book—who are not Jesus-followers. Let me ask you a question. If such an alien experience of forgiveness and consolation is available to Jesus-followers, what could possibly be in the way of you enthusiastically pursuing this path? What could possibly be keeping you from further intellectual pursuit of Jesus? Seriously, what has your current philosophy of life, or lack of any specific philosophy of life done for you? How's it going for you, really?

This does not resolve all of the complicated issues and conflicts of faith, and in particular the historic Christian faith. This does not in anyway suggest that churches aren't riddled with hypocrites. I confess, I am one of the many.

This does not in any way try to defend the Crusades, or the ongoing mistreatment of many people groups committed in the name of Christ. We Christians have huge issues. I get that totally.

"Many paths to God, to love," you say? To tell you the honest truth, looking around the globe today and even throughout human history, I only see shallow fingerprints of anything that looks like many paths to love. Which of those so-called multiple paths have truly helped you, restored your wholeness, and peace, and value and worth to you? If you find a better path than the one described here. Run into it with all of your energies and being.

Or have you been looking for love and justice in all the wrong places until now? Consider that there is a solid path that is open to all Plaintiffs who are willing to run to Jesus with cries of help. Come as you are into His arms and be filled. Join the rest of us recovering Plaintiffs who have come to see that this path is transformative. Just a thought.

Biblical Forgiveness That Does Not Cause You to Lose Any More Dignity

Plaintiff, the Bible never requires you to "forgive" unrepentant, unremorseful perpetrators. God never does. So why would God require His people to be more magnanimous then Himself? You will never, ever be required to give up your rights to justice. God does not. If God could just wave His hand and forgive sin—then why did Jesus have to pay such a deep price?

Plaintiff, biblically the weight of forgiveness is *not* carried on your shoulders. In fact, the burden of forgiveness is carried by God Himself. It is God who has the capacity to fill cups after all. God as the Judge of the Universe alone can bring about an objective and thorough justice. He has promised already to purge evil, to punish the unrepentant and to restore all diminished parties to wholeness. Forgiveness is innate to God's very DNA. Biblically speaking, Plaintiff, you cannot forgive. But you can access such a forgiveness that is a fruit of God's Spirit.

Six Propositions

In summary, there are six Cupological propositions that undergird this book's philosophy of Biblical forgiveness:

> **Proposition 1:** All violations—no matter how small—cause cup-reduction.

> **Proposition 2:** There can be no forgiveness until the cup-reduction has—at least imperfectly—been remedied.

> **Proposition 3:** All Plaintiffs are made in the image of God and therefore are of great value and worth. So any cup-reduction is beyond the capacity of any human or court to fill.

> **Proposition 4:** God promises a filling for all cups through a just consolation. Consolation entails evil being purged, the guilty punished, and the Plaintiff restored to fullness.

Proposition 5: By faith, through the Holy Spirit, Plaintiffs can to a large degree begin to experience refilling of their cup *now*.

Proposition 6: Cups refilled by the Holy Spirit have a fresh, new, powerful vantage point to consider appropriate and safe next steps. Only whole cups—or cups made experientially more whole again—can really forgive. An experience of forgiveness and the motivation to pursue a safe and dignified reconciliation are—at the end of the day—fruit of God's Spirit in you.

Reflection Questions for Individuals or Groups

1)   The author implies that those who have been diminished by crimes can by faith run to God in order to be re-filled in some dynamic equivalence. What are your thoughts about this possibility? Doesn't it sound just too easy?

2)   From examples in your own life, compare what is being illustrated in Figure 6 (above) versus Figure 7 (above). Some have commented that at first blush this is very counter-intuitive. What do you think?

3)   Based upon your answers to Questions 1 and 2, what would you say to the coffee lady? Describe the concept of *consolation* to her in your own words? How do you think she might respond? What might a miraculous *eucatastrophe* from God look like to her?

PART TWO

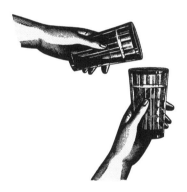

Forgiveness in the Old Testament

5

Cupology and Consolation in the Old Testament

Plaintiff, as we go through the Old Testament's understanding of forgiveness hear this up front:

- You will never be asked or commanded by God to forgive the one who hurt you until you have experienced some sort of the full-orbed justice that we defined in the last chapters.

- You will never be asked to give up your right to any justice.

- You will never be required or even encouraged to reframe the crime or the criminal

- You will never be cajoled or expected to feel empathy for an unremorseful Defendant.

But isn't God compassionate? Aren't His mercies renewed every morning?

Sure. Absolutely. That is truth. But what does God's compassion really look like? Where the rubber meets the road, what does His mercy look like for guilty offenders? For beat-up plaintiffs? Remember Ex 34:6-7? God is proclaiming his brief autobiography to Moses—and to us. Who is God?

> "The Lord, the Lord, the compassionate and gracious God, slow to anger, abounding in love and faithfulness, maintaining love to thousands, and forgiving wickedness, rebellion and sin. Yet he does not leave the guilty unpunished; he punishes the children and their children for the sin of the fathers to the third and fourth generation."

There is no conflict at all within the nature of God between His compassion and his rich complete justice. He does not make a choice between them when people sin (i.e., commit a crime against Him). God requires objective and compassionate justice and consolation.

Today, in the Western world, we regularly pit compassion against justice. Justice (usually imagined as exclusively retributive) has no heart—it goes by the letter of the law. Our modern human judicial institutions can express mercy only by alleviating the letter of the law justice requirements. Right? These are modern human concepts of justice and mercy that are to some degree out-of-sync with God's nature. God is *fully* merciful and *fully* just—with no compromise implied whatsoever.

Plaintiff, the God of the Old Testament *never* requires more of you than He requires of Himself. God *never* looks at those who commit crimes against Him and just "chooses to forgive." He *never* gives up His right to justice. He *never* gives to the guilty an altruistic gift of forgiveness—not in the modern sense. *Never*.

He *never* reframes the criminal and crime seeking to understand the sinner's motives and context—hoping that He would begin to feel empathy for them. He already perfectly knows their motives. "No one is righteous, no not one." "No one seeks God" (Rom 3:11). He knows the rebellious self-centered heart of His wayward corrupted image bearer. As the Judge, the one who wrote the law as a reflection of His Nature, He will adjudicate all sinners according to the same standard. If you are guilty of unrighteousness, rebellion and sin, by word, deeds or motivations, then the law requires the same penalty—*death*.

> "For God will bring every deed into judgment, including every hidden thing, whether it is good or evil." (Ecc 12:14)

But can't God just choose to forgive? Just wave His hand over the whole mess and say,

"You are guilty as sin—you deserve death—but in my empathy and mercy, I can see that it was just your upbringing. You didn't have a perfect childhood, you were raised on the harsh streets, this is all you knew. It was the anger in your heart—not you. So I gratuitously ignore the law and just forgive you."

No absolutely not!

Plaintiff, this is such good news. Why? Because if God Himself does not gratuitously forgive criminals through a unilateral altruistic gift, how can you ever be asked to be more magnanimously "merciful" than God? You are made in His image and likeness, and it is not in you.

But wait? Where is mercy? Where is God's compassion? His kindness? I beg your patience. I promise to get to these questions later in this chapter.

Horizontal Forgiveness in the Old Testament

Most people are surprised to find that examples of horizontal forgiveness *between* people are virtually absent in the Old Testament. In fact, in the entire Old Testament there are only seven references to people explicitly forgiving other people, and none that reflect the modern victim-centered, empathy-driven (VCED) approach.

Proverbs twice suggests that for one person to forgive sins[36] of another is an act of love (10:12; 17:19). Joseph's brothers out of fear lied that their father had given them a message to Joseph just before he died, "I ask you to forgive the sins[37] of your brothers" (Gen 50:17). Pharaoh (Ex 10:17) pleads to Moses to forgive his sins.[38] In 1 Sam 15:25, Saul pleads for Samuel's forgiveness.[39] Abigail begs David to forgive the sins[40] of her foolish husband (1 Sam 25:28). Shimei (2 Sam 19:18-19), in fear of David's retribution bids him to forgive (literally to not remember[41]) his betrayal.[42]

That's the entire Old Testament record of explicit examples of—or directions on—"horizontal forgiving."

---

36 lit., to cover the sins: *casa pesha*
37 lit. to lift the sins off: *nasa pesha*
38 lit. to lift the sins off: *nasa chata'a*
39 lit. to lift the sins off: *nasa chata'a*
40 Lit., to lift the sins off: *nasa pesha*
41 Hebrew: *chashav.*
42 Hebrew: *zachar*

The five references in historic narratives are hardly examples that can star in how-to books. There is no moral at the end of the account where we can say now, "Go and do likewise!"

The two instances mentioned in Proverbs do not give us any real guidelines to speak of at all. We only learn that forgiveness is a really good thing.

But how do Plaintiffs forgive? How are Defendants freed from guilt and shame? Not a great deal of immediate help, it would seem.

Doesn't this feel like a massive gap? Vertical forgiveness—God's desire to forgive rebellious humanity—is virtually everywhere in the text. There is no more important topic in the 39 Old Testament books than how the crimes of mankind against a Holy God can be forgiven.

Isn't this interesting? In the entire Old Testament, there are only seven largely unhelpful passages that speak to the topic of forgiveness *between* individuals.

Here is my observation. Though there are only seven texts that reflect what we *typically mean* by "forgiveness," there are multiple passages that deal with resolution of crimes involving Tolkien-esque *consolation* driven by God himself on the behalf of His helpless, unforgiving people. The point is this. The Old Testament writers imagined forgiveness differently.

Cupology: Torahic Case Law about Breach of Trust

We do have one thing in common with our predecessors. Three thousand years ago, people were still people. They still took advantage of each other, still selfishly used and mistreated others, still were greedy and still defrauded others when they thought they could get away with it. Forgiveness is as necessary now as it was 3000 years ago. Leviticus 6 gives us a great insight into some typical case law in Moses' day.

"The Lord said to Moses: 'If anyone sins and is unfaithful to the Lord by deceiving his neighbor about something entrusted to him or left in his care or stolen, or if he cheats him, or if he finds lost property and lies about it, or if he swears falsely, or if he commits any such sin that people may do—when he thus sins and becomes guilty, he must return what he has stolen or taken by extortion, or what was entrusted to him, or the lost property he found, or whatever it was he swore falsely about. He must make restitution in full, add a fifth of the value to it and give it all to the owner on the day he presents his guilt offering. And as a penalty he must bring to the priest, that is, to the Lord, his guilt offering, a ram from the flock, one without defect and of the proper value.'" (Lev 6:1-6)

Jud v. Azariah

So just for fun let me put together a fictional incident that would be covered by this case law. Being a pious Jew, Jud had been planning all year to go to the annual Feast of Booths in Jerusalem. A shepherd by trade, he would have to barter a significant portion of his annual profits he earned from the milk of his goats and the wool of his few sheep to be able to rent a booth and to feed his family while in the Royal City of God, Jerusalem. He would pick his best goat for an offering and of course he would have to find someone to care for his remaining sheep and goats the month that he and his family were away.

His neighbor Azariah wasn't going this year and was very happy to care for Jud's farm for a slight fee of course. They made a covenant in the presence of witnesses and Jud was now free for the two-day difficult journey to Jerusalem. A month later, when Jud and his family returned to their small farm, they were met with some very bad news. According to Azariah, a couple of Jud's prize goats came down with something and died suddenly. Azariah burned them whole—of course not wanting the illness to spread. What else could he do—the deaths were not his fault.

Jud was normally a very trusting man, but as he inquired deeper, he felt that Azariah's story didn't hold water. The first clue was that new cashmere sweater that Mrs. Azariah was sporting—that looked suspiciously like one of Jud's former prize black goats. He also had a visit from another neighbor that spoke about a huge BBQ dinner that was held at his farm a few weeks past.

Jud had heard enough and confronted Azariah with his suspicions. Azariah denied the charges and even swore in front of witnesses an oath that he had been absolutely faithful with his charge.

In today's context, Jud might be encouraged to come to grips with the hurt and anger caused by such betrayal, such a loss, such perjury. He might be reminded that as bad as the crime was, he too was not perfect by any stretch of the imagination. He had made many bad decisions in the past and had for the most part experienced broad forgiveness.

"Remember Jud, you just participated in the Day of Atonement at the Temple of God Himself. Didn't you witness the slaughter of the goat offering by the High Priest representing God's payment for your crimes? You didn't pay for them did you? The goat did, right? God's mercy for your many sins. Wouldn't it be a good thing, then, to forgive Azariah's alleged great sin since you have been forgiven much?"

Somewhere in the counseling, he would be instructed that he must intentionally decide to forgive Azariah.

"Jud you must unilaterally choose not to pursue justice anymore. Give up your right to restitution and vindication. You can't have both forgiveness and justice. Stop ruminating on the betrayal. Choose to forgive. Maybe, Azariah desperately needed the money. Maybe he was too ashamed to be able to admit his crimes. Maybe something else was going on that you just aren't aware of. Can you walk a mile in Azariah's sandals? God is compassionate, Jud. So can't you likewise feel compassion on your fellow Jew and forgive Azariah?"

A compelling modern case for an ancient emptied cup. Right?

Old Testament Forgiveness: God Never Gives Up His Right to Justice

The problem with the modern victim-centered, empathy driven (VCED) approach is that there is *no evidence* of it in the Old Testament.

Moses would have never advised Jud to unilaterally forgive Azariah. Judaism is adamant about the absurdity of requiring a Plaintiff to forgive an unrepentant Defendant. Rather, the Plaintiff for their own well-being and the well-being of the entire community (including the Defendant) is expected to take the Defendant to court.

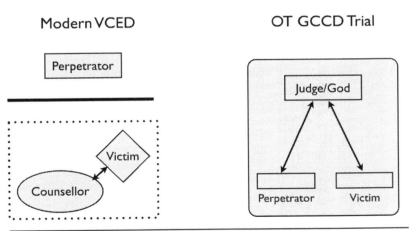

Figure 8- Contrast the Modern VCED Models with the OT GCCD Trial Motif

On the left is an illustration of the typical modern western VCED approach. Usually, the Plaintiff is separated from the Defendant and spends significant time with a trained therapist or counselor. In contrast to the VCED modern approach, the Old Testament approach (on the right)

might better be labeled God-centered, consolation-driven (GCCD). It involves both Plaintiff and Defendant (the latter implicitly or explicitly) in the presence of God. Both were required by law to have their day in court before God or a God-designated judge. Both Plaintiff and Defendant were required to participate in the entire process and to ultimately submit to the judgment of the court (Judges 4:5; 1Ki 3:16-28).

If you were alive in the Old Testament times, Plaintiff, you would absolutely *not* give up your right of justice at all. It would be absurd for you to even think of it. It was your right to have your day in court before God. The ideal goal for all involved was a larger consolation: an accurate, fair verdict that vindicated and restored the innocent, evil purged from the community, the unrepentant punished and the repentant Defendant restored. It was God-centered and consolation driven (GCCD).

So Azariah allegedly committed a crime against Jud. Jud had no absolute evidence, but did confront Azariah with his suspicions. Azariah denied the crime. Perhaps he shifted the blame, certainly wasn't repentant at all. No resolution. What could Jud do? He would send a message to the elders and schedule their day in court.

Maybe the trial took place in a special room designated for that very purpose adjudicated by the elders of their city or village—people that they both knew and respected. Or maybe this particular trial was to be adjudicated before the King himself, or by one of the many Judges who oversaw Israel.

Either way, it was Jud's covenant right and privilege to bring the matter to the community officials. This was his legal and culturally designated path to vindication and restoration. On that day, Jud was a person of great honor and value standing before the God who covenantally loves him, who knew exactly what went down, what was taken, and what the costs truly were to Jud. Jud was not alone.

Guilty!

Let's just say for argument that after hearing both sides of the events considering all the evidence on both sides and interviewing all witnesses, the judge determined that Azariah was guilty. There in the presence of Plaintiff, Defendant and witnesses, the judge would officially point his finger at the Defendant and publicly proclaim "Guilty!" Serious *Aaaah factor!* For Jud, right?

The Judge would then order that Azariah pay Jud back for his loss—the full market price of the stolen goat plus the 20% penalty fine.

Good enough? It's a start of course. But God is much bigger than that. Better, God's consolation is bigger than that. In any trial held among

God's people, God is both the ultimate Judge, prosecuting attorney *and* Co-Plaintiff. All crimes are ultimately against Him. When David was dealing with his horrific capital crimes of rape and murder, he concluded:

> "Against you [God], you only, have I sinned and done what is evil in your sight, so that you are proved right when you speak and justified when you judge." (Ps 51:4)

Of course David's crimes against his neighbors were immense and worthy of death. But compared to his crime against His Lord? He is aware of the vast difference between horizontal and vertical crimes.

The human Plaintiff was never alone in God's courtroom. They were always co-Plaintiffs with God. Therefore it makes sense then in Lev 6 that the guilty Defendant must also publicly admit his crime against God Himself.

> "And as a penalty [the guilty Defendant] must bring to the priest, that is, to the Lord, his guilt offering, a ram from the flock, one without defect and of the proper value." (Lev 6:6)

Don't mistake this for the pagan notion of God being a narcissistic wounded demi-god who needs an offering to get out of his petty depression or to assuage his anger. God is not such an adolescent human creation such as Zeus or Artemis. God does not need such offerings to be made whole, or to be joyful again. God is whole. The sin does not diminish God one little bit.

Therefore, the prescription at the Temple is less about God and more about healing and restoration for the community. God's ultimate goal is oneness between Himself and His wayward self-focused and idolatrous people—including both the Defendant and the Plaintiff. The entire justice process is His prescribed means to achieve that goal.

So in addition to Azariah paying Jud the value of their loss plus a healthy fine, Azariah must also bring a very costly guilt offering to the Temple. An innocent animal is slaughtered by Azariah as a legal substitute for his own debt to God. The law requires death, God's mercy affords a substitute atonement—a substitute death.

> "He is to bring to the priest as a guilt offering a ram from the flock, one without defect and of the proper value. In this way the priest will make atonement for him for the wrong he has committed unintentionally, and he will be forgiven." (Lev 5:18)

> "In this way the priest will make atonement for him before the Lord, and he will be forgiven for any of these things he did that made him guilty." (Lev 6:7)

As the sacrificial ram perishes, so do all of Azariah's legal consequences in the presence of God. After this bloody ritual the Priest would perhaps proclaim over Azariah, "It is finished!" The debt has been paid, the community can begin the long and often arduous task of developing trust and intimacy again. It is the beginning of closure and hope for the Defendant. God Himself is satisfied with the sacrifice. The co-Plaintiff is also required to be satisfied. Granted, trust takes longer, but this is a huge first step.

The High Holy Days

In ancient Israel, the culmination of all individual guilt offerings made throughout the year by all of the "Azariahs" is the annual great Day of Atonement (Yom Kippur; see Leviticus 16 for details). Ten days before Yom Kippur—on Rosh Hashanah—God the Judge rises to His celestial bench and calls a vast trial to order. It was understood, that on that special day, all of mankind passed in front of God to be judged for their annual good and bad deeds.

Those who have been *perfectly* righteous were declared innocent. Those who have not been *perfectly* righteous in all of their dealings with God or others were declared guilty. By the way, if you have been paying attention you can already see what is happening here. *All of humanity is declared guilty.*

Perfect righteousness is a very, very high standard. The court recorder, looking at millennia of annual trial verdicts could report, "There are none righteous, no not one" (Rom 3:10). This trial is a bit of a formality really. Nevertheless, the guilty have ten days until the Day of Atonement to repair the wrongs.

Sounds good on paper, right? But, even if they wanted to, no one could fully pay their sin-debts. It was impossible. I would suggest that the ultimate goal of this trial and verdict was to open the eyes of the repentant Defendants of their desperate need for God to intervene on their behalf and to Himself atone for their sins.

At last on Yom Kippur, as all Israel gathered at the Temple, God *imposed* His forgiveness upon all repentant Defendants. There He accomplished on behalf of the unrighteous what they could not achieve on their own. God provided atonement for the sins of repentant Defendants.

Once justice had been fully served, God declared the repentant unrighteous "righteous."

The High Holy Days represented a celestial trial. On Rosh Hashanah, God considered *all* the evidence and declared *all* humanity guilty for crimes against God, humanity and creation. The correct sentence was death. But

71

on Yom Kippur, God provided a substitute atonement that was chosen to carry away the sins of the repentant Defendants.

Technically, those guilty Defendants who either were "high-handed," or those who chose to be righteous by their own efforts, would receive *no* experience of *consolation*. No forgiveness for their sins. Those who were truly repentant had their sins and the consequences of their sins lifted and carried away by God Himself.

Leviticus 16 details the Yom Kippur proceedings. The High Priest on the behalf of the repentant unrighteous would take two spotless goats from among the many offerings brought by the people. The first goat was slaughtered as a corporate "sin offering," in this case a sacrificial substitutionary atonement for the repentant.[43]

The second goat, the so-called scapegoat, was then brought before the High Priest. He laid both hands on the scapegoat confessing the sins of repentant corporate Israel. Liturgically the consequences of sin (i.e., shame, guilt, fear, disenfranchisement) of all the repentant guilty were then committed to the hapless shoulders of the scapegoat and carried away, never to be seen again. "The goat will carry on itself all their sins to a solitary place" (Lev 16:22).

By means of the two goats, the sins of the guilty were purged (*kipper*) from both the Temple and the people. On that day, at that trial, God purged, lifted and carried the consequences of sin (i.e., shame, guilt, fear, disenfranchisement) away. The entire Yom Kippur liturgy was summed up this way.

"On this day atonement will be made for you, to cleanse you. Then before the Lord you will be clean from all of your sins" (Lev 17:30).

---

[43] Keil, C. and F. Delitzsch, Commentary on the Old Testament in Ten Volumes. (Grand Rapids: William B Eerdmans, 1978) Vol 1, 278-9. The blood of the sin offering was sprinkled on the atonement cover and in front of it. This drama imagined the cleansing of the stain and stench of sin's residue away from before the face of God. Ancients (e.g., Israelites and Babylonians) imagined that sin left a residue in the temple, in the presence of the deity that was offensive. Per Jacob Milgrom, (J. Milgrom, *Leviticus*, Minneapolis: Fortress Press, 2004), the polluting of the adytum is caused by Israel's' presumptuous, wanton sins. The likely consequence of the pollution is that God could choose to abandon His sanctuary. (Milgrom, 1061). On Yom Kippur, these "impurities are purged to keep them from provoking the indwelling God to leave" (Milgrom, *Leviticus*, 1083). The trial liturgy on Yom Kippur is all about whether God will stay or leave Israel's midsts. So Hebrew "*kpr*" refers to "wiping off," removing or purging the uncleanness that came from sin. The goat is the wiping material so to speak and is disposed of outside the camp. As long as impurity persisted, God remained offended, so to speak and the danger of his wrath and possible alienation was imminent. This ancient view of Yom Kippur is somewhat different from that which came to predominate in later Judaism, especially in the centuries following the destruction of the Second Temple of Jerusalem in 70 CE. Atonement for the sins of the people eventually replaced the purification of the sanctuary per se as the central theme of Yom Kippur.

On the Day of Atonement, the guilty Defendant and the Plaintiff both passively/helplessly would watch as God himself (represented by his high priest) on behalf of the repentant Defendant and for the sake of the Plaintiff, purged the remaining legal debt demanded by Law. At this point in the liturgy, the Defendant and Plaintiffs were to accept and believe that the voracious appetite of God's Law was fully satisfied. It is a faith statement that should lead to obedience.

What happened next was brilliant. After the High Priest declared that the Law proclaimed that the trial was finished, the now *former* Plaintiff and *former* Defendant have only a few days to get ready for the great feast of Sukkoth (the Feast of Booths) where symbolically all of purged Israel would sit and eat at a common peace meal in the presence of the redeeming God. This is God's end game: consolation's fruit.

God desires oneness among His people. The Feast of Booths is a very Tolkien-esque liturgy symbolizing God's ultimate desire that all of His people, former Plaintiffs and Defendants alike should live happily ever after.

The Modern Arabic *Sulh*

In modern rural Arabic communities, it is not uncommon to see something similar played out. When a crime takes place, the Plaintiff initiates the *sulh*, the legally prescribed settlement process. The *sulh* is very public, inclusive of the whole affected community, and is structured as a legal ceremony—complete with due diligence, trial, judge, Plaintiff and Defendant.[44]

In the *sulh*, both parties are required to submit to the jurisdiction of the *jaha*, a team made up of wise and respected community leaders and elders. According to Islamic law, the *sulh* is legally binding upon the all of the participants.

The *sulh* could be either "total" or "conditional." The former officially ends all conflict as both parties resolve to end all disputes and not to hold any grudges in the future. The "conditional *sulh*" binds the parties to abide by a peace defined by specific conditions.

In the *sulh*, the family of the Plaintiff calls for a truce (*hudna*) and engages the *jaha* to accept the role of mediators. The *jaha* then engages in detailed fact-finding, interviews and other due diligence, defines the compensation (largely symbolic) from the offender's family to the Plaintiff's, and initiates the reconciliation ceremony, the *musalah*.

---

[44] G. Irani, G., and N. Funk. "Rituals of Reconciliation: Arab-Islamic Perspectives." Paper presented at the Kroc Institute Occasional Paper #19:OP:2, August 2000.

The "Feast of Booths-esque" *musalah* typically takes place in the village square. The families of both the Plaintiff and the offender line up on both sides of the road and exchange greetings – the latter offering apologies to the former.

Next, the two families shake hands, sealing the *sulh* settlement. It is often appropriate, as an act of atonement and humility, for the offender to directly approach the Plaintiff's family. This is supervised by the *jaha* and is an important exercise of repentance and, on the other hand, of the capacity of the Plaintiff and family to forgive.

Then it is not uncommon for the family of the Plaintiff to go to the family of the offender to receive a cup of bitter coffee—followed by a shared meal hosted by the offender's clan.

The goal of the *sulh* is not to punish the offender but to prevent escalation of dispute, restore dignity to the individuals who suffered loss, and, most importantly, to restore peace and stability to the community.

This captures much of the feel of the Old Testament consolation process. The obvious missing element is the mysterious movement of God in the community and in the hearts of the Plaintiff and Defendant.

Yom Kippur and the Plaintiff

So lets assume that Jud went to Yom Kippur that year. He had already been vindicated in the courts. Azariah has already paid full restitution. And yet, Jud's cup still feels diminished. The nagging consequences of those secondary crimes still lingers. He remains victimized. Plaintiff, you know exactly how he feels.

What can he do? Well Jud could throw himself by faith on the promises of God. He can choose to believe in the future final justice of God. He can believe that God will not let these feelings of diminishment last for all eternity. Even in the Old Testament, there was a proclaimed hope of total future consolation accomplished fully by God on the behalf of all broken cups.

Even the cynical author of Ecclesiastes gets God's future grace, "God will bring every deed into judgment, including every hidden thing, whether it is good or evil. (Ecc 12:14). The Prophet Isaiah imagines a time when God will push Jud's narrative to the inevitable happy ending.

On that day, all of creation will be full cups and all will fully rejoice. Why? Because the Great All-Seeing Judge will be on the earth. He will see that all evil is purged, and all injustices fully and finally dealt with. At last there will be *shalom*.

"A shoot will come up from the stump of Jesse; from his roots a Branch will bear fruit. The Spirit of the Lord will rest on him — the Spirit of wisdom and of understanding, the Spirit of counsel and of power, the Spirit of knowledge and of the fear of the Lord — and he will delight in the fear of the Lord. He will not judge by what he sees with his eyes, or decide by what he hears with his ears; but with righteousness he will judge the needy, with justice he will give decisions for the poor of the earth." (Isa 11:1-9)

Hope in future promises is good, right? But alas, poor Jud. The future is the future and the present is the present. Jud's heart would want more now. At the end of the Old Testament, God's people were still largely emptied cups waiting for this long promised day of fulfillment.

So is Jud only relegated to a hope of a future fulfillment? Not exactly. God's nature includes a deep drive to intercede on behalf of His people. God forgives in the future, but God also offers a powerful experience of that future forgiveness now.

Reflection Questions for Individuals or Groups

1)   Are you surprised that there are so few examples of horizontal forgiveness in the Old Testament? Why do you think that this might be the case?

2)   The author suggests that there is a severe fundamental contrast between the Old Testament and modern socio-psychiatric approaches to forgiveness. In your own words, describe the similarities and differences. How would you describe the Old Testament approach to someone who has endured a victimization today?

3)   At the beginning of the chapter, the author writes that the Old Testament would never demand the offended parties to forgive unrepentant perpetrators. The offended parties must experience real justice first. What are your thoughts and feelings about that assertion?

6

God's Present *Eucatastrophic* Imposition

In today's judicial process, when the trial is over, justice is over. The guilty Defendant may serve time, or pay a fine, but for the most part, justice is done—whether they are remorseful or not.

In the Old Testament, the judicial process *is just getting interesting* after the official human trials are completed. Remember, in Tolkien's understanding of how great fairy tales end, there is always a *eucatastrophic* intervention that changes the story from a tragedy to a fairy tale that can at long last end, "And they all lived happily ever after." God's most important interventions appear to happen outside of the official justice procedure and liturgy.

Let me ask you, Plaintiff. If you could counsel Jud post-trial, post-Yom Kippur, what would you tell him to ask the judge for? Jud had been fully vindicated at trial before the human judge. Azariah had been declared guilty and had agreed to do all that he was commanded: repay you the value of the goat plus a penalty and expeditiously bring a guilt offering to the Temple. Jud should be getting that *Aaaah! Factor* about now, right?

Honestly, what else would you like to see happen?

Well if I were in Jud's sandals, I would want Azariah to not only accept the guilty verdict, I would want him to actually *feel* the guilt. I would want to see real signs of remorse and Godly sorrow. I would want him to really feel badly that he dishonored me.

Are you following me? I would also want my life put back the way it was. I would want my diminished cup restored, not just for the primary crimes (dealt with by the human judge) but also the many secondary crimes. I want to be made whole again. Isn't this what you want too? Or is it too much like a fairy tale to even imagine anymore?

Good news! This is exactly what the Old Testament Plaintiffs and Defendants were to expect. Why? Because it was understood that such a trial was in the presence of God. It is expected that God is not just the Judge who only sits passively behind the bench rendering judgment. He is also the God who intervenes.

In fact, He *eucatastrophically* imposes his will. God can actually change hearts, change a person's motivations and desires. He can change people's perspectives regarding their actions. I see evidence of at least six ways in the Old Testament that God has intervened in the affairs of humanity apart from the letter of the law human procedures. Without such imposition by God there could be no *present* experience of our promised *future* happy ending for God's foolish beat-up people. God's forgiveness process can involve some or all of the following *eucatastrophies*:

For the Plaintiff
   1. God can restore him or her to a miraculous sense of wholeness.

For *all* Defendants,
   2. God can forcibly give him or her new hearts that feel Godly sorrow, and conviction for their crimes.

For *repentant* Defendants
   3. God Himself can pay his or her unpaid justice.
   4. God Himself can remove the destructive shame and guilt from his or her heart.

For *unrepentant* Defendants
   5. God can punish him or her for their crimes.
   6. God can choose to redeem and restore him or her against their wills.

1) God Can Restore the Plaintiff to a Miraculous Sense of Wholeness.

The Levitical law provided the means and methods by which the community could shape a semblance of corporate justice and fairness. But in the end, guilty Defendants like Azariah *could* just go through the motions and do all the law officially required without being truly reformed.

Remember, even though the court required Jud pay back for the primary crime, it has no power or jurisdiction over the losses due to the secondary crimes. The 20% penalty is a mere drop in the bucket—a symbolic admission of the presence of costs to the Plaintiff beyond the scope of the trial.

God requires absolute justice—a perfect justice for all crimes, primary and secondary. Every loss must be restored for His justice to be satisfied. God can and will go beyond the court proceedings.

> "For the Lord your God is God of gods and Lord of lords, the great God, mighty and awesome, who shows no partiality and accepts no bribes. He defends the cause of the fatherless and the widow, and loves the alien, giving him food and clothing." (Dt 10:17-18)

So Jud, hear this. God loves you too much to let you absorb the losses. Someone without your permission violated your cup, and diminished your level, your sense of well-being, of value and worth, and your name. Maybe you have been hoping that human courts could fix what Azariah broke. But they are not designed to do so. They do not have such power.

Your loss—because you are an image of God—is far greater than any court could repay. You may have hoped that if only Azariah would repent and give back what they took, then you might feel restored? No. Not even if he did so with 20% interest, it is not enough. You are judicially short-changing yourself. You are a majestic image of God, a masterpiece. The Defendant dishonored the image of God. A fine, no matter how painful won't cut it.

God can restore you and pay back what Azariah cannot. This is what God regularly does. In the future it will be accomplished perfectly and for all eternity. But in the present, God freely and regularly intervenes to restore the broken. God wants to restore to you what Azariah took.

"I will Repay…"

In Joel's familiar prophecy to a ravaged Judah, he uses the bold, stark imagery of the land devastated by a swarm of locusts—an event deeply feared in the Middle East. We are not sure if the "locusts" were actually the crop-destroying bugs or more likely metaphorical entities that robbed Judah of their comfort and livelihood. Either way, Judah is left victimized. Their cup was drained dry. But God promises that He can turn the disastrous devastation into a spiritual renewal—a source of real rejoicing and thanksgiving. Then He goes one more step—He miraculously by some dynamic equivalence gives them back the fruitfulness of the locust ravaged years. He promises to refill their emptied cups—that is, remove the driving motivation for their deep identity shame.

"Be glad, O people of Zion, rejoice in the Lord your God, for he has given you the autumn rains in righteousness. He sends you abundant showers, both autumn and spring rains, as before. The threshing floors will be filled with grain; the vats will overflow with new wine and oil. "I will repay you for the years the locusts have eaten...never again will my people be shamed." (Joel 2:23-26)

"I Will Restore the Fortunes ..."

"This is what the Lord says: 'You say about this place, 'It is a desolate waste, without men or animals.' Yet in the towns of Judah and the streets of Jerusalem that are deserted, inhabited by neither men nor animals, there will be heard once more the sounds of joy and gladness, the voices of bride and bridegroom, and the voices of those who bring thank offerings to the house of the Lord, saying, 'Give thanks to the Lord Almighty, for the Lord is good; his love endures forever.' For I will restore the fortunes of the land as they were before,' says the Lord.'" (Jer 33:10-11)

"The Lord Will Restore the Splendor..."

"The Lord will restore the splendor of Jacob like the splendor of Israel, though destroyers have laid them waste and have ruined their vines." (Nahum 2:2)

In Old Testament thinking, in the presence of God, Plaintiffs are never alone. You are not limited by your capacity to forgive, *or* to be healed. You are not dependent upon the Defendant, their decisions or lack of decisions or their capacity to repent either. God is in the middle of the proceedings. God alone has the power to fill your cup—heal your wounds—give you a new heart filled with a renewed sense of worth and value, joy and gladness. This is what God does.

Christian Plaintiff, it is your right and privilege to run to the Judge God and plead with Him to give you a *present* experience (albeit imperfect) of your perfect *future* restoration—beginning now.

As God fills your cup, you may be quite surprised at what you may begin to feel. Based upon the verses mentioned above, you could feel a release of shame (Joel 2), an irruption of gladness (Joel 2), joy (Jer 33) and a restoration of your old glory (Nah 2). You may even begin to feel very differently *toward* yourself, *toward* the person who hurt you, and even *toward* God.

If God fills your cup Plaintiff, imagine how easy it would be to begin to feel a substantial empathy for the repentant Defendant—and even perhaps begin to feel authentic forgiveness toward them? This type of restoration is to be expected as you come officially into the presence of the Judge God.

2) For all Defendants, God Can Forcibly Give Him or Her a New Heart

In human trials, the Defendant is not required to feel or express remorse. No court could ever make a Defendant feel guilt or remorse. Not really. They can go through all of the motions of the punishment without feeling any real sorrow for what they did. In God's courtroom more is expected. God's process of forgiveness can entail a miraculous intervention by God in the very soul of the Defendant.

Solomon and God's Imposition

Listen to the expectations of the wisest man, King Solomon as he dedicates the permanent Temple to God's glory. He requests that when there are official trials for horizontal crimes held in the Temple, God would interpose on two fronts.

> "When a man wrongs his neighbor and is required to take an oath and he comes and swears the oath before your altar in this temple, then hear from heaven and act. Judge between your servants, condemning the guilty and bringing down on his own head what he has done. Declare the innocent not guilty, and so establish his innocence." (1 Kings 8:31-32)

Just a side observation. Isn't this curious? We would never have a trial in our church building would we? That would seem so strange. Isn't church about worship and communion, fellowship—positive community-building things?

But here, in the Holy Temple of God in Jerusalem, we are led to understand that there were regular trials—judicial proceedings that considered such things as losses of goats. It would seem that the Ancients understood that such judicial practices were actually acts of obedience and very sophisticated worship to God.

So imagine with me. Remember Jud and Azariah? Jud makes an appointment with the priests at the Temple of God in Jerusalem for his case to be heard before God's face. Jud makes his charges, presents all of the evidence against Azariah. Then it is Azariah's turn. He stands in the Temple, in the presence of the God-Judge and swears that he didn't steal Jud's goat—that there was no breach of contract. In other words, he flat out lies in the presence of God—a very dangerous thing.

We already know that Azariah had wronged Jud. He was guilty of breach, theft, of lying, and now he dares to stand in front of God and swears falsely. You get the scene?

So Solomon, foreseeing such a trial, boldly requests that the Judge Himself (God) not just sit back passively but rather intervene. Here is my loose translation of the beginning of the King's prayer:

"God, hear both of the cases, all of the testimony, all of the evidence and then do something. Judge your servants."

What does Solomon have in mind? It is as if he is saying:

"God condemn the guilty (literally "wicked the wicked"). Humanly speaking, it is difficult to discern who is lying and who is telling the truth. So, God make it obvious."

Can God do this? Sure. Remember in 2 Chr 26:19 when King Uzziah disobeyed God and was struck with leprosy? Or for that matter Miriam in Num 12:10? She, too, became leprous "like snow." That is pretty clear. So Solomon requests that God make it clear somehow to everyone who is guilty.

But there's more. He asks that God bring down on the head of the guilty party what he or she has done. I suggest that this is a euphemism for God making the guilty feel all of the consequences of their crimes: all of the shame, and the guilt. Once again, here is my expanded version of Solomon's prayer:

"God, convict them to the bone. God bring down upon his head what he or she has done. God, declare the guilty, guilty. Cause the merited punishment to fall upon him or her. God, don't let him or her get away with the crime and duplicity. Bring Godly sorrow and conviction to bear upon him. Cause them to see—to deeply feel—what they did to the Plaintiff and how wrong it was. Make them feel what you feel God."

Let me ask. Are we at all comfortable with asking God to do this anymore? Plaintiff, have you ever asked God, boldly asked God with some expectation, that He actually might answer your prayer,

"God make the person who hurt me feel the weight of their guilt and shame. Break their heart to see what they have done, convict them deeply for their actions?"

Solomon makes a similar outlandish prayer on the behalf of the Plaintiff. "Declare the innocent 'not-guilty.'" (1 Ki 8:32) To flesh it out a bit more:

"God, righteous the righteous (literally). God publicly vindicate them, make it clear to them and to everyone that they are innocent, they are the Plaintiff here. But don't stop there. God 'establish their innocence.'"

I would suggest that this is the opposite of the actions that God took to convict the Defendant. Here is what Solomon is saying:

"God make the Plaintiff feel vindicated, feel whole, feel honored, feel like a person who should be treated with honor. If they were raped, God make them feel clean and pure again, a person of honor again. If they were slandered, give them back their name. If they were robbed, fill their cup with some dynamic equivalence. God you make people's names great. So God, act! Put on the wronged party, his rightness. Give them Your *Aaaah! Factor*."

Remember Plaintiff, this does not negate the law's requirement that the guilty pay you back for what they did—for what they took from you (as evaluated by the human court). The Leviticus case law is *still* sacred and *still* requires that the Defendant pay back the loss plus a fine.

These restitution laws are under the authority of the human court—humanly speaking doable by the guilty Defendant whether they are remorseful or not—and arguably do not need God to intervene.

Solomon is asking God for more than this. He asks God to do on the behalf of the Plaintiff what only God can do. Here is what he is really saying:

"God convict the heart of the guilty Defendant. Give them deep alien godly sorrow. Make the Plaintiff feel vindicated. Make them right again."

Isn't this stunning, Plaintiff? Solomon wisely understood that God the Judge is not distant or passive. In His courtroom, He interposes His will into the judicial proceedings and works miracles. It is God's role to "actively interpose, and judge his servants, to punish the guilty and justify the innocent."[45]

This concept might be a tad uncomfortable to modern sensibilities. Today we virtually idolize our so-called "free" wills. Much of that pedestal was erected during the Enlightenment[46]—hardly something that is hyped much at all in the Old Testament.

In contrast, the Bible is not shy to speak of *God's* free will by which He regularly intervenes in the affairs of man, with or without permission. Plaintiffs, this is great news. God can cause the Defendant—even the most stubborn and resistant of Defendants—to actually feel debilitating guilt and sorrow.

Judge Judy could never do that. Jud may have understood that as he began the process of taking Azariah to court before God. Perhaps Azariah was not willing to confess. He was not remorseful at all. There was no obvious experience of guilt and shame. The process was God-ordained to be the surgical instrument of God opening Azariah's heart to experience godly sorrow. Godly sorrow is from God. In a later time, Paul will speak of this same *eucatastrophic* sorrow:

> "Godly sorrow brings repentance that leads to salvation and leaves no regret, but worldly sorrow brings death. See what this godly sorrow has produced in you: what earnestness, what eagerness to clear yourselves, what indignation, what alarm, what longing, what concern, what readiness to see justice done. At every point you have proved yourselves to be innocent in this matter." (2 Cor 7:10-11)

Ezekiel and God's *Eucatastrophe*

The Prophet Ezekiel speaks of the same *eucatastrophic* intervention by God when he prophesies to guilty Defendant Israel who, like Azariah, is also stubbornly defensive and unremorseful for their many, many sins.

Let me put this in context. For their crimes of self-sufficiency, regularly turning away from God and rabidly pursuing other gods, God convicted

---

45 Keil, C.F. and Delitzsch, F, 129.

46 The Enlightenment is the very important period in the history of western thought and culture, stretching roughly from the mid-decades of the seventeenth century through the eighteenth century. The Enlightenment was characterized by dramatic revolutions in science, religion, philosophy, society and politics, which swept away the medieval God-centered world-view and ushered in our modern human-centered western world. At the core of the Enlightenment was the absolute primacy of human reason and the importance of free will.

them to 70 years of exile. This was a clear punishment from God's hand against a guilty people.

But, tragically, it seems that even after the 70-year exile, Judah's heart remained as hard as a rock. They still didn't get it. They were still defensive, unmoved, unremorseful, and still high-handed. So what did the Judge do? He forcibly, without asking for permission, stepped all over their self-destructive "free" will. He promises a holy *eucatastrophic* operation that would give them a new heart.

"I will give you a new heart and put a new spirit in you; I will remove from you your heart of stone and give you a heart of flesh. And I will put my Spirit in you and move you to follow my decrees and be careful to keep my laws...Then you will remember your evil ways and wicked deeds, and you will loathe yourselves for your sins and detestable practices." (Ezekiel 36:24-32)

Plaintiff, can you hear this? God has this kind of authority and power. He can give even the most hard-hearted defensive destructive perpetrator a new heart and a new spirit. That celestial surgery changes everything. This *eucatastrophe* of God sets the narrative on a whole new trajectory.

What would be noticeable post-heart-operation? A Defendant with a new heart and spirit would naturally begin to see what they did and hate themselves for doing it (vs. 31). Isn't that one thing you deeply desire Plaintiff? They would feel shame and disgrace for the choices they made— for their destructive actions against you. Wow! Praise God. This is the original gift that keeps on giving.

The new heart also has a new motivation to obey the Law of God. Remember the Law? Love the Lord your God with all your heart and mind and soul (Dt 6:5). Love your neighbor (including their former Plaintiffs) in the same way (Lev 19:18). Get it? They will be filled with an alien new love for you, Plaintiff—a new miraculous core desire to treat you as a person of great honor—very different from what they did before.

This is one aspect of God's stunning mercy and grace—a gift for both the guilty Defendant and the innocent Plaintiff. A new heart. Tolkien spoke about a *eucatastrophe* that totally changed the trajectory of a tragic story—morphed it into a great narrative of justice and restoration. In His presence, such miracles are to be expected.

Azariah and Godly Sorrow?

In the Leviticus 6 case it would seem that God did impose such a sorrow upon the heart of the Defendant. The passage describes the Defendant's state of mind at the end of trial phase as "when he thus sins and becomes guilty."

To unpack it a bit, I would suggest that two things are happening here. The judges have determined that the Defendant was in the wrong, literally, he or she sinned. There was an official verdict, "Guilty!" The Defendant was declared guilty of breach of contract and possible cover-up. But, it is most likely that the "guilty" represents more than just a forensic decision of the court. The Defendant has "become" guilty.

I strongly suggest—though it is not specifically mentioned—that God intervened and the fruit of this intervention was the presence of real remorse. In modern terminology, something happened, and now the Defendant actually feels guilt.

King David poetically captures what such an imposed guilt feels like. "My guilt has overwhelmed me like a burden too heavy to bear" (Ps 38:4). David felt the heaviness, the deep presence of shame, guilt, perhaps a poignant sense of disenfranchisement, and fear of being caught. It is an unbearable burden.

This is a very sophisticated notion of what guilt and shame due to sin *feels* like. We all feel such guilt at one time or another. God can plant this guilt in the heart of sinners even without their permission. Godly sorrow comes from God. It is one of the miracles that God can accomplish in the heart of the guilty Defendant in His presence.

The Old Testament view of God is not only as the ultimate Judge but a present, very pro-active God who freely interposes His will in the hearts and lives of his struggling people. God is not limited by the letter of the Law. He can miraculously give the Azariahs of the world new alien hearts that are very different from their old ones. With this new heart, Azariah would *necessarily* experience deep guilt and shame for his crimes against Jud.[47] As you can imagine, such a holy operation changes everything about the trial.

---

[47] There is a common phrase in the Old Testament describing guilty Defendants using the verb *nasa* (to carry) linked with one of the common nouns for sin forming an idiom that takes on the meaning of bearing the responsibility and consequences of their sins. The idea is that they have been found guilty of a specific crime against God, persons or creation and so now they must pay the price themselves –carry the sin on their shoulders. The NIV glosses over the idiom sometimes "bear the consequences of his/her sins" (Num 5:31; Ezek 23:49; 44:10, 12), "bear the responsibility for offenses (Num 18:1;), being "responsible for your guilt" (Num 30:15 "suffer for your unfaithfulness/sins" (Num 14:33, 34;), "share the guilt" with others (Ezek 18:19; 20). In one instance, *nasa* is combined with the word for disgrace (*kelimma*)—you will bear your disgrace (Ezek 16:54). The image is of a condemned criminal with no other recourse available to them other than paying the penalty and consequences of the crime themselves. This is the ancient version of "You do the crime --you pay the time." The most prevalent experiential consequence of the crime is guilt—guilt leads to fear, shame disenfranchisement and deep identity issues if left undealt with.

3) For a *Repentant* Defendant God Can Himself Pay His or Her Unpaid Justice

In most justice systems, the guilty Defendant has no other choice other than carrying their guilt and shame with them for the rest of their life. This is true for Azariah as well. Let's assume that God did give him a deep experience of sorrow, conviction for the crimes that he committed. No doubt, he would be much more highly motivated to pay the judicial fines. He could go and tearfully bring a guilt offering to the Temple. He could openly express deep, deep remorse to Jud and the community. But in a real sense, none of those things are effective at relieving his guilt—not really. *Only* God can remove the experience of guilt and shame.

God's Forgiveness and Entrenched Shame

A friend of mine, P., was caught in a police sting targeting Internet child molesters. Though married, P. had been having an Internet affair with another woman for many days. He agreed to meet with her in an obscure park nearby. When P. arrived at the location, he was arrested and charged with aggravated assault involving a minor. The Judge threw the book at him. Guilty of all charges! Three years in jail as a sex-offender.

Don't get me wrong. Whether he was aware of the underage status of the woman or not, P. *was still* a sex offender. He was guilty of adultery against his wife—a horrific crime. He was caught red-handed.

When I met him shortly after his arrest, he was deeply devastated by the inner-experience of his guilt. He was a living and walking picture of shame. Neither the subsequent trial, nor his heartfelt confession of adultery to the court and to his wife alleviated his bone-crushing shame and guilt. It seemed to P. that he would have to carry the guilt of this crime for the rest of his life. The guilt and shame were firmly and irrevocably on *his* shoulders.

In many ways, P.'s need speaks to one of the very core elements of God's "forgiveness." God's forgiveness is not a transaction where God merely chooses to release the person from justice due. God's forgiveness is much bigger and more invasive that that. The only exclusive Hebrew verb for forgiveness is *salach*, and it is only used of God. God is the God who forgives sin.

> "Praise the Lord, O my soul; all my inmost being, praise his holy name. Praise the Lord, O my soul, and forget not all his benefits—who *forgives* (*salach*) all your sins and heals all your diseases, who redeems your life from the pit and crowns you with love and compassion, who

satisfies your desires with good things so that your youth is renewed like the eagle's. The Lord works righteousness and justice for all the oppressed." (Ps 103:1-6)

Salach is only ever used of God and God's specific intervention into the lives of repentant Defendants. Humans do not *salach*. It is an attribute, an action of God alone. Technically speaking only God *salachs*.

What is the unique nature of God's *salach*? In Psalm 103, God's *salach* is placed in parallel with God unilaterally healing the Defendant's diseases, lifting them from the pit and crowning them with love and compassion, and even satisfying their desires.

When I consider what "diseases" P. might be suffering from, I would imagine that self-destructive shame, guilt and fear would top his list. What would P. have given to have been lifted out of his pit and experience love and compassion again? This might initially be beyond his wildest dreams—but again, that is why he needs the *eucatastrophic* imposition of God before he has any hope of a happy ending after all of his horrific destructive choices.

I have often glossed over these verses thinking "Oh, what a nice God we serve." But in reality, this is a troubling verse. God is doing these honoring things on the behalf of guilty Defendants (sinners)—those who clearly do not deserve such honor. He is doing this on the behalf of idolaters, adulterers, liars, betrayers, murderers, sexual predators and the like. What in the world is God doing intervening on behalf of the P.s of the world? Where is justice for those who were victimized if the perpetrators are treated so well by God? It seems so one-sided. Doesn't God love the offended party?

But wait a minute. Lets just sit back and think about it some more. We are all P.s aren't we? Isn't this the gospel message? Sure, maybe we all don't commit adultery in the same vile way that P. did, but if we were honest we are far greater sinners than we ever want to admit.

The gospel is that God doesn't save good people. No, God saves messed-up faulty people. From God's point of view, we are all self-centered rebels who have used others to satisfy our own desires. We have all treated other people badly. We are all sinners who need a God who intervenes powerfully to take our justice upon His shoulders and set us free from our destructive shame and guilt. This is part and parcel of God's process of forgiveness, God's *salach*.

God's *salach* is two-fold. It not only fully takes care of our sin, but it also restores us to a position of righteousness and glory.

Look, Azariah's punishment is pretty straightforward. He stole a goat from Jud and lied about it. Justice seems pretty straightforward—humanly speaking anyway. But what could P. possibly do to pay back for his crimes? He betrayed his wife's trust in him, despised his vows, subjected his whole family to deep painful disgrace, financial and emotional hardships, and years of ongoing trouble. How could he possibly pay this debt?

Biblically, the celestial penalty for P.'s crimes was death (Rom 6:23). Committing adultery is one of the Ten Commandments, after all. God hates unfaithfulness. P. could not ever pay enough goats to assuage God's justice due his sin. So God, in his merciful imposing forgiveness, provided an alternative to P's death. P. could by faith put his crimes upon a willing substitute. In the eyes of God the death of such a substitute fully satisfied the demands of the Law. Only then, as hymn writer John Newton sings, "Justice smiles and asks no more."[48] The theological label that best describes such a transaction is "substitutionary atonement." This Bible concept is stunning good news for guilty Defendants whose sins condemn them before God.

The Suffering Servant

The Old Testament clearly looks forward to God's ultimate provision of a worthy substitutionary atonement. The Prophet Isaiah foresaw the coming of a person, not a goat, who would at last accomplish justice for all *repentant* Defendants. It is one of the most hopeful and familiar passages in the entire Bible. Listen carefully and try to not trip up on its familiarity.

> "Surely [the Suffering Servant] took up our infirmities and carried our sorrows, yet we considered him stricken by God, smitten by him, and afflicted. But he was pierced for our transgressions, he was crushed for our iniquities; the punishment that brought us peace was upon him, and by his wounds we are healed. We all, like sheep, have gone astray, each of us has turned to his own way; and the Lord has laid on him the iniquity of us all." (Isa 53:1-12)

Isaiah introduces guilty Israel to such a substitute—the Suffering Servant Messiah. This Messiah will take upon himself and carry away all of the infirmities and sins of the people (Isa 53:4, 12). This Messiah will legally substitute himself for the repentant Defendant and fully submit to the court and its just and right verdict.[49] He takes full legal responsibility for the sins and all just consequences due.[50]

---

[48] Newton, J. *The Works of The Rev. John Newton. 2*(III). (New Haven, CT: Nathan Whiting, 1826), 597).

[49] Heb: *paga*; Isa 53:12.

[50] Heb: *saval*; Isa 53:4, 11.

Listen to the courtroom smell of Isaiah's imagery. He is speaking to Plaintiffs and Defendants alike. For you Plaintiff, this atonement has power to heal the wounds that you have had to carry—all of the consequences of the secondary crimes.

But it is also great news for the repentant Defendant. Azariah, you can't ever pay what the law fully demands even for the smallest of your crimes against an image bearer of God. So by faith, look to your substitute sacrifice, the Suffering Servant who was killed for your transgressions and iniquities. His death can bring you wholeness/peace/shalom to you too. His death alone can really bring freedom from any present or future justice.

4) For a *Repentant* Defendant God Can Remove His or Her Guilt and Shame

God alone can "remove" shame and guilt from the heart of the repentant Defendant. In fact, only God has the stuff to do this. Counselors—no matter how good they are at counseling, cannot. Only God can.

By the way, this is one of the wild crazy benefits of being a Christian. We can have our shame and guilt removed. This is so important to me, personally. Not just because I still do shameful things, but this was the gate through which I came to be a Jesus-follower.

I was 21, living in Houston Texas. Art, a friend at work, tricked me into going to an Institute for Basic Youth Conflict at a nearby auditorium. Art told me (partially true) that it was a seminar on communication.

What Art could not have possibly known was that shortly before that I had been caught red-handed doing something that I was deeply ashamed of. I had done shameful things before, but this time, I couldn't shake the guilt and shame. Day and night, I felt a heavy weight on my shoulders: emotionally, spiritually and physically. I felt trapped, diminished and troubled.

During the Thursday night lecture, the speaker (actually just a projection of the speaker on a huge central screen in the auditorium) asked if there was anyone in the auditorium who was feeling guilt and shame. Well, there was at least one of us. He continued by asking, "Do you want to be rid of the shame and guilt?" I silently answered "Hell yes!" What he said next was amazing good news to me. It was something like this:

"Imagine yourself walking up to the Cross of Jesus with a huge heavy backpack on your back filled with your shame and guilt. You have tried to get rid of it—with no success. Look up in to the loving merciful eyes of your dying Savior and let Him take it off you and put it on Himself. Fall to your knees and accept His salvation on your behalf."

You may say that this sounds too easy—to Pollyannaish. But a miracle happened that day in that auditorium. My chains fell off. My burden was lifted. Our God does this.

If P. were here, he would testify to the same stunning truth of what God can do. Shortly after going to jail, God miraculously intervened in P.'s heart. Across from me at a hard colored plastic table in the meeting room of C cell block, P. confessed Jesus as His only Lord and Savior. What was P.'s immediate awareness of the power of God in his life? He was immediately set free from his debilitating shame and guilt. It was palpable. I have to imagine that the guards who were watching over us had to see it too. It was as if God—right then and there—physically took the shame and guilt off of his shoulders and put it on Himself.

Though P. still had three years to serve in jail, in a larger sense he was set free. He didn't deserve that freedom from God. He was guilty of great sin and destruction—but he was now an adopted child of God in fully restored fellowship with His heavenly Father. Our Father does this. This is core to His entire forgiveness process.

What can the Defendant do to facilitate such a glorious heart operation. In one sense, nothing. Try removing your own shame and guilt. It is impossible. Particularly if it is acute. In another sense, there is nothing that we can do other than to, by faith, throw ourselves upon God's active forgiveness intervention on our behalf.

Like P., Azariah could also humbly run to God to beg him for his mercy and compassion. He could ask that God would—by His power alone—remove the sins and consequences of sin (shame, guilt, feeling abandoned by God).

"Have mercy on me, O God, according to your unfailing love; according to your great compassion blot out my transgressions" (Ps 51:1).

God Alone Forgives

God's process of forgiveness includes His ability to actually remove our shame and guilt. In addition to the singular Hebrew word for forgiveness (*salach*)—used of God alone—there are many other forgiveness figures of speech that imagine this "guilt-ectomy" operation by God. We are told that God Himself can "wash" sin off a condemned sinner.[51] So imagine, P. is so consumed with destructive shame and guilt that he feels covered with filth, unclean. God has the desire and power to wash those feelings away. He can "empty"[52] the internal consequences of sin that has consumed every

---

[51] Heb: *kavash, taher*; Mic 7:19, Ps 51:2).
[52] Heb: *naqa*

ounce of P. He has the wherewithal to "purge,"[53] "blot out,"[54] "cover"[55] and "wipe away"[56] debilitating Godly sorrow. Can God really do this? Absolutely. He desires that we be set free from our sins and the consequences of our sins—now.

I particularly love the most common of forgiveness figures of speech. The verb *nasa* captures the concept of "to lift off." God naturally desires to reach down to the repentant sinner burdened by the weight of the consequences of their crimes and literally "take the burden off" their shoulders.[57]

P. cannot do it on his own. He tried, but he was left in a dark tailspin of depression. But God can accomplish on the behalf of *repentant* Defendants what they could never do. Shame and guilt are removed as far as the east is from the west.

Job and God

Job knew of God's desire to do this.

"Why do you not pardon my offenses and forgive my sins? For I will soon lie down in the dust; you will search for me, but I will be no more." (Job 7:21)

Job is saying something to the extent, "God, if I have indeed sinned unaware, why don't you just take them off my shoulders. I can't be free unless you intervene and do it." Though innocent, Job understands that only God can truly release us of sin's shame, guilt, and fear. He alone can pay for unpaid sins, and He alone can remove our experience of shame and guilt from us.

P. needed a forgiving God. P. needed a deep miraculous *eucatastrophic* forgiveness. Don't miss what I am saying, he still desires forgiveness from his wife and children. This has yet to occur. But what he experienced from God alone has powerfully set P. free from his debilitating shame. Now he can actually actively pursue his wife's forgiveness. P. has tossed his unpaid judicial debt upon the shoulders of Jesus. P. has believed that God has accepted Jesus' death as full and complete payment for his many unpaid legal debts. P. got it that in the eyes of the Judge, he *was* guilty as sin—but now through Jesus, the Suffering Messiah, his punishment has been fully paid.

---

[53] Heb: *kaphar*; Jer 18:23
[54] Heb: *macha*; Jer 18:23
[55] Heb.: *casa*; Neh 4:5, Psalm 32:5; 85:2.
[56] Heb: *macha*; Isa 43:25. 44:22; Jer 18:23; Psalm 51:1, 9; 109:14; Neh 4:5.
[57] Heb: *nasa*; Ex 32:32; 34:7; Num 14:8; Mic 7:18, Psalm 25:18; 32:1, 5; 85:2.

Get it? P. experienced a *eucatastrophic* washing away of the vast shame and guilt he was carrying. His shame was "blotted away," "purged," "lifted off his shoulders," "cleaned away," and "fully covered." God can do this.

I want to point out that P. did serve his complete multi-year sentence in prison for his crimes. Now he is beginning the very hard work to regain his wife's trust and love. But He is different, a new creation. Now he is not debilitated by shame as he was formerly. He has had that shame lifted by Jesus. So he is now pursuing reconciliation as a *free* man. He knows that what he owes his wife, he can never ever pay back. Its just that now, P. believes that God *can* restore to her what P. took on his behalf. He has that hope.

In a word, P.'s shame was *forgiven*. When the Bible speaks of God's forgiveness, it refers to more than God waving His hands over a sinner declaring that justice is satisfied. God's forgiveness entails much more than that.

It entails pro-sinner actions that restore him or her to full card-carrying adopted child status. No more sin on the books; guilt and shame unleashed and sent far, far away. God Himself must clean the sinner's heart—purge it of debilitating shame and guilt. Such is God's forgiveness. No wonder only God forgives. God's forgiveness is beyond our capacity.

5) God Can Punish *Unrepentant* Defendants

Up until now, I have framed how God's invasive forgiveness naturally falls upon *repentant* Defendants. Perhaps they see their guilt and humbly run to God to set them free from their shame.

But, you may ask, "But what about the Defendant who is not given a new heart and so refuses to accept or admit guilt and refuses to submit to the court?" Modern therapists would likely instruct you—for your own good—to forgive them anyway. But that is not the record of the Old Testament. Previously we have been talking about Defendants who as a result of the trial actually accept their guilt and express true "godly sorrow" (2 Cor 7:10-11). But what if even after they have been declared guilty by God's ordained court, they still refuse to own their sin?

In Num 15:30-31, God can't be any clearer.

"But anyone who sins defiantly, whether native-born or alien, blasphemes the Lord, and that person must be cut off from his people. Because he has despised the Lord's word and broken his commands, that person must surely be cut off; his guilt remains on him."

The English adverb "defiantly" attempts to capture the Hebrew phrase, *beyad ramah*, literally "with a high hand."[58] You get the image. This high-handed Defendant stands unbroken, unrepentant, angry, resistant toward the judge and indifferent to their Plaintiffs. Inwardly perhaps, they raise their fist to his face defiantly. Since they choose to reject God's process of healing and consolation, they must then bear the consequences of the crimes on their own shoulders.

What consequences? These could include guilt, shame, disenfranchisement from God and the community—a type of relational exile. This is a very sophisticated understanding of shame and guilt, and unresolved sin. Until there is a change of heart, the Defendant will remain a miserable human being. In one sense, the community can act to cut them off, to exile them in their anger and rebellion. But in another sense, any physical excommunication is just making official what the Defendant's angry heart is already experiencing.

For the high-handed Defendant, there is no present experience of hope, freedom, redemption or humanity for that matter. They are an exiled person—a person out of relationship with community—a living hell. There is also no reconciliation possible until the Defendant is restored and redeemed.

Shortly after Cain murdered his brother Abel, God gave him multiple opportunities to see and admit officially that he was a murderer. The dialogue in Gen 4:9-16 could be a scene in a modern courtroom where the District Attorney is examining the Defendant on the stand. If there was a confession of guilt, and remorse, I have little doubt that God would have lifted Cain's guilt off his shoulders, and freed him from his shame and exile. But Cain was high-handed. In verses 11-12, God sentences Cain to lonely

---

58 In the Old Testament, the opposite of high-handed sins are "unintentional sins." Crimes specifically mentioned as part of this category are accidental or non-premeditated murder (Num 35:11, 15, Josh 20:3, 9), inadvertent sin or sin due to ignorance of the law (Lev 4:22, Num 15:22), withholding critical testimony in a trial (Lev 5:1), the touching of anything ritually unclean (Lev 5:2-3), or taking an oath thoughtlessly (Lev 5:4). This is a pretty broad list of crimes. The heart of the matter is that when the person sees that they committed a crime, they want to repent (literally, they experience guilt, e.g., Lev 5:1-4). I suggest that the core essence of unintentional sins are sins which occur out of ignorance, deception, foolishness or weakness which reflect no intent to renounce the sovereignty of God. In other words, the sin was indeed still a sin of the will, but the will's desire was not specifically to challenge the authority of God. One of the signs that the Defendant's sin is "unintentional" or can legally be treated within the category of unintentional sins is that he or she are observably repentant and remorseful. The high-handed sinner is anything but repentant and humble before God. For repentant guilty Defendants the Judge Himself has provided relief. God prescribes for the repentant Defendant who realizes their guilt and desires to be restored the "guilt-offering."

exile and hard labor. Cain records, "My punishment is more than I can bear" (Gen 4:13).

Literally, I cannot carry the consequences of my crime. There is no freedom for Cain. Cain must live a subhuman disenfranchised existence.

6) God Could Choose to Redeem and Restore *Unrepentant* Defendants Against His or Her Will

Is there any hope for the high-handed? The answer is "Yes, of course!" God can *eucatastrophically* impose His will upon them, give them a new heart that responds differently—that actually loves others.

Just so we never put God in a box, there are cases where God does just this. He imposes His desired restoration and release from the ravages of shame and guilt upon *unrepentant* sinners—*without* their permission. It seems that the Judge is not limited to the guilty Defendant's repentance. God can even forcibly interpose repentance into their hearts.

Gomer and God's Unwanted Eucatastrophe

What might such rescue and redemption look like? Feel like? The prophet Hosea's wife Gomer was a provocative example of God's healing and restoration of a person who obviously didn't want to be forgiven and healed.

Gomer (metaphorically representing unfaithful Israel) was the caricature of an unfaithful wife—humanly speaking—far beyond the possibility of any redemption. She unrepentantly pursued other lovers in a self-destructive cycle of using and being used. Never did she turn to her original husband or show any remorse at all. Nor does the reader expect she ever would. She was a horribly fractured cup, and if the truth were known, she was very self-destructive as well. She never appealed to God for rescue, or redemption. She would not, or perhaps humanly speaking, could not.

So what did God do in her case? God *eucatastrophically* pursued her. He—in a positive sense—*forced* his will upon her. In the end, he unilaterally restored her former glory and re-wed her to himself.

> "Therefore I am now going to allure her; I will lead her into the desert and speak tenderly to her. There I will give her back her vineyards, and will make the Valley of Achor a door of hope. There she will sing as in the days of her youth, as in the day she came up out of Egypt."
> Hos 2:14-16

How did Gomer respond? It is not in the text. I can only assume that God's holy *eucatastrophic* intervention was successful, and that her new heart responded to God brilliantly. I assume that with such a new heart that naturally loves God, she will begin to actually act like God's faithful and loving bride, and see things differently. With such a new heart, I have no doubt that she will look back and be so glad that God didn't wait for her to be repentant. Once again, God's forgiveness is a bit scandalous—good but scandalous.

Summary

Plaintiff, I want to stop here and ask a question. Doesn't all of this ring true to you? Isn't this what your heart and head have been telling you all along? I have spoken to many frustrated Plaintiffs who have finally seen that much of their well-meaning forgiveness efforts have failed because they were fighting against their heart's natural and right demands for consolation.

Plaintiff, your soul—created in the image and likeness of God—demands that the imbalanced scales get balanced. Isn't it true that one of our children's first full sentences are "But, that's not fair!" We have an inherited deep sense of fairness—and a need to resolve any unfairness. What happened to you was not fair. To give up on the imbalance seems highly offensive, right?

But, we modern Christians have been indoctrinated that such a loving, compassionate justice is somehow bad and un-godlike. As I have taught this in a number of Christian settings, there are always a few well-meaning, nice Christians who feel the need to strongly push back at this point. They say,

"This seems a bit petty, a bit unlike Jesus. Aren't we just supposed to make a decision to be merciful, to absorb the loss? (At this point they usually bring up the parable of the foolish servant—more on that later). Aren't we told by Jesus to forgive seventy times seven? To turn the other cheek?"

Yes of course. But here is the rub. At issue is not whether we are to forgive, or to love our enemies. No, at issue is the *process*. We have been taught and largely have embraced the modern concept that to forgive, we must first give up our right to justice.

The Bible knows nothing of such a process of forgiveness. I will speak more to this in the upcoming chapters on forgiveness as presented in the gospels and epistles. But suffice it to say here that we have largely misunderstood the importance of a just and fair consolation to any real and lasting forgiveness. Such a consolation requires a *eucatastrophic* intervention by God Himself on our behalf. We cannot do it on our own.

96

Listen to the cries of your heart, Plaintiff. Imagine what you feel when someone who really hurt *you* indifferently says, "Sorry. My bad"—or they defend themselves, make excuses or worse, blames you. There may be a part of you that thinks you still have to take some imagined high road and accept this. It would be the peacekeeping thing to do, the "Jesus thing." But at another level, you *know* that you are risking re-victimizing yourself. It is more than an act of sacrificial love. It is intentional self-victimization. Your heart will fight against you ten times out of ten.

Are you open to hear that much of your well-meaning VCED forgiveness efforts have been only heroic works of the flesh—childlike, a well-meaning mimicry of the real thing? Unsatisfying counterfeits. Much of modern forgiveness, while arguably helpful, ironically can be a further offense to you, and a denial of the immense moral cost of the offense. Keep doing that and you will lose moral authority in your life.

Consider God Himself. God never forgives anyone until there has been full justice paid. God never, ever surrenders the right to get even. He never cancels expectations. He never just releases the person from the debt that is owed. Sins need to be paid for first. Isn't that great news? God, the Great Celestial Judge, requires absolute payment for all crimes—*all* crimes (Ex 34:6-7). There is actually *no* Biblical evidence of God giving up His right to justice, ever. This is *not* to say that God is not love. His justice is never accomplished apart from his love and compassion (Ex 34:6-7). And it is also true that His compassion and love are never manifested apart from His requirement of justice either.

Whoever God is, there is one thing for sure: He is both abounds in love and forgiveness, yet still requires perfect judgment. He forgives wickedness, rebellion, and sin, but he does not leave the guilty unpunished. God's forgiveness requires complete and perfect justice. There is no conflict between the two in God's character. God's forgiveness is a function of perfect justice.

Biblical Mercy

The Bible does *not* pit justice and mercy against each other. Biblical "mercy" is not God feeling some modern concept of empathy for the guilty and then reducing the sentence or considering time off for good behavior. Biblical mercy is the capable substituting for the incapable, the good for the bad, the righteous for the unrighteous, the innocent for the guilty.

Real mercy cannot stomach merely setting the law aside, or a mere waving of His hands proclaiming forgiveness. Mercy requires that the law be fully satisfied first. The criminal (or a legal substitute) must die. Only then can a convict become a citizen again.

97

If the Plaintiff is not required to forgive unrepentant Defendants, what is he or she to actually do?

Reflection Questions for Individuals or Groups

1)   Read the rest of Solomon's great Temple dedication prayer in 1 Kings 8. Isn't it surprising that such a mundane paragraph on false oaths is included? It seems so non-glorious, so out of place in the context of a temple dedication. Why did Solomon prioritize such matters in this very historically important dedication prayer?

2)   Does it seem strange to imagine that people would have brought such pedantic legal matters to the Temple? Modern Christians would never bring such matters to our sanctuaries, would we? Our sanctuaries are designed for worship, and singing and gathering, not for legal matters between two people, right? Discuss your thoughts about the appropriateness of the Temple for such legal matters.

3)   The author suggests that God freely intervenes in legal matters brought before Him, sometimes *without* specific permission of the participants. In essence, God can work *against the wills* of participants to accomplish justice. Do you agree? Why or why not?

7

Plaintiff's Role in the Old Testament Consolation Process

Forgiveness in the Old Testament is much broader and more magnificent than we imagine forgiveness today. It was a very sophisticated intervention ultimately by God on the behalf of his hapless people, Plaintiffs and Defendants alike, who just can't seem to get along.

The Levitical law prescribed an institutional judicial process whereby Plaintiffs can get relief. If the Defendant was declared to be guilty, in addition to bringing full restitution to the Plaintiff plus a severe penalty, they were required to bring a guilt offering to God.

As helpful as this was, it was still very limited. Into this bare-bones judicial process, God could lavish His glorious power of forgiveness. God could do what our human institutions cannot do even on their best days. God could make the Defendant deeply feel guilt, feel the wrong for what he or she did. God could make the Defendant actually want to honor the Plaintiff. God alone could fully pay the Defendant's judicial bill, completely satisfying justices voracious hunger. God alone could physically remove the Defendant's guilt and shame. Lastly, God alone could ultimately restore what the Plaintiff had taken.

This is not only what God could do, this is what God's nature desires to do. God sets the prisoner free, restores the victimized to glory and redeems the guilty. In a phrase, God forgives the unrighteous. All who He *eucatastrophically* forgives are forever changed in the process.

So what was the Old Testament Plaintiff to do to kick off the process? What was their official part in God's forgiveness? I see three distinct assignments for the Plaintiff. As soon as they are aware of a specific crime, they are charged to

- Initiate God's forgiveness process through the established courts,

- Run to God for a present experience of healing and restoration to wholeness, and

- Pray that God would forcibly change the heart of the Defendant.

All pretty doable, right? All of these assignments retain all of the remaining dignity of the Plaintiff, no matter what the crime was. It is low risk and puts the Plaintiff in no real danger. Rather, it invites the Plaintiff into a process that is ultimately restorative and honoring. Remember in an earlier chapter where I spoke about *Procedural Justice*? Plaintiffs long to participate in a fair human judicial process that treats them as a person of honor—a process that is before an objective judge and gives them the right of "voice." The Old Testament was aware of the benefits to the Plaintiff long before social scientists "discovered" it again.

How to Forgive the Unforgiveable

Years ago I met a very successful business man, who later became a dear friend. Joe had sunk all of his savings into a new townhouse development in a fast-growing upscale area of the city. He was set to make a huge fortune. But then things horribly unraveled. One evening at home, one of his adult sons viciously attacked Joe, pummeling him to an inch of his life. It turns out that the key instigator was his wife, who had incessantly goaded the young man to attack his father. It came out later that the wife had been having multiple affairs behind Joe's back, and had been blackmailing their children for a decade to not tell Joe. It was a disastrous situation. The good news is that in the midst of the worst of these inhumanities, Joe accepted Christ as his Savior and was dramatically transformed.

But the bad news for Joe is that the attack had severely damaged his mental processes and so there was little chance that he could manage such a complicated investment opportunity. He lost all of his investments. His family eventually isolated Joe, largely because of his newly found faith. As you can imagine Joe was very angry at his son—enraged at his wife who was now openly flaunting her latest boyfriend. He had lost so much: his health, his wealth, his family. He had to move into a very basic government-financed apartment—painfully near his old bankrupt development.

So what should Joe do? Humanly speaking the situation was very bleak. Imagine what he was feeling. His son was arrested and charged with attempted murder. His wife's role was never proven by the authorities and so she was off scot-free. What could forgiveness possibly look like? It is unimaginable.

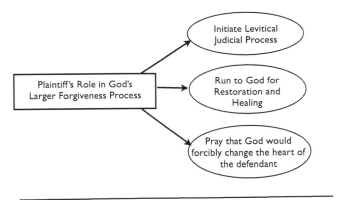

Figure 9- OT Path of Consolation from Victim's Perspective

If this had taken place in pre-exilic Old Testament times, Joe would be required to do three powerful things. Very straight-forward, very doable. Three tasks that do not re-victimize Joe any further. In fact, they are honorable God-honoring tasks that reflect deep faith in God as the good Judge over all. Joe would have been charged to

- Initiate God's forgiveness process through the established courts,

- Run to God for a present experience of healing and restoration to wholeness, and

- Pray that God would forcibly change the heart of the Defendant.

Initiate God's Forgiveness Process[59]

"I am the Lord your God.
Do not steal.
Do not lie.
Do not deceive one another.
Do not swear falsely by my name and so profane the name of your God.

I am the Lord.

Do not defraud your neighbor or rob him.
Do not hold back the wages of a hired man overnight.
Do not curse the deaf or put a stumbling block in front of the blind, but fear your God.

I am the Lord.

Do not pervert justice; do not show partiality to the poor or favoritism to the great, but judge your neighbor fairly.
Do not go about spreading slander among your people.
Do not do anything that endangers your neighbor's life.

I am the Lord."
(Lev 19:9b-16)

In this passage, we are pummeled with a broad array of laws related to community. Just in case we forget—the Judge reminds us, four times, that He is the Lord, not us. We must obey these holy laws not because they are good things, but because the Creator God says so. If you do not, you should expect a day in court before the Judge Himself. What things?

Do not steal, lie or deceive others (11).

Do not swear falsely, do not defraud your neighbor, don't hold back wages (12).

Don't show favoritism in court (15).

Don't do anything that endangers the life of your neighbor (16).

Don't spread slanderous gossip (16).

---

[59] This is not to say that Defendants cannot initiate the process. The emphasis in the Old Testament is that Plaintiffs are called to make sure the process moves forward.

Plaintiff's Role in the Old Testament Consolation Process

Excellent laws. It would be a different world if we did these things by nature. Plaintiff, the crime committed against you perhaps fall in this list. Joe could certainly accuse his wife and son of a couple of these. Based upon the evidence, the two had very little positive defense to speak of. Ignorance is not a legitimate defense. So let the trial before God begin.

In the case of "Joe" v. "Wife and Son," the primary crimes would include adultery, betrayal, lies, deceit, attempted murder, anger and hatred, and so many others. Joe's son and wife did not love their "neighbor" in this case. They didn't honor Joe or bless Him. They conspired to murder Joe. "Guilty!"

But the list of secondary crimes that were committed against Joe is even more extensive including: loss of livelihood, identity, health, comfort, sense of safety, autonomy, joy, family, and many more no doubt.

If Joe would listen to modern VCED proponents, he would no doubt be told that he should not pursue "justice"—rather he should deny himself that right for the sake of forgiveness. He would have been told that love and forgiveness are two sides of the same coin.

> "Joe you must choose to give your despicable wife and murderous son the altruistic gift of forgiveness disregarding your right to justice and reparation. Joe just put yourself in their shoes and see the instance from their point of view. Reframe the criminal and the crime and then choose to feel empathy for them—the latter displacing the normal hatred that you naturally feel."

Right? As we have seen, that is not what the Torah teaches at all. The author of Leviticus seems to expect that these laws will be transgressed and so gives clear commands to the victimized when the crimes inevitably happen—because they will. Plaintiff,

> "Do not hate your brother in your heart. Rebuke your neighbor frankly so you will not share in his guilt. Do not seek revenge or bear a grudge against one of your people, but love your neighbor as yourself. I am the Lord. Keep my decrees." (Lev 19:17-19)

Leviticus gives the Plaintiff three negative commands (Thou shalt nots...) and one positive command (Thou shalt...)—three things that you are *not* supposed to do in response and one overarching thing that you are *to* do—because He is the Lord and He says so. Plaintiff, I hope you are sitting down. These commands to you have *equivalent authority* to the previous "do nots."

Plaintiff "Thou Shalt Nots!"

Here it is. Plaintiff, no matter what happened to you, how badly you were treated, used or abused, no matter what was taken from you, God commands that you to not hate the person who treated you so badly (vs. 17). *Second*, you must not seek revenge. And *third*, you must not bear a grudge against them. What!? This doesn't seem right, does it?

Do not hate [the one who hurt you so badly] (vs. 17).

Lets face it, if you are anything like me, I tend to really, really dislike people who treat me badly—OK my heart even has a tendency to hate them. Whew! I said it. The Hebrew word *sane'* (hate) is very telling.

Sane' expresses an emotional attitude toward persons and things which are opposed, detested, despised and with which one wishes to have no contact or relationship. It is therefore the opposite of love. Whereas love draws and unites, hate separates and keeps distant. The hated and hating persons are considered foes or enemies and are considered odious, utterly unappealing.

In general, I am a pretty good guy, but I would readily admit that I understand *sane'*. When someone with no remorse robs me, I don't want them anywhere around me. It's my heart. By the way, Jesus agrees with my assessment of my heart's capacity to be angry to the point of hatred. Listen to this passage from Mark 7:

"For from within, out of men's hearts, come evil thoughts, sexual immorality, theft, murder, adultery, greed, malice, deceit, lewdness, envy, slander, arrogance and folly. All these evils come from inside and make a man unclean." (Mark 7:21-23)

My heart can be a virtual hate and anger factory. I remember one evening, my wife and I were having an "intimate heightened discussion;" if yelling and name-calling could be described as intimate. Speaking for myself, my heart was in full factory mode—evil thoughts, malice, murder, despising ripping off my heart's assembly line. I thought that my small children had gone to bed. That was the law in the Senyard household.

But there was a cautious knock on our closed bedroom door. Irritated, I firmly walked over to the door, flung it open and there they stood—two of my young children—no doubt very troubled at the yelling—but from my point of view, in clear disobedience to the LAW! So what did a good guy like me do? Of course, I yelled at them to get back into bed "NOW!"

I am not sure if it was the volume of my command, or the angry contorted look on my face that communicated to them that this was a bad time to ask how we were doing. They turned on their tiny little legs and scurried off to their rooms and stayed there the rest of the night. Tragically, it took me another two days to really embrace how badly I treated my kids. I initially felt justified that they had disobeyed me and ignored the rules to go to bed. They pushed buttons in my heart that were already smashed to the wall—and felt the full thrust of my angry heart. I finally profusely repented to them for my totally misplaced anger and the consequences.

So if anger, despise and hatred naturally come out of my heart when I am treated unjustly, how then can I hope to obey the law and "not hate?" Don't get me wrong, I am still responsible for my choices and actions, but I can't seem to stop the vileness that surprisingly will lash out of my heart in these cases. When someone hurts me, my immediate knee-jerk reaction is anger, a desire for revenge—unhindered these could quickly mature into hatred. Forgive the grammar, at some level I can't not-hate them. It's my heart. I want to believe that I will grow to the place where love oozes out when someone hurts me. But my heart will need a deep and ongoing overhaul for that to happen regularly.

What the Lord commands in Lev 19 is impossible humanly speaking. My heart has the surprising bent to be immensely angry at even tiny cute little Defendants who virtually did nothing at all to earn it. Imagine what my heart would do to someone who really beat me up, or robbed me of something important. My heart is a hate factory. If someone treats me badly, disrespects me or victimizes me—it is only natural for hatred to pour out—whether I am able or willing to admit it is another topic altogether.

Sometimes when I officially welcome visitors to my church I say something to the effect of,

> "Welcome visitors to our church. I hope that you have felt honored and very welcomed. But give us a couple of weeks and we will eventually do something offensive. Welcome."

It is tongue-in-cheek of course—but pretty accurate I think—not just for our church—but for the entire human race.

Don't hold grudges (Lev 19:18)

Seriously? My heart not only naturally holds grudges—but I can put them into cold storage for a very long time—just ask my wife. But the Lord commands that I am not to "hold in" anger. Every Plaintiff understands the "holding in" of anger, right? I know that I am not supposed to let the bitterness, anger and hatred burn in my heart. The experts have a word, "ruminate," that speaks of how we Plaintiffs tend to mull over the crime over and over, like a cow chewing it's cud resulting in fresh expression of anger and victimization. So how do I *not* hold a grudge? I have tried to stop it. You probably have too—and like me, failed, and that's one reason you are reading this book.

Do not seek revenge (Lev 19:18)

Really, Moses? This happens to be another key go-to strategy of my heart. I was watching a recent historical fiction TV drama on the Hatfield and McCoys. I totally understood how things went from a mere slight to murder to all-out-war so quickly.

I know in my head that revenge does not work. Forgiveness guru Lewis Smedes (author of The Art of Forgiving) points out that revenge is not resolution—vengeance never satisfies justice anyway. "Vengeance is a passion to get even. It is a hot desire to give back as much pain as someone gave you. The problem with revenge is that it never gets what it wants; it never evens the score."[60] And yet, my heart leans into it anyway.

So how do I obey the Lord's command? *I can't!* That's the point. I can try really hard. I imagine a weight lifter straining against gravity to dead-lift huge barbells over his triangle neck and baldhead—veins bulging. He closes his eyes and holds his breath—anything that might help him focus on the seemingly impossible task of lifting the weight over his block torso.

We Plaintiffs sometimes imagine that if we just strained hard enough, our heart "muscle" would just not hate, not hold grudges, not seek revenge. Scientists understand that our physical hearts are "involuntary" muscles—meaning that they contract apart from our conscious control. Likewise, our emotional heart is not under our head's jurisdiction. The history of mankind is littered with story after story of our out-of-control hearts. So we can grunt and strain, but our heart unaffected still spews out hatred, anger and vengeance—even when our head says "No."

It is true that sometimes the angry feelings seem to go away, but if the truth were known, they effectively just go deeper into the complex systems of crevasses of my wounded heart. Psychologists speak of this as repression. They bide their times to erupt when the right strings are pulled and buttons pushed, even by innocent, frightened children. Neither denial nor repression constitute real obedience to the Lord's command.

---

[60] Smedes, L., as quoted in M. Henderson, *Forgiveness: Breaking the Chain of Hate*. (Wilsonville, Book Partners, 1999), 2.

Plaintiff "Thou Shalts"

So lets check the score. The ones who treated Joe so badly are guilty of crimes against Joe and the Creator God. Score one for Joe. But, the moment that Joe's heart felt anger, hatred, desire for vengeance, he also sinned against the Creator God. Score one for Joe's Defendants.

Leviticus is not finished. OK, so we failed with regard to the negative commands. Maybe we can do better with the positive one?

Love Thy Neighbor

Nope. The law says, "Love your neighbor as yourself." Love is an emotion—similar to anger, hatred, unforgiveness, vengeance. All of these are mostly under the control of the heart—not our reason. I can't make my heart love any more than I can stop it from being angry.

Let's face it, our love is very conditional. If someone treats me well, I tend to like them more. We are all that way. Love is a function of the object's lovability and attractiveness, not the subject's ability to love. We are made in the image of God to love beautiful, lovely things. So we most naturally will not love those who have hurt us and treated us so badly.

But the Bible is clear, love your neighbor (including the one who hurt you) as much as you love yourself. This passage should be very familiar to most of us. It is expanded on in the New Testament by Jesus, Paul and James (Mt 22:39; Mk 12:31; Lk 10:27, Rom 13:9; Gal 5:14; James 2:8)— Love your neighbor as yourself!

Just to underline this particular command God repeats "I am the Lord." This is an important command. This is a *big* deal.

So Plaintiff, even if you could miraculously pull off not hating your Defendant, you are still not in-line with the law. Plaintiff, you are positively commanded to love your Defendant as yourself. Plaintiff, you can "choose to obey" all you want, but the right posture at this point is to state the obvious. As I carefully explained this approach to my friend Joe, his response was absolutely correct. "I can't forgive them for this, much less love them. I can't do it." Exactly!

"Yakach" your offender

So then, what are you supposed to do—specifically? What do you do to be in line with the law of God? How do you "not-hate?" It is an emotion after all—not a choice per se. How do you legitimately turn-off a powerful emotion without slipping into denial and repression? How do you turn-on "love" toward someone that hurt you so much, who treated you so insignificantly? Plaintiff, good news! You can't. Or you won't. Either way the result is the same.

But, buried alongside of the aforementioned "do's" and "do nots" is one more very helpful "do." Plaintiff, this one you *can* do. You are commanded to initiate the God-ordained justice process. God commands you to *"yakach"* your offender (vs. 17). The Hebrew verb *yakach* can mean to rebuke, chasten, or make a defense against. It can also include the narrower technical notion of taking the person to court (i.e., making formal legal charges against them).

The grammatical structure[61] that the Law uses is interesting. It is appropriate to read it, "Rebuke, rebuke," "intentionally rebuke," or "really rebuke" the offender. You get the sense that this is really important, so listen closely.

Your role here is to intentionally deal with this matter. If you don't— and this is very interesting—you risk carrying some of their guilt on your shoulders. "Rebuke your neighbor frankly so you will not share in his guilt" (Lev 19:17). According to the Old Testament law, love and rebuke are two sides of the same coin. Fascinating. This is very strange to our modern sensibilities. Such rebuke is the front door of the God-divined process of forgiveness.

According to the law, Plaintiff, once you are aware of the hurt, anger and hatred toward the Defendant and crime, you are to embrace your rightful responsibility in the community of God to initiate the God-ordained justice process (in pre-exilic Israel it was to get a court date with the elders in the city gate, or before the priests at the Temple perhaps). You are not to ignore your role, or to give up the right of justice. You are to wisely and safely confront your Defendant. In a larger sense, you are initiating your day in court. In the Old Testament community, such actions were commonplace. Elders sat regularly in the city gates to oversee such actions.

How is this fleshed out today? More about that once we look at the consolation process in the Gospels and Epistles.

Run to God for Restoration and Healing

In modern forgiveness models, Joe would be required to dig very deep and find by any means empathy for the one who hurt them—whether his wife and son were repentant at all. What do the modern models mean by "empathy?" Empathy involves a fresh feeling of compassion toward the one who hurt you. This compassion stems from the Plaintiff at last

---

[61] Infinitive absolute

beginning to see the events from the Defendant's point of view, ideally creating a powerful positive emotional identification with them.

The Old Testament does indeed command compassion toward one another, but it is far more realistic about the success of deeply wounded people ever accomplishing deep compassion for unrepentant people who have hurt them deeply. The situation is very similar to what we said about God's command to love your neighbor as yourself. It is indeed commanded, but the first step to accomplish the law is to admit that your heart will *not* do it.

Joe, your heart is pretty beat-up and angry, empty of love—and so has nothing to really offer people who have hurt you. You are still commanded to be compassionate, but you have nothing in the tank other than hurt, anger and revenge.

I could have counseled Joe for years to dig really deep to feel compassion for his wife, to see the attempted murder from her point of view and to gain an emotional connection with her—and get nowhere.

The Old Testament is much more realistic. Joe, before you have any hope of feeling positively toward your wife, you first need to by faith run to God and experience *His compassion for you.* You are invited to run to the great stream of living waters to have your very empty cup filled—first (Jer 2:13).

Unlike you, Joe, God has endless quantities of compassion. Perhaps the closest Hebrew word to the English "empathy" would be *raham. Raham* is a "feeling of love, loving sensation, mercy (originally designated the seat of this feeling, meaning bowels, inner parts of the body, the inner person)."[62]

In *normal* human relationships, *raham* can refer to acts of compassion and favor from one person toward others (Prov 12:10). It can be a sacrificial, positive act toward another that requires the giving up of rights.

In 1 Kings 3:26, in an official legal dispute before the Judge King Solomon over the identity of an infant, the true mother "filled with compassion for her son" was willing to give up her child rather than have him killed. In normal mutually positive human relationships, *raham* is an internal motivation that most naturally leads to pro-social actions on the behalf of the well-being of the "other."

When *raham* is stifled, the result is the negative anti-social emotions of anger and rage (Amos 1:11). But as in the case of love, we are naturally compassionate to people who we like, those who respond positively. If they are destructive, abusive, our enemies, it is just flat out impossible for our

---

[62] L. Koehler, L. and W. Baumgartner. *The Hebrew and Aramaic Lexicon of the Old Testament (HALOT).* (New York: E.J. Brill, 1996), 1219.

hearts to be compassionate. On the other hand, God is by nature *raham* always[63].

> "And he passed in front of Moses, proclaiming, "The Lord, the Lord, the *compassionate* and gracious God, slow to anger, abounding in love and faithfulness, maintaining love to thousands, and forgiving wickedness, rebellion and sin. Yet he does not leave the guilty unpunished." (Exod 34:6-7)

In this important self-testimony of his own innate nature to Moses, God proclaims that He is by nature *raham*. God is uniquely always *raham* toward his covenant people (Ps 51:1; Isa 63:7; Dan 9:9; 18; Lam 3:22-23). It is his *raham* that motivates him to never abandon His people permanently (Neh 9:19, 31).

God's *raham* humanly speaking leads to a variety of "other-directed" actions: blotting out the consequences of sin on behalf of the guilty penitent (Ps 51:1; Ps 103:10-12), turning his face (of favor) to helpless Plaintiffs (Ps 69:16-19; Ps 77:9; Ps 79:5-9), drawing near, redeeming and rescuing helpless Israel who were being disciplined because of sin (Neh 9:27-28), forgiving sin (Dan 9:9), restoring Plaintiffs to honor (Hos 2:19; Ps 103:4), restoring to life (Ps 119:77; Lam 3:22), and restoring the exiles to the land (Jer 42:12).

In stark contrast to modern socio-psychological definitions regarding "empathy," there is no record of God's *raham* ever moving him to explore the Defendant's motives or reframing the crime.

Joe, There is Another Pathway to Forgiveness

Allow me to speak to Joe directly here.

> "Joe, if you rely on your own strength, chances are you will likely *not* feel real compassion for your wife and son. But, you can run to God, admitting your lack of such empathy, and get filled up to all the fullness

---

[63] *Raham* is often linked with *hesed* (covenantal love), *hanan* (mercy) and even *mishpat* (justice). In the post-exilic book of Zechariah, *raham* is linked to *hesed* as the expected fruit of God's new kingdom. As God's people are filled with *raham* and *hesed*, they will not oppress the helpless segment of society (widow, fatherless, the alien and impoverished), nor think evil of each other (Zech 7) and they will adjudicate true justice among them. It should be noted that though God's innate *raham* is consistent, the people do not always experience God's *raham*. They experience his *raham* toward them when they repent and turn from their evil ways (Isa 55:6-7; Zech 1:4,16; 2 Chr 30:9), cry out to him (Neh 9:27), turn toward him, look to Jerusalem, the temple and cultus (1 Kgs 8:58), or are obedient (Deut 13:17). In an interesting metaphor, Hosea speaks of God's *raham* becoming viscerally aroused (11:8)— perhaps referring to the people's present experience of the ever-present *raham* of God.

of God's compassion (Eph 3:19). As God begins to fill your empty cup, you might even begin to feel something brand new, something miraculous and strange. You may even begin to feel toward your wife and son the way that God feels toward them. This *eucatastrophic* reframing is very powerful to watch unfold."

"Joe, one of the other "fruit" of God's *raham* is a new powerful motivation to forgive. In Isaiah 55, *raham* is placed in paralleled with God's forgiveness.

"Seek the Lord while he may be found; call on him while he is near. Let the wicked forsake his way and the evil man his thoughts. Let him turn to the Lord, and he will have *mercy* on him, and to our God, for he will freely pardon." (Isa 55:6-7)

"So Joe, run to God and access his compassion by faith. This *is* doable. Just follow in King David's humble footsteps. Listen to David's cry in Psalm 69:

"Answer me, O Lord, out of the goodness of your love; in your great *mercy* turn to me...Come near and rescue me; redeem me because of my foes. You know how I am scorned, disgraced and shamed; all my enemies are before you. Scorn has broken my heart and has left me helpless; I looked for sympathy, but there was none, for comforters, but I found none." (Ps 69:16-20)

"David knew that he could not depend upon his enemies for sympathy and comfort. He had learned that God is his ultimate source of rescue, redemption, intimacy and mercy. David is *not* trying to pursue empathy for his enemies, or examining his own psychological defenses, or seeking to appreciate the reason for the offender's actions. He runs to God boldly to have his diminished beat-up cup filled. It is God alone who can heal, redeem and restore a Plaintiff's lost glory. The Defendant just can't do it."

"Joe, even if your wife is powerfully touched by God, transformed into a deeply remorseful person, and even profusely repents of her wrongdoing—your beat-up cup will still remain greatly diminished. She does not have pockets deep enough to pay you back for what she took from you. But, the good news is that God can restore you—far more than you can comprehend. His celestial pockets are more than deep enough."

Pray That God Will Forcibly Intervene and Change the Heart of the Defendant

Plaintiff, God has the power to change hearts. You cannot. The law cannot. The courts cannot. As we have discovered, your Defendant cannot change his or her own heart. So, if you want them to be filled with a godly sorrow for what they have done to you, your only hope is to run to God in prayer and ask that he would intervene and miraculously change their hearts (See Gen 43:14; 2 Chr 30:9; 1Kgs 8:50; Ps 106:46; Dan 1:9; Neh 1:11; Jer 42:12).

The Psalmist credits God with the ability to *make* the captors feel pity for the captives (106:46). "[God] caused [His people] to be pitied by all who held them captive."

Daniel also credits God alone with causing officials to show him favor and sympathy (Dan 1:9). Solomon prays that God would not only forgive the sins of Israel, but also cause their conquerors to show them mercy. The Old Testament places your Defendant's heart and motives finally in the hands of God. It is definitely in God's wheelhouse to *make* the heart of the Defendant favorable to you—feel remorseful for what they have done—even feel God's honor toward you.

Plaintiff, contrary to the VCED model, the God-centered, consolation-driven (GCCD) approach does not put the entire burden of forgiveness upon you. As a free agent to whom honor is now due, Joe can pray,

"God, make my wife feel my pain, my loss. Cause my son to authentically regret what he did. Make him want to repent. Give him a shot of the honor that you feel toward me."

Quite a stunning miracle—more than a mere parlor trick. It is a covenant privilege that the elect can pray for God to change the heart of their Defendants.

The Old Testament *Consolation* Process

In the Old Testament, the Plaintiff was never required or encouraged to unilaterally forgive the person who hurt them until that person was truly repentant. There is no text that teaches that forgiveness is limited to the Plaintiff's ability to empathize with the Defendant.

The Old Testament teaches that for every crime, there must ultimately be complete *consolation*. There must be a trial, evil purged from the land, the diminished party restored to wholeness, repentant Defendants forgiven and restored, and the unrepentant punished.

God's role in the forgiveness process is critical. Only God can change hearts. Since the Defendant has little control over their own heart, they desperately need God to interpose to give them a new heart.

Likewise, since the Plaintiff has little control over what oozes out of their heart, they desperately need God to intervene and give them a new heart. Only God can pay back what was taken. Only God can ultimately pay for both the primary and secondary crimes. In a phrase, only God forgives.

Plaintiffs have three honorable and critical assignments. *First* they are to initiate the trial by making charges against the unrepentant Defendant for the alleged crime. In Israel, such trials were commonplace and quite safe.

Second, since the Defendant didn't have the power to make them whole, the Plaintiff is charged to run to God to be made whole. Third, the Plaintiff is charged with requesting that God give the offender a new repentant heart.

Final Thoughts

As I have taught this Old Testament model in a variety of settings, I usually get push-back in two areas. *First*, many well-meaning Christians cringe at all of the references to trial, justice, punishment, etc. It seems so un-Christ-like. *Second*, many very beat-up Plaintiffs are quite uncomfortable about all of the Old Testament emphasis on God healing and restoring Defendants.

Why All the Trial Language?

Right now, I assume that some Plaintiffs who read this may be frustrated and confused. You have likely been taught that it is a loving act to release the Defendant from fault. Isn't this godlike? To forgive? To pay the debt owed to yourself? To turn the other cheek, seventy times seven times?

Yes and no. We are to forgive—but we must first define what the Bible means by the word. What is the God ordained *process* of forgiveness?

You can trust God to have your back, Plaintiff. Certainly the God who created you knows. Truly the God who is both just and compassionate would have you free of your wounds and more alive than you are right now. Logically, the God who loves you, would not leave you in the dark with regard to how such freedom and restoration can take place right now.

It is the purpose of this book to flesh out the path of forgiveness that God has defined in both the Old and New Testaments. The approach might be initially counter-intuitive, perhaps even confusing, largely because we have for the most part been taught a very different approach by almost every expert out there.

Cupology 101 is in fact very straightforward and wildly simple. Plaintiff, don't give up. This does not negate all of your efforts to-date. Not at all. This will build upon them.

Tolkien and Consolation

In the first Chapter, I introduced JRR Tolkien's concept of *consolation*.

> "*Consolation* requires that the right order of the world is restored; this means punishment of the evildoer, tantamount to the elimination of evil from the hero's world—and then nothing stands any longer in the way of the hero's living happily ever after."[64]

Basically it is a bi-directional resolution of all conflict that happens in great and lasting stories. The characters of the story are going about their lives and something happens, something unexpected, undesired, unwanted, a *dyscatastrophe*. The story's antagonist either robs them of something or forces them to carry an unwanted burden. The readers react with "That's not right!"

For the conflict to be resolved two things must happen. Tolkien argues that even children expect such a bi-fold resolution of the conflict. First, there must be legitimate, fair, impartial retributive justice. The antagonist must have their day in court, be found guilty and punished appropriately by the law. "Whew!" says the reader relating to the Plaintiff. At last, there has been justice. The world is back in order again.

But wait—there is something missing in the two-fold consolation process. Remember? Something was taken from the Plaintiff, or a burden was placed upon the Plaintiff's shoulder. Consolation requires that the Plaintiff is restored to wholeness again. Tolkien observes that great fairy tales have a *eucatastrophic* turn where someone or some power intervenes and changes the fate of the protagonist. Remember the kiss of the prince in Sleeping Beauty? Such a turn is required if they ever hope to live happily ever after.

Similarly, Plaintiff, your very being, your deepest core DNA requires and demands such a two-fold consolation—justice and restoration. The Old Testament concurs completely. So often, when we separate the altruistic gift of forgiveness from justice's firm embrace, we tragically short circuit the resolution of the story and, in fact, narratively inject another conflict—but sadly in this case, we are our own antagonists.

---

[64] B. Bettelheim, *The Uses of Enchantment: The Meaning and Importance of Fairy Tales.* (New York: Vintage Books, 1977), 144.

Forgiveness can and will happen, but *after* we have experienced justice and restoration. First there is the consolation and the process of consolation divined by God Himself.

Why All of the Emphasis on Healing the Defendant?

This is a very good question. Most forgiveness books focus almost exclusively on the healing of the Plaintiff. The Old Testament models are very concerned for the healing and wholeness of the Plaintiff. But they are *equally* concerned with redemption and restoration for the repentant Defendant.

This is actually—if you can step back and see the larger picture—very good news. This is the whole point of the Bible isn't it? We are all bad guys, Defendants relative to God. We have all sinned and broken covenant, betrayed God over and over again. The story is mainly about how He moves into creation again to unilaterally redeem Defendants.

To put it another way, heaven will be filled with redeemed and restored Plaintiffs as well as redeemed and restored Defendants. If I were honest on any given day, I take on the masks of both.

In the bigger picture, I will stand before God as the Plaintiff for many crimes committed against me. But I will also stand as the Defendant for the many crimes that I have committed against others. God loves both Plaintiffs and repentant Defendants. But His approach is different for each.

So Plaintiff, the crimes committed against you initiated a resolution process toward consolation directed by God. It involves—simplistically put—two journeys, yours and the Defendant's.

For you Plaintiff, consolation involves:

- An experience of justice (i.e., appropriate punishment for the Defendant),
- A restoration to wholeness,

and

- An experience of reduced negative and increased positive emotions toward the Defendant (i.e., forgiveness).

But for the Defendant, consolation involves:

- The very same justice,
- An experience of remorse and repentance for their crimes,
- An experience of positive emotions toward the Plaintiff,

and

117

- An external removal from their shoulders of the shame, guilt, fear and disenfranchisement that comes as a consequence of committing crimes.

When God sees the repentant Defendant weighed down by shame, guilt and fears, He sees both his or her crimes as well as the horrible dehumanizing consequences of sin. From another point of view, God feels the need for perfect justice for the crime and the consequences of the crime, and second, He sees the need for healing and restoration for all involved: Plaintiff, Defendant and community.

Must the Plaintiff Forgive an Unrepentant Defendant?

Remember, there is no evidence in the Old Testament of our modern transactional "forgiveness"—that unilateral altruistic gift that is required by the Plaintiff to the perpetrator whether there has been justice, or remorse, or even an admittance of wrongdoing at all.

Modern Judaism concurs. Humanly speaking, for forgiveness and reconciliation to take place, the offender must become worthy of forgiveness by means of apology, remorse, and restitution (if appropriate) before God and others. The highly influential twelfth-century Jewish Rabbi Maimonides (Dorff, 1998) defined appropriate offender *teshuvah*. *Teshuvah* must include:

- Acknowledgement that one has done something wrong,

- Public confession of one's wrongdoing to both God and the community,

- Public expression of remorse,

- Public announcement of the offender's resolve not to sin in this way again,

- Compensation of the Plaintiff for the injury inflicted accompanied by acts of charity to others,

- Sincere request of forgiveness by the Plaintiff,

- Avoidance of the conditions that caused the offense, and

- Acting differently when confronted with the same situation.

Only after the offender has appropriately done *teshuvah* is the offended party duty-bound to accept the person back into community, to forgive them, and to work toward full reconciliation.

Schimmel agrees with Maimonides and defines the Jewish tradition as an "obligation to a repentant offender."[65] Schimmel criticizes the Western therapeutic models, which he describes as having an unstated radical Christian understanding of forgiveness, but which misunderstand that God offers atonement for sins only on the basis of a sinner's (offender's) repentance. Instead of de-emphasizing the role of the offender, Schimmel says that humanity is called to imitate God who "punishes unrepentant sinners and forgives repentant ones."[66] He suggests that the "radical" Christian concept of forgiveness that demands that the offended party forgive an unrepentant sinner is "morally wrong."[67] He interprets such New Testament passages as Matt 6:12-15 and 1 Cor 13:4-8 and concludes that it just "isn't clear if God expects us to forgive others who hurt us even if they have not apologized or repented."[68]

In the Judah of Jesus' day, the command to forgive assumed that the offender has already performed *teshuvah*. And so in Schimmel's view, Jesus' rabbinical admonition that we are to forgive even seventy times seven times actually refers to a case where an offender has truly repented for their crimes over and over again and yet the offended party just *will* not forgive them. In classic rabbinical thought, the remorseful offender only needs to truly repent three times. If the offended party remains unforgiving, then they have actually committed a separate crime against their former perpetrator.

Jesus is *not* teaching plaintiffs to ever forgive unrepentant perpetrators. That would be a very foolish and even destructive thing to do.

Conclusion

So here's the point. While the Old Testament is virtually silent with regard to our modern notion of a victim-centric empathy driven socio-psychotherapeutic forgiveness, it is unreservedly unabashed in defining and fleshing out the appropriate and loving ways for the Plaintiff to "rebuke" Defendants.

In fact, Plaintiffs who do not take advantage of godly means and methods of resolution of the breach caused by the crimes against him or

---

[65] S. Schimmel, *Wounds not Healed by Time*. (New York: Oxford University Press, 2002), 46.
[66] Schimmel, 69.
[67] Schimmel, 70.
[68] Schimmel, 78.

her, may legally share the guilt of the original crime. Ironically, to emotionally forgive Defendants may even biblically be a law-breaking act.

The key to deep heartfelt forgiveness is God's active participation. God is expected to not only serve as the judge and co-Plaintiff, but he is also the key change agent of the whole affair. It is safe to say that there can be no real forgiveness apart from God's *eucatastrophic* imposition. There is no possibility of justice, or restitution. No possibility of any eventual real reconciliation. Only God forgives.

But this is good news. God does forgive.

Reflection Questions for Individuals or Groups

1)   The author suggests that the role of the Plaintiff in the Old Testament was three-fold: a) To initiate God's forgiveness process through the established courts, b) To run to God for a present experience of healing and restoration to wholeness, and c) To pray that God would forcibly change the heart of the Defendant. Take one of these three charges to plaintiffs and apply it to a real injustice in a modern context. What might it look like to do this today?

2)   Schimmel argues that *no* Jewish Rabbi in first century Israel would *ever* counsel any Plaintiff to forgive unrepentant perpetrators. He labeled such a suggestion as morally wrong. Jesus, then, did not mean that Plaintiffs should forgive an unrepentant perpetrator seventy-times seven times. If this is true, then what did Jesus mean?

3)   Imagine a recent unresolved crime committed against you, where the unremorseful perpetrator still denied responsibility. Perhaps they blame someone else. Maybe they have made some excuse—but they are not repentant. Now imagine what would happen if God intervened and made them truly remorseful of their crime. Specifically how would that change matters? Do you believe that God intervenes in such relational matters today? Why or why not?

PART THREE

Forgiveness in the New Testament

8

Forgiveness in the Gospels

Now when he saw the crowds, he went up on a mountainside and sat down. His disciples came to him, and he began to teach them, saying: (Matt 5:1-2)

Thus Matthew begins the narrative of the popularly named "Sermon on the Mount." It reeks with Old Testament connotations.

Jesus' Radical Message of Forgiveness

On a steadily rising slope on the northern coast of the Sea of Galilee, Jesus spoke to a gathering of plaintiffs; a beat-up occupied and despised people.

"News about [Jesus] spread all over Syria, and people brought to him all who were ill with various diseases, those suffering severe pain, the demon-possessed, those having seizures, and the paralyzed, and he healed them. Large crowds from Galilee, the Decapolis, Jerusalem, Judea and the region across the Jordan followed him. Now when [Jesus] saw the crowds, he went up on a mountainside and sat down. His disciples came to him, and he began to teach them, saying:

125

Blessed are the poor in spirit, for theirs is the kingdom of heaven.
Blessed are those who mourn, for they will be comforted.
Blessed are the meek, for they will inherit the earth.
Blessed are those who hunger and thirst for righteousness, for they will be filled.
Blessed are the merciful, for they will be shown mercy.
Blessed are the pure in heart, for they will see God.
Blessed are the peacemakers, for they will be called sons of God.
Blessed are those who are persecuted because of righteousness, for theirs is the kingdom of heaven.
Blessed are you when people insult you, persecute you and falsely say all kinds of evil against you because of me.
Rejoice and be glad, because great is your reward in heaven, for in the same way they persecuted the prophets who were before you."
(Matt 4:24-5:12)

These were people who were largely religious, largely Jewish. They wanted to know how to please God so that they could be blessed by Him.
"Teacher, what do we need to *do* to get God to powerfully return to His people and restore us to greatness? What must we do in order to get God's attention so that He might free us from the strangle hold of Herod and pagan Rome?"

Embedded in the Sermon on the Mount, are these very familiar words very much related on the topic of this book.
"This, then, is how you should pray: "'Our Father in heaven, hallowed be your name, your kingdom come, your will be done on earth as it is in heaven. Give us today our daily bread. Forgive us our debts, as we also have forgiven our debtors. And lead us not into temptation, but deliver us from the evil one.' For if you forgive men when they sin against you, your heavenly Father will also forgive you. But if you do not forgive men their sins, your Father will not forgive your sins."
(Matt 6:9-15)

This "Lord's Prayer" has brought such comfort and guidance to so many Jesus followers since it was written. But I would suggest that we have largely misunderstood its purpose and role in the larger story of Jesus' life, death and resurrection. It *is* supposed to be comforting, but not in the manner that we usually mean.
Let me unpack it a bit. Highlighted among the lists of commands that Jesus gives are these verses on forgiveness.

"Forgive us our debts, as we also have forgiven our debtors…For if you forgive men when they sin against you, your heavenly Father will also forgive you. But if you do not forgive men their sins, your Father will not forgive your sins." (Matt 6:9-15)

Jesus is starkly clear in His meaning. Plaintiff, you *must* forgive what people owe you. If you do not then *why would you expect God to ever forgive you?*

Whew! At first blush this does *not* sound like really good news to plaintiffs, does it? Rape survivor, if you want to know God's blessing, you first have to totally forgive the rapist? You Galileans who had your sons unjustly slaughtered by Herod's troops, if you would please God you first have to truly forgive Herod. You must forgive Rome and the Roman occupiers who kicked you out of your homes and farms. Otherwise, God will never forgive your sins. Is this really what Jesus is saying?

Tragedy at Nickel Mines

Shortly before 10 a.m. on October 2, 2006, milk truck driver Charles Carl Roberts IV entered the one-room West Nickel Mines School (PA) with a Springfield XD 9 mm handgun, a .30-06 bolt-action rifle and a 12-gauge shotgun along with reportedly 600 rounds of ammunition. By the time the police busted down the door, Roberts had murdered five girls ages 6-13—shot execution style, and seriously wounded 5 others. He then turned his pistol on himself.

At the time, I was the pastor of a church only 2 hours east of Paradise Township. The horror of the event shook eastern Pennsylvania to its core. Were there signs? Warnings? Some, perhaps. Roberts had lost a child, a premature death some three years before. The survivors told of Roberts saying that what he taking revenge upon God for the loss of his daughter, "I'm angry at God and I need to punish some Christian girls to get even with him... I'm going to make you pay for my daughter."

All of this unresolved anger. No experience of Tolkien's consolation. Even his wife had no idea that he was a volcano ready to blow. But none of these excuses offer any relief, any respite to his murder survivors or their families—none at all. Robert's actions were vile, despicable, with total lack of concern for anyone—total indifference to human life. This was a horrific unimaginable *dyscatastrophe*. No happy ending could possibly be expected in this dark narrative.

And yet, what happened next was stunning—deeply convicting to both the religious and non-religious communities of Eastern Pennsylvania. The Amish of Paradise Township heroically chose to forgive Roberts. They raised money for his family and personally brought them flowers and meals, recognizing that they were diminished too. About forty Amish even came to Roberts' funeral and embraced his wife and children as fellow survivors.

The media were stunned at such an unexpected magnanimous superhuman gesture. "Within the first week there were 2,400 stories about forgiveness on the Web from news media around the world," said Donald Kraybill, senior fellow at the Young Center for Anabaptist Studies at Elizabethtown College in Lancaster County, PA. "I was just astonished that forgiveness became news."[69]

In a public statement of gratitude to the Amish, Robert's widow wrote, "Your compassion has reached beyond our family, beyond our community, and is changing our world, and for this we sincerely thank you."[70] Another friend of the murderer's family concurred,

> "All of the expressions of forgiveness provided a great freedom that enabled them to move on with healing despite all the sadness and sorrow. It gave them hope for the future and released them from the heavy burden."[71]

"Hope?" "Release from the heavy burden?" These are "happy ending" descriptors that one would expect once the *dyscatastrophe* was eclipsed by a greater *eucatastrophe*. But there has been no such consolation yet. In the end, despite all of the well-meaning efforts of the Amish toward the perpetrator's family, there remained unresolved guilt, shame and disenfranchisement in the heart of the perpetrator's family, and there remains a huge humanly unfillable hole in the souls of the Amish community. This is *not* consolation.

Plaintiff, stay with me here. I need to lay out the well-meaning logic of the Amish. In my experience, this is where the heads of most modern Jesus-followers go. It seems so biblical, so Christ-like. But in the end, it misses the available miraculous *eucatastrophic* ending prepared by God and purchased for us by Christ. It misses the present foretaste of the future already purchased by Christ. It's narrative does not end "and they all lived happily ever after."

Why did the Amish take such steps to forgive and embrace the murderer's family? Paradise Amish leaders provided an explanation in an unsigned letter:

---

[69] http://www.post-gazette.com/stories/local/uncategorized/nickel-mines-legacy-forgive-first-503952/#ixzz21rhlmUef
[70] D. S. Kraybill, S. Nolt, and D. Weaver-Zercher. *Amish Grace: How Forgiveness Transcends Tragedy.* (San Francisco: Jossey Bass, 2007), 47.
[71] Kraybill, 47-8.

"There has been some confusion about our community's forgiving attitude, [but] if we do not forgive, how can we expect to be forgiven [by God]? By not forgiving, it will be more harmful to ourselves than to the one that did the evil deed."[72]

This conclusion is mainly drawn from their very-literal reading largely of the two very difficult verses immediately after the well-known Lord's Prayer.

"For if you forgive men when they sin against you, your heavenly Father will also forgive you. But if you do not forgive men their sins, your Father will not forgive your sins." (Matt 6:14-15)

The Amish believe that in order to be forgiven by God, they must forgive their oppressors. This is what was at stake at Nickel Mines. According to one Amish writer,

"When we pray the Lord's prayer, we ask the Father to forgive us as we forgive others. Forgiving and being forgiven are inseparable. The person who does not forgive others will not be forgiven...The person who refuses to forgive others has cut himself off from love and mercy. We must forgive, accept, love, if we want God to forgive us our daily trespasses."[73]

Are the Amish right in their interpretation and their application of Jesus' words in the Sermon on the Mount? It would appear that Jesus is saying *exactly* what the Amish suppose—that forgiveness from God *is* conditional on active forgiveness of those who hurt you. By the way, as I explore this question, I am in no way diminishing the heroic faith of the Amish. These are well-meaning Christian brothers and sisters who in a very difficult situation maintained the integrity of their faith to a level that caught the attention even of the world. Even the cynical media saw integrity of belief and actions coming from Nickel Mines.

The question is not whether or not the Amish were being faithful to what they believe. The question is "do they interpret Jesus' words rightly?" My answer is probably going to surprise many readers. I say "yes and no."

---

[72] Kraybill, 95.

[73] Kraybill, 96. Kraybill et al., observe that "Amish assumptions about forgiveness flip the standard Protestant doctrine upside down. The more common understanding asserts that because God has forgiven sinners, they should forgive those who have wronged them. In the Amish view, however, people receive forgiveness from God only if they extend forgiveness to others."r

First of all, yes. The Greek is pretty clear after all. In the Lord's Prayer we do specifically ask that God treat us in the very same way that we treat other people.

"Forgive us our debts, as we also have forgiven our debtors."

Just in case we miss the importance that God puts on such horizontal forgiveness, Jesus clarifies the matter beyond debate.

> "For if you forgive men when they sin against you, your heavenly Father will also forgive you. But if you do not forgive men their sins, your Father will not forgive your sins." (Matt 6:9-15)

This is admittedly a very troubling passage—for all of us. I would have preferred Jesus speak about some other area of the Christian life—other than forgiveness. Forgiving is very, very difficult for me. I do not do it well at all. When someone hurts, me, slanders me, undermines me, or betrays me, my heart naturally lashes out.

Remember from a previous chapter that our hearts are not muscles controlled by our reason. Our heart largely does exactly what it wants to do. This lack of control is universal. It would have been so for every person who in desperation for relief came to hear Jesus speak on the north shore of the Sea of Galilee.

Of all the subjects that Jesus could have expanded upon, he chose the topic of forgiveness. Why? I would suggest that He picked the area where *we regularly fail the most.* Forgiveness is beyond difficult. It is impossible for us. Are we supposed to forgive others? Of course. Its Biblical. But we don't. We won't. Not the forgiveness that God has in mind.

The Amish and the Sermon on the Mount

Hold that last thought. Go back and listen to the rest of Jesus' sermon. Remember He is speaking to frustrated Jews who have not found healing by religiously working hard to obey the Torah. The Law did not accomplish wholeness for them—no matter what they did. What does Jesus do? At first, Jesus seems to pile-on those who were already victimized. It turns out that they were bigger failures than they had ever imagined.

Jesus, in no uncertain terms, informs these fractured emptied cups that anyone who breaks even the smallest of all of the commandments is least in the Kingdom (vs. 19).

It gets worse. God apparently hates anger at a brother as much as He hates murder—and boy does He hate murder! This one had to hurt—assuming that guys haven't changed throughout the centuries. He made lust as big a sin as adultery (vs. 27).

To the beat-up who had come to Jesus for healing, many of who had no doubt been horribly abused, He says that they should not resist an evil person rather they should turn the other cheek (vs. 38-9). Imagine telling a rape survivor that they should just turn the other cheek? Seriously Jesus can't mean what they think it means, can He? In fact, says Jesus, the Torah minces no words. God's people are to love their enemies (vs. 43). What? Egypt? Rome? Herod?

Now at this point, you may be saying to yourself that I must be taking these instructions out of context. Not really. I am making a very important point, based upon my in-depth analysis of the text, as to how we are to understand the Sermon on the Mount.

Jesus makes two additional points. Listen.

"Unless your righteousness exceeds the righteousness of the scribes and Pharisees you will by no means enter the kingdom of heaven."

What? This would have been a body blow. Everyone knew that only the righteous could get into God's kingdom. Certainly not the wicked. God would look favorably upon the man or woman who does those things that please Him and who turn away from those things that anger Him.

The gold standard of righteousness would have been the exemplary pious lives of the scribes and Pharisees. Be careful here. We tend to project the bad and arrogant behavior exemplified by some of the scribes and Pharisees upon the whole group. But that is unfair. These were, generally speaking, pious men and women who lived their lives totally committed to pleasing God. These were the professionals. No doubt there were bad arrogant power-hungry eggs in the carton, but many were doing everything they possibly could to obey God's written word so that they could please Him, earn His favor and expect blessings. So if I may draw a parallel, they were the Amish of 2000 years ago.

Strikingly, Jesus said that all of that sacrificial piety was not enough. Not even close. What? Certainly something is wrong here. Jesus presses his point further—beyond complaint and argument. Just in case you are one of those who imagines that they can pull the rest off. Are you sitting down?

"Therefore, you shall be *perfect*, just as your Father in heaven is perfect"(vs. 48).

What would be the most normal and reasonable human response to this? I can hear the composite voices of so many that I have shared this with.

"But that's impossible!"

131

"What's the point, then, of even trying?"

"I just want to give up, then."

Or the biblical cries of the heart,

"Those who heard this asked, 'Who then can be saved?'" (Luke 18:26)

"Once I was alive apart from law; but when the commandment came, sin sprang to life and I died." (Rom 7:9)

Meaning in today's vernacular, "I thought for a while that I could do, in fact *was* doing everything that God required. I had almost convinced myself, then someone in authority re-explained the law more clearly. It turns out that I wasn't close at all. I was way off the mark."

Right! Exactly! Only the most arrogant person could possibly hear this sermon and say, "Got it, I will start on Monday morning." The person who would dare to say that just wasn't listening—or was listening and not really hearing.

Imagine the vast blindspot—large enough to drive a truck through—of the person who prays, "God help me be perfect?" Seriously? Granted, it sounds so godly, so pious. But isn't what the person is really saying is "I am doing pretty well at this 'doing perfect' thing. God, I just need you to top it off a bit. Then I'm good."

Perfect is perfect. If you do 99%, you fail.

So the Amish are absolutely correct in one sense. It is indeed what Jesus says.

"You want to please God? You want to earn God's blessings and favor? You want to earn God's forgiveness on your own? Then you had better *really* forgive from your heart (1 Pet 1:22) those who hurt you—100% perfectly."

But what the well-meaning Amish miss is that no matter how sincerely they try to forgive Roberts, they will not forgive. *Not to the level that God and the Law demands. It is humanly-speaking impossible.*

To be fair, the Amish at Nickel Mines did forgive in some ways, but horribly failed to forgive in others. In *Amish Grace*, the authors come to the same conclusion.

"Did the Nickel Mines Amish really forgive Roberts within twenty-four hours of the shooting? If forgiveness is defined as forgoing the right to revenge, the Amish clearly forgave Roberts immediately. If forgiveness also includes overcoming resentment and replacing it with love, then the answer must be yes and no....Some bitter feelings lingered."[74]

One Amish minster shared,
"I'm concerned these families will struggle with the forgiveness issue for a long time. They will have to forgive again and again and again, and accept [the loss] again and again."[75]

Decisional versus Emotional Forgiveness

Forgiveness experts often separate "decisional" and "emotional" forgiveness. Christian forgiveness expert Dr. Everett Worthington notes that real forgiveness takes place when the offended party is able to replace their negative unforgiving emotions with positive other-oriented emotions. He referred to this as "emotional replacement hypothesis." [76] Unforgiveness, then, is more than a decision, it is ultimately an emotion—a whole body experience—inevitably linked to patterns of neurochemical releases that shape the emotions.

"It is only as those negative emotions are replaced by such positive emotions as empathy and compassion that the individual will experience forgiveness."[77]

In Worthington's helpful terminology, the Amish heroically forgave *decisionally*, but not necessarily *emotionally*. Arguably, they made a choice to forgive in the only way that they could.

Those victimized *can* choose to forgive by decision.
They *can* choose to move to embrace the perpetrator.
They *can* make corporate and individual commitments to keep decisionally forgiving the perpetrator.

But,

---

[74] Kraybill, 134.

[75] Kraybill, 135.

[76] Worthington, *Forgiveness and Reconciliation*, 24. Emotional forgiveness is the emotional juxtaposition of positive other-oriented emotions against negative unforgiveness, which eventually results in neutralization or replacement of all or part of those negative emotions with positive emotions. The positive emotions that lead to emotional forgiveness have been identified as empathy, sympathy, compassion , romantic love, and altruistic love. (Worthington, *Forgiveness and Reconciliation*, 58)

[77] Worthington, E., as quoted in P. Hill, J. Exline, and A. Cohen. "The Social Psychology of Justice and Forgiveness in Civil and Organizational Settings." In *Handbook of Forgiveness*, edited by E. Worthington, Jr., 477-490. (New York: Routledge, 2005), 478.

The victimized *cannot* make their heart not feel bitterness, sadness, anger, desire for justice and vengeance.
They *cannot* make their heart emotionally forgive.

No one can just choose to vacate such powerful emotions such as hatred, anger, bitterness from their heart—as if there were an emotional cleaning device that would on-demand come and pump all the negative emotions out of their septic tank heart.[78]

So here is the obvious next question. When Jesus says that His followers must forgive crimes, is He speaking just about decisional forgiveness? Or is He commanding His followers that we must also emotionally forgive? Let's go back to the Lord's Prayer.

"Forgive us our debts as we forgive others."

Logically, if we take the second forgiveness to refer to decisional only, then we must also translate the first forgiveness as decisional. Is this what we want of God, that He would merely choose to decisionally forgive, lean toward us, treat us well, but all the while harboring bitterness, resentment and anger toward us? No of course, not. We want God to emotionally forgive us right now—as we are—based upon Jesus' work on our behalf. So what Jesus is really saying in the Lord's Prayer is this,

"God emotionally forgive us our debts, as we also have emotionally forgiven our debtors…For if you emotionally forgive men when they hurt you, rob you, rape you, abuse you against your will, your heavenly Father will also emotionally forgive you. But if you do not do both from your head and heart, then neither will your Father feel positive emotions toward you—only negative."

---

[78] Research has shown that there are unwanted negative consequences in strong cultures—like the Amish--that implicitly or explicitly require victims to immediately and unconditionally forgive crimes. In her 2005 book *Legal Affairs*, Nadya Labi explored the reports of sexual abuse in several Amish communities and concludes that the Amish strict practice of decisional forgiveness has led to some horrific situations. The Amish ethic of forgive-and-forget "often enables offenders to continue their abusive practices." (Nadya Labi, "The Gentle People", Legal Affairs (January-February 2005, 25-32), as quoted in Kraybill, 138.) Such decisional forgiveness that ignores the offender taking responsibility for his or her actions can be very dangerous to any potential healing. Ozick concurs. She charges that such unilateral forgiveness which arguably ignores justice constructs can "brutalize" just as vengeance does. "Forgiveness is pitiless. It forgets the victim. It negates the right of the victim to his own life. It blurs over suffering and death. It drowns the past. It cultivates sensitiveness toward the murderer at the price of insensitiveness toward the victim" (Ozick, C. "Notes Toward a Meditation on 'Forgiveness'," in The Sunflower: On the Possibilities and Limits of Forgiveness (New York: Schocken Books, 1997), 217. The forgiveness process must not undercut the victim's ability to release pent-up emotions such as anger, fear, self-loathing, resentment, and rage (See Legaree et al., *Forgiveness and Therapy*).

So now how well did the Amish do? What grade would God give them? While their actions are heroic and faithful, they still do not get a passing grade. I am sure that the Amish at Nickel Mines heroically tried to emotionally forgive Roberts. They no doubt asked for God's help to forgive such a horrific crime. But to the extent that they couldn't forgive Roberts emotionally, they failed to do *all* that Jesus commanded. If we take the text literally—as the Amish do—the Biblical standard is total emotional forgiveness. This does not make them bad humans, only humans.

Adynaton

So back to the Sermon on the Mount. It now seems clear that Jesus is using a figure of speech called *adynaton* (plural *adynata*). The word comes from the Greek *adunaton* that literally means "without power." The Romans parallel is telling—*impossibilia*. You get the idea? It is a form of hyperbole that uses exaggeration so magnified as to express a virtual impossibility.[79] Or better, in this case, the teachings should cause the listener to throw their hands in the air in total helplessness exclaiming, "But who could possibly do these things? I have no hope at succeeding. There must be a Plan B somewhere, or I am toast."

Don't misunderstand what I am saying. Jesus' commands are not outlandish, or beyond the prescription of the Torah. It is just the opposite. He is accurately expounding the heart of the Law. He wrote the Law after all and so it is His right to clarify what it demands. *The Law of God demands perfection.* In one sense, it is not impossible to accomplish (Dt 30:11-14)—but we *will* not. Practically speaking, it is as good as impossible.

In light of these *adynata*, what should our response posture be?
"But Jesus, this is impossible for me. I cannot--or will not do this. I need another way to get God's favor. I *need* a Savior."

Exactly! Now let's unpack the rest of the Lord's Prayer. I would suggest that it is loaded with *adynata*.

Hallowed be Your [God's] name

In Mt 6:5-7, Jesus has already criticized the professionals for pursuing their own glory even as they outwardly prayed to God.

---

[79] http://www.wordnik.com/words/adynaton

"And when you pray, do not be like the hypocrites, for they love to pray standing in the synagogues and on the street corners to be seen by men. I tell you the truth, they have received their reward in full." (Matt 6:5)

If the professional pious are so hypocritical—that even while they pray to God, secretly they want the praise of men—what hope do the rest of the population have. Lets face it, our hearts at a certain deep level are no different than the other hypocrites. My heart wants—demands—my own experience of "hallowing."

How many times have I heard Christians complain that they are not getting anything out of their prayer life? Think about it with me. If my prayer was that God gets the entire honor from everything that I do, what difference does it make if I don't get a good feeling when I pray? If I were being honest, I pray partly in order to *feel* some personal sense of "hallowed be *my* name." If I don't get that spiritual hit on a regular basis, I will become discouraged and my prayer life will languish. So can I really say that in my heart of hearts that I really mean,

"God forget about my experience, the important thing here is that you receive proper glory? I am good with doing this forever if need be. Don't worry about me."

I am supposed to really want God to be honored over and above my own honor—*no matter what I feel*. But if the deep heart truth were really, really exposed, even as I say the prayer, I really want to share God's honor. So I *can* (and am supposed to) give God 100% of the glory, but I will not. My heart's severely honest testimony probably sounds more like this,

"God, hallowed be Your name of course. But now that I have said that, can you please hallow my name in front of my friends. Just a little bit, please?"

Your Kingdom Come, Your Will Be Done

God is God after all. If anyone should get His way, it should be Him. But I want *my* will to be done too. So even though this prayer is extremely kosher, if the truth were known, I want God's will to be done, as long as it is in sync with mine.

When Jesus prays, "Not my will but your will be done," as He accepts the torture and death of Golgotha (Luke 22:42), we are exposed to a submission that is superhuman. His submission takes our breath away and exposes our own cowardice and unbelief.

My heart naturally prefers and regularly demands that my own will be done. In our largely consumeristic society, we idolize our preferences— often making them equal to God's. Submission is a very dirty politically-incorrect word in churches that pray this prayer regularly.

It is the nature of our flesh. Our hearts naturally prefer that our will be done. Christian, when you pray this prayer, you are giving God your immediate approval to do anything that He may choose to do. What would you think if His will was to put you through great Nickel Mine-esque suffering? What if He asked you to give all of your wealth away—to your competitor? Jesus is telling the truth about God's standards for His people. The Biblical standard is that those who are called by God are to be willing to obey Him all the time. But we won't. So once again, we *can* submit 100% of the time, but we *will not*.

Give us this day our daily bread

I would think that this *adynaton* is obvious. Do you and I really mean to say this?

> "God, I am so dependent upon you right now that I am not worried about my next meal, or the next. I am fully trusting in you. No complaints here. See, I haven't stored up food for my next meal or the next. I am hour by hour at your disposal and provision."

Pantries and savings are not evil per se, but our hearts do tend to idolize our storehouses—our wealth. We too often tend to depend upon our savings and investments, our ability to provide for ourselves more than we daily depend upon God's goodness. Right? Jesus lived a life that modeled "give us this day our daily bread" dependence upon the care of His father. Like in the other cases, we *can*, but we *won't*.

Now is it becoming clearer what Jesus is trying to get those Plaintiffs to see? "You are worse off than you can ever imagine. You need a really big Savior." Now listen to the verses on forgiveness one more time.

Forgive us to the same degree that we forgive others

God help us. Please God, do not answer this prayer, please. We will all perish. God, I need you to forgive me far more than I forgive others. I hold grudges. God please do not hold grudges against me. I pull away from people who hurt me. God do not pull away. I can be passive-aggressive. God please, I do not ever want you to be passive-aggressive toward me. Forgive us Father far beyond our practice. We have no idea what forgiveness looks like, or really costs. Even if we did, our hearts would betray us and spew out hatred, anger and desire for revenge.

So this doesn't sound like good news—at least at first blush does it? What hope do we have to forgive others? In the next chapter, we will look at the familiar parable of the Wicked Servant.

Reflection Questions for Individuals or Groups

1) Before beginning to read this book, how would you describe your personal forgiveness experience? Would you have considered yourself successful? Was your forgiveness typically more *decisional* or *emotional?* Discuss.

2) Dialogue with the author about his take on the Lord's Prayer. Do you agree? Disagree? Why?

3) In attempting to understand and apply Jesus' harsh words in Matthew 6,

> "Forgive us our debts, as we also have forgiven our debtors…For if you forgive men when they sin against you, your heavenly Father will also forgive you. *But if you do not forgive men their sins, your Father will not forgive your sins.*" (Matt 6:9-15)

The Amish scholars conclude,

> "When we pray The Lord's Prayer, we ask the Father to forgive us as we forgive others. Forgiving and being forgiven are inseparable. The person who does not forgive others will not be forgiven…The person who refuses to forgive others has cut himself off from love and mercy. We must forgive, accept, love, if we want God to forgive us our daily trespasses."[80]

Do you agree or disagree? Put in your own words what you believe that Jesus meant.

---

[80] Kraybill, 96. Kraybill et al., observe "Amish assumptions about forgiveness flip the standard Protestant doctrine upside down. The more common understanding asserts that because God has forgiven sinners, they should forgive those who have wronged them. In the Amish view, however, people receive forgiveness from God only if they extend forgiveness to others."

9

Forgiveness and the Parable of the Foolish Servant

"Then Peter came to Jesus and asked, "Lord, how many times shall I forgive my brother or sister who sins against me? Up to seven times?" Jesus answered, "I tell you, not seven times, but seventy-seven times[81]. "Therefore, the kingdom of heaven is like a king who wanted

---

[81] It is widely noted that in Rabbinical writings, it was limited to three times. "One who asks pardon of his neighbor need do so no more than three times..."(Yoma 87a; Hil. Teshuvah 2:9; Orah Hayyim 606:1). But notice the context is very different. It is written that the repentant perpetrator need only go and confess and request forgiveness from their victim three times. After that (in most cases) the unforgiving victim has now sinned against the perpetrator. The standard among the rabbis was not that the victim should forgive unremorseful three times. "Forgiveness must be deserved, and it is earned only after a victim has received restitution and has been appeased. The righting of wrongs and the exacting of

to settle accounts with his servants. As he began the settlement, a man who owed him ten thousand bags of gold was brought to him. Since he was not able to pay, the master ordered that he and his wife and his children and all that he had be sold to repay the debt. "At this the servant fell on his knees before him. "Be patient with me," he begged, "and I will pay back everything." The servant's master took pity on him, canceled the debt and let him go. "But when that servant went out, he found one of his fellow servants who owed him a hundred silver coins. He grabbed him and began to choke him. "Pay back what you owe me!" he demanded. "His fellow servant fell to his knees and begged him, "Be patient with me, and I will pay it back." "But he refused. Instead, he went off and had the man thrown into prison until he could pay the debt. When the other servants saw what had happened, they were outraged and went and told their master everything that had happened. "Then the master called the servant in. "You wicked servant," he said, "I canceled all that debt of yours because you begged me to. Shouldn't you have had mercy on your fellow servant just as I had on you?" In anger his master handed him over to the jailers to be tortured, until he should pay back all he owed. "This is how my heavenly Father will treat each of you unless you forgive your brother or sister from your heart." (Matt 18:21-35)

This is a very troubling parable, particularly the last sentence—leading to the typical moral that many, perhaps even most, preachers attach to the parable:

"Plaintiff, you had better choose to forgive the perpetrator. Just remember how much you have been forgiven by God and out of gratefulness to God pass it forward. You are only being commanded to forgive a relatively small amount compared to God's over-the-top magnanimous gift to you."

But, listen carefully Plaintiff; if that was indeed the moral, you had better forgive *completely—100% of the time*. Good luck with that. If you don't really forgive from the heart, you could lose your present experience of your once-for-all-time salvation. If you fail you will subject yourself to very painful discipline by God.

Is that really what He means? Let's look more closely. This is great storytelling. The original audience would have gotten it. The foolish servant cannot pay that debt. Some have calculated that the amount owed was around $170 million in today's dollars. But the idea is that it is an

justice are prerequisites for achieving forgiveness ("Forgiving the Unforgiveable? Jewish Insights into Repentance and Forgiveness" JSAFE website, author unknown.)

unbelievable amount—to enter into the spirit of the parable, let's say it was $100 billion trillion. It is an absurd debt. Only a king of outrageous substance and wealth could stomach such a bill. The audience would certainly be thinking that this guy is dead, one way or another. No human king would put up with such gross irresponsibility.

Cupology Case Study #6- The Magnanimous King and the Foolish Servant

Imagine a majestic multi-gallon pitcher that should be full but only has a couple of inches of water in it. Then imagine alongside of it there is an infinitesimally smaller, fragile, leaky cup with only a couple millimeters of water. There is no way that the picayune cup—the wicked servant—could possibly refill the pitcher; even if he tried for days or weeks. It is laughable.

The servant is not only a very bad investor, but he is way out of touch with anything close to reality. He doesn't seem to understand how big the debt is. He thinks he can work it off. He needs a little more time.

But here the story takes a surprising turn. We would expect the king to say, "Off with his head!" But not this surprising King. It is not anger that manifests from His being, but rather *splagchnizomai,* compassion (translated in most versions as "pity"). Best defined, *splagchnizomai* is the gut-wrenching emotion that God alone feels when he sees His image-bearer suffer.

Splagchnizomai is only innate to God, not to fallen humanity. So we speak of it as "pity" or "compassion," but it is so much more. Who is this King in Jesus' parable? It is a metaphorical image of God the Father.

This *splagchnizomai* is huge and very strange. The listeners would expect that the King might—just might—give the guy another chance. That would be very magnanimous—off the charts, really. But no! Not this outrageous King. *He forgives the debt.* Literally, he moves the debt away from the servant. Technically speaking, He makes a gift to this totally undeserving servant of $100 billion trillion. Wow! So the story has a happy ending. Everybody gets it. He cuts a check to Himself from His own limitless glory. Now, the foolish servant is totally off the hook.

What happened? Go back to Cupology 101 for a second. As we look closer at the large pitcher, we now see that it seems to be attached to an open faucet by a very substantial hose. Now we can see that this pitcher will never run dry. It is not in its nature. In fact, its nature is to always overflow with precious liquid, overflow over and over again filling the myriad of cups that surround it. It does not ever empty. It is rather the only external source of abundant liquid to other needy cups.

So Plaintiff, get this. We are the foolish servant of the King. We have amassed great, unpayable debts—i.e., sin. It is beyond our reach to pay. Laughably, we are so thickheaded that we will argue that we can do it.

"God, we can pay it all back. Give us another chance! We plead with you, Thou O Holiest One. We'll go to church. We'll read our Bible. We will really love our spouses (if that what it takes), and we will tithe 15% . . . yeah, that ought to do it."

It is truly boneheaded. We can't imagine the immense unpayable debt that each of us has accrued. Even if we are perfect from this point on (how likely is that?), we still have already amassed such a huge debt that we will never even make a dent in it. But legally, the debt must be taken seriously. This King doesn't brush it under the carpet in an act of what we call "mercy" today. Instead, shockingly he pays it on our behalf. This is way beyond what we ever deserved.

Notice that the King doesn't just help the foolish boneheaded servant— give him a little leverage, a little more time, some investment ideas, etc. The King pays it all. It is finished.

This is the heart of our salvation. Our salvation is just not about what we *do* to pay back our sins, but what the King pays on our behalf. This is exactly what happened on the Cross for us 2,000 years ago. So this *splagchnizomai* is not over the top or unusual for this outrageous King. This is His DNA. This is the very nature of this King. Praise God.

How Does the Foolish Servant Forgive Others?

Jesus the tremendous storyteller is not yet done. The readers probably had guessed where Jesus was headed. It is a moralistic tale, right? The out-of-sync servant would *certainly* be so grateful, so overwhelmed by the magnanimous, outrageous actions of the King toward him, that he would of course go and do likewise. He would forgive all of the debts against him. He would pass it forward, right? Wrong!

The next conflict exposes something else about the boneheaded servant. Though his debt on the King's book is perfectly paid, he remains an empty leaky cup. Imagine the scene with me. The huge King is overflowing with substance and *splagchnizomai*, an endless amount. But now look over at the servant of the King? He is not overflowing. Not at all. In fact he is just the opposite. He hasn't really changed much. He is still a small fragile empty cup.

So he does exactly what empty cups do. He tragically turns to another leaky empty cup who owes him pocket change, a laughable picayune debt, not enough to even come close to filling his emptiness. He violently demands justice—full payment. The picture is absurd. It's a parable.

The moral of the tale is this: the foolish servant is *not* the King. Remember the DNA of the King. The King out of His vast endless supply of *splagchnizomai* readily pays the debt of the other. His servant could choose to likewise dismiss the debt of the other servant. But he does not—will not. Why? Because he is not filled. His emptiness is blinding. So desperately feeling the lack, he grabs the fellow servant cup who owes him a tiny debt. He even has the guy arrested until he can pay. It's crazy.

The foolish servant *is* right about justice. Justice must be paid. But he is totally out-of-sync with the King's heart. There is no deep, residing desire to pay for others. So he is debt-free related to the King, but his heart is still empty. No Kingly DNA. This is largely why we have such difficulty with forgiveness. We need to squeeze others to fill our empty cups. It seems so "right" to us. But there are consequences,

"This is how my heavenly Father will treat each of you unless you forgive your brother from your heart." (Matt. 18:35)

I would suggest that the harsh discipline is not designed to motivate the empty cup to obey the King's example—but to see at last that they *will not* obey the King's example. Their hearts will ten times out of ten demand full payment from those who owe them. Why? They are empty. That is what emptied cups do. So, even if they decide to do the right thing out of obedience or fear, their heart still holds an emotional demand of the other for months or years.

Moral of the story? Remember, the moral is not that violated, bone-empty cups have to perfectly forgive the person who has hurt them—or else God will beat them up even more. The better moral is: *Full vessels freely forgive debts. Empty vessels can—but will not.*

So in the end, the boneheaded servant even though his debt has been fully paid to the King, ends up tortured and miserable, disenfranchised from his gracious King.

Christian, if only our debts are paid for, i.e., we live out of forgiveness alone, we still will act "empty." We are commanded to forgive over and over—but we won't. In fact, we really, really don't want to. Why? *Splagchnizomai* is not in our DNA.

So what could the boneheaded servant have done? The answer seems to scream out from the middle of the words of Jesus.

"You bonehead, run to the always overflowing magnanimous King and ask to be made full! The minute amount that was owed to you by your fellow servant is not going to fill you. Period. If you want to be filled, you must go to a source that is larger than yourself. Full vessels

145

act differently. Feel differently. Filling is what the Magnanimous King does. Run to the spring of living water."

Plaintiff take some time to dwell on Jesus' familiar words about how vines work.

> "Remain in me, and I will remain in you. No branch can bear fruit by itself; it must remain in the vine. Neither can you bear fruit unless you remain in me. I am the vine; you are the branches. If a man remains in me and I in him, he will bear much fruit; apart from me you can do nothing" (John 15:4-13)

It is stunning what dry branches can do if they are drinking out of the fullness of the vine. Without the vines *splagchnizomai*, the branch can't do anything vine-esque. But if the branch has any hope of loving others, it is because it has drunk out of the fullness of the vine-that-loves. That branch that is immersed in the juice of the vine appears to pick up some of the wild attributes of the vine. It is even willing to die for friends—i.e., pay the debt on behalf of those who owe them.

How do empty cups and dry branches get to this point? They must see with fresh awareness that they *cannot* do such things on their own. They *will* not do it because they are commanded—or because they will be punished if they don't. They will not do it because it was done for them first. They are empty cups and must admit their emptiness and run to be filled.

As in the Sermon on the Mount, Jesus uses *adynata* to elicit a severely honest emotional response from the audience that He deeply loved. How else would they come to see the human impossibility of accomplishing what they were supposed to accomplish? He knows them. He knows the fractured human spirit. They will just keep on keeping on, keep trying harder until in frustration they will at last give up. What conclusion might they come to?

> "So I am supposed to forgive seventy times seven times. Now I get the heavenly joke. Unless I am regularly filled with the DNA of the King, I will never pull that off. Not even close. My cup is pretty empty on a daily basis. I leak. Whether I want to admit it or not, I am far more like the empty boneheaded servant than the ever-full magnanimous King. So based upon my efforts, the best that I can earn is celestial discipline. I desperately need help beyond my capacity. I am commanded to forgive perfectly, but it is not in my capacity to forgive until I first experience a *eucatastrophic* restoration."

Back to Nickel Mines

Now we can go back to the Amish. In one sense, they read the passage correctly. But in another, very important sense, they functionally appear to have overlooked the mystery of the *adynata*.

Good news, Amish brothers and sisters. Your present experience of God's forgiveness does not depend on *your* piety, or *your* hard efforts to forgive Roberts. At best you can only decisionally forgive Roberts—a far cry shy of the demands of the Law of God. Roberts violently diminished your cups, robbed you of your children, your peace, your joy and your wholeness against your will. Emptied cups cannot forgive. Not really.

It may be helpful to slightly adjust Jesus' parable to fit your circumstances. Same magnanimous King, same foolish servant. Same transaction of the King to absorb the servant's debt himself. But then something goes terribly wrong.

As the debt-forgiven servant is leaving the presence of the King, he is violently attacked by another cup. What precious little liquid he had left is now all gone. What should the servant do? In the hospital, the servant ponders his options. He had just left the presence of the magnanimous King and had a vast debt totally forgiven him. So he concludes that he should mimic the King's gratuitous gift and choose to give up his right of justice.

Isn't that what the King would want him to do? He doesn't have much substance left and so the forgiveness is lacking depth, but he chooses nonetheless to press on.

So I ask you. Is this what the magnanimous King would have the servant really do? To mimic him? No, of course not. The King would be horrified that the servant that He loved wouldn't feel comfortable coming to Him to be filled again. The King can do it. He can restore what the bad cup took. This is what the King does after all. It turns out that this King is also very concerned with justice. He is very concerned with how his servants treat each other. Only when the servant cup is not only debt-free but also filled to the fullness of the DNA of the magnanimous King, wonderful and glorious things can happen.

Jesus tells his disciples that it will all become clear once His Spirit arrives. Then they will understand this miraculous gift of "filling." Filled with the *splagchnizomai* of the magnanimous King, even the disciples will begin to do miracles. Not just mere parlor tricks like parting the Red Sea or walking on water, but really surprising stuff like forgiving someone who hurt them:

> "I tell you the truth, anyone who has faith in me *will do what I have been doing. He will do even greater things than these*, because I am going to the

Father...And I will ask the Father, and he will give you another Counselor to be with you forever...When he, the Spirit of truth, comes, he will guide you into all truth." (John 14:12-26, 16:13)

What you cannot do Plaintiff, God can do through His Spirit in you.

Jesus' Work on the Behalf of the Defendant

But what does Jesus say about the Defendant? I want to stick with the parable a bit longer. There is a loaded phrase that Jesus tosses out there that captures in essence Jesus' role as the Savior of repentant sinners.
"The servant's master took pity on [the wicked servant], canceled his debt and let him go."

This is what Jesus was incarnated to accomplish on behalf of repentant Defendants. He came to cancel the vast debt that repentant Defendants owe the magnanimous King. Like the foolish servant, you have amassed an unpayable debt (i.e., sin). You do not have the capacity to even begin to pay the King back, ever, no matter how hard you try. So what does the King do? He pays your debt for you.
In the Old Testament, there was a foreshadow of Jesus' role as debt-payer in the annual sacred ritual of Yom Kippur. Each year in the presence of the magnanimous King, the great collective debt of all of the repentant wicked servants was ritually placed upon the goat. As the goat was slaughtered in their place, the High Priest proclaimed "It is finished." But these bloody rituals only foreshadowed a single final substitutional atonement. The author of Hebrews captures this brilliantly. All of the endless sacrifices that were annually made were
"...only a shadow of the good things that are coming—not the realities themselves. For this reason it can never, by the same sacrifices repeated endlessly year after year, make perfect those who draw near to worship. If it could, would they not have stopped being offered? For the worshipers would have been cleansed once for all, and would no longer have felt guilty for their sins. But those sacrifices are an annual reminder of sins, because it is impossible for the blood of bulls and goats to take away sins." (Heb 10:1-4)

Ultimately Yom Kippur pointed to the substitutionary death of Jesus that can wash even the guiltiest conscience clean
"Therefore, brothers, since we have confidence to enter the Most Holy Place by the blood of Jesus, by a new and living way opened for us through the curtain, that is, his body, and since we have a great priest

over the house of God, let us draw near to God with a sincere heart in full assurance of faith, having our hearts sprinkled to cleanse us from a guilty conscience and having our bodies washed with pure water." (Heb 10:19-22)

This theology of atonement is echoed by Menno Simons, the theological patriarch of the Amish,

"Through the merits of [Jesus'] blood we receive the remission of our sins according to the riches of Thy grace. Yea through this blood on the Cross He reconciled all upon earth and in heaven above. Therefore, dear Lord, I confess that I have or know no remedy for my sins, no works nor merits, neither baptism nor the Lord's supper...but the precious blood of Thy beloved Son alone which is bestowed upon me by Thee and has graciously redeemed me, a poor sinner, through mere grace and love, from my former walk."[82]

So this is the means and method of God's canceling of your debt. But have you ever wondered about Jesus' sparse description of the foolish servant's response to the Kings stunning unbelievable generosity? I would have at least mentioned the servants surprise, gratefulness, expression of joy and freedom? Nothing? So for the rest of this chapter, I want to give the Defendant a picture of what that foolish servant *should have* felt in response in the wake of such magnanimous grace.

Les Miserables

The 1998 movie, Les Miserables (starring Liam Neeson and Geoffrey Rush) beautifully captures what it should feel like to have such a vast debt paid. Les Miserables is set in the early 1800s in post-revolution Paris. As the movie opens, the main character, Jean Valjean (Liam Neeson) is sleeping on a cold city bench—a vagabond—an outcast of society.

Why? He is a convict—a perpetrator of a minor crime against the French law. He had just finished serving his sentence for stealing bread as

---

[82] In an insightful overview of early Anabaptist's understanding of the atonement, Frances F. Hiebert concludes that "For Anabaptists, atonement is not God's act of forensic justification in which the sinner is declared righteous without actually being made so. It is the transformation of the believer's life, an ontological change brought about by the work of Christ and the faith of the believer." Where some strains of reformational theology arguably overemphasized the "legal or forensic fiction that the work of Christ makes God justify people even when they are actually unchanged" the Anabaptists recognize "the dynamic role of the Holy Spirit as absolutely essential to the work of Christ." (Frances F. Hiebert "The Atonement in Anabaptist Theology," Direction, Vol 30 No. 2 Fall 2001, 122-138).

a boy. The French law was very exact. A crime—even one so human as a hungry boy stealing a loaf of bread is still a crime and must be paid! And so he did. Nineteen years in chains—hard labor.

But now? He had put in more than enough time. He has been released from jail. But, is he free? No. He is physically free, but not really free. The law still permanently records him as a convict. He is given a yellow passport and must report to a parole officer or face going back to prison for the rest of his life.

He *is* a thief. The law says that it is not only what he *did* but who he *is*. He will live now for the rest of his life with the record of the law—"Guilty!" This is what the law does. It is exact, specific and can show no—what we commonly called "mercy." In one sense, the law says that he can never be innocent again. His crime, even though he has completed his legal sentencing, has altered his identity.

There is a great deal of confusion here in the West related to law and mercy. In *our* court systems there is room for what we popularly call "mercy." First, there is "sentencing" mercy. Based upon the circumstances, a lesser penalty can be chosen. But Biblically, the law only knows "guilty or innocent." It asks, "Did you steal?" If yes, then you are guilty. It marks you with a permanent marker as a thief. Secondly, there is "societal mercy." Society can determine that a person has paid the debt, reformed, repented and can give second chances. But law, in its purest form, must be seen more as an exact science. Guilty is guilty. Valjean is a thief according to the law. He bears a yellow passport. He is not a full citizen anymore. One of the consequences of his crime that he must shoulder himself is that he has lost citizenship. He is sub-human in that society.

In the first scene, we see Valjean wandering from place to place, no relationships, no family, and no community. The burden that he is carrying is palpable. He is disenfranchised and must remain so. Maybe it would be helpful to remember the lepers in the Old Testament, or the untouchable class in Hindu countries. Valjean is an outsider.

Even though the law will not, a Christ-like Bishop shows "mercy" to Valjean. He takes him in—as he is. Surprisingly, the Bishop doesn't treat Valjean as a criminal, but instead treats him with dignity afforded to a full citizen. The Bishop feeds him, provides a bed for him. But the unreformed Valjean robs the Bishop of precious silverware and runs. The police capture Valjean and return him to the Bishop for accusation. In a surprising turn (Tolkien's *eucatastrophe*), the Bishop not only does not press charges, he tells the police that the silver was a gift to Valjean. Valjean doesn't understand the Bishop's "mercy." How could he? He is a creature shaped by the objective indifferent "merciless" French law. According to that law, he is guilty and deserves punishment.

But the Bishop understands one element of the law that Valjean has not yet been exposed to. The law doesn't care who pays for the crime—just that the crime be paid for. Of course, this is a type of Biblical redemption (more on this later). The Bishop says to Valjean, "With this silver I bought your soul. I ransomed you from fear and hatred and now I give you back to God."

This is hailed by many as the redemptive scene in the film. The Bishop—as a Christ-figure--at least on the surface pays for Valjean's immediate sins. He pays the full price of the theft of the silver from the cupboard. He pays the debt the law requires and so Valjean is free from the law's grasp. The Bishop's actions are a wonderful type of the redemption earned by the work of Christ at Golgotha. Having said that, notice that the redemption was largely incomplete.

Why incomplete? First, though the Bishop has accomplished much in his behalf, he did not, nor could he truly set Valjean free from the law. The Bishop had no power or authority to change Valjean's identity from thief to citizen. The law still proclaims Valjean "guilty." That hasn't changed! The Bishop's redemption kept Valjean out of jail for his most recent crime, but did not set him free. Second, Valjean was not restored to citizenship. He still carries the yellow card. The Bishop offered what we would label as grace or mercy—but could not offer a new identity.

Not to take anything away from the actions of the Bishop, Valjean needs more in order to be truly free. In the movie, Valjean still had to live in the shadows—isolated, his true identity covered up, wearing masks for his own safety, afraid of being recognized and caught. By who? The law! This is a great image of the consequence of sin pre-consolation. David in Psalm 25:18 refers to this burden as affliction and distress. Valjean is still burdened by such a guilt.

What then can the thief Valjean do? This is often what guilty, burdened Defendants try to do. They try to take matters into their own hands. They tend to do whatever it takes to become a new person on their own. Valjean creates a mask—a new life. A pseudo-consolation. He changes his name, gets forged citizenship papers. In a sense then, the thief Valjean "dies." He begins a new life, new identity with a clean slate-- and eventually becomes the successful Mayor of Vigo. Arguably, in the short run it seems to work. To the community, Valjean is no longer Valjean the thief. He is Le Mayor, a gracious gentleman. But the law is not fooled. Dress up a convict all you want—reform all you can—but the record clings to you like a dirty shirt. The law is a stickler and is not so easily fooled.

But all the readers know that it is a very unstable house of cards. All the viewers know that he will get caught.

A few years ago, we went to pick up my then-teenage son John after two weeks of summer camp. Whew! There was a real smell on him—deeply penetrating his skin and clothes, It took days of washing after washing to clean out. It clung to his skin and clothes. Similarly, the consequences of sin (e.g., shame, guilt, fear of being caught) clings to the heart of guilty unwashed Defendants. Legally, the stench of their crimes clings to them until they die.

Deep down, Valjean knew that all of his rebirth actions were not enough. Valjean lives the bulk of his adult life in fear of being exposed. Though wealthy, he lived as a recluse and a hermit. Reformed? Perhaps—but nevertheless, in fear of the law. Is Valjean really a new man? No. It is the law that measures the man.

The law—represented by Vigo's Chief Inspector Javere (Geoffrey Rush), a former prison camp guard--recognizes Valjean. Javere loves the law, every jot and tittle. Valjean is a criminal and must be held accountable. The law is not concerned with reformation—only justice. Valjean just can't understand why the law cares anymore.

"Why couldn't you just leave me alone? I am nothing—I am no one. I am just trying to live in peace."

Javere, the incarnation of the law can only reply, "I won't stop... I won't let you go!"

The law by nature cannot hear of mercy apart from perfect justice. The law cannot forget. The law is the law.

In a remarkable scene, through a complex turn of events, Valjean is actually given an opportunity to kill Javere. Wouldn't that be great? If I was given a sledgehammer and was able to crush the tablets of the 10 commandments? No more law. Then maybe I would be free—right? There are some speed limit signs that I would just love to rip out of the ground – stomp all over them and toss them into the yards of the bureaucrat who put them there. Maybe you teens can relate to this one. "If I could just get out of my parents' house and restrictions—and religion—then I would be free." Right? Isn't this what the Jews and Romans did on Good Friday 2000 years ago. Let's kill God's Son, the judge himself, and then we are free.

But you cannot kill the law. It is bigger than you or I. It is one of the principles of creation. It is the structure of the heart of God. And this is good news. The law is a very powerful, unyielding antagonist, but it is just as powerful an advocate! The law is great if it is on your side!

One of the Old Testament's ultimate end game is beautifully portrayed in the last scene. There we see Javere and Valjean on the banks of the Seine River, all alone. Valjean is tired and old—worn down by the lifelong chase—by the weight of the disguises, the shame, guilt and fear. Valjean, the thief, is now rightly in chains. Javere has a gun to his head. The law will be satisfied. The debts will be finally paid by death. Javere deliberately explains to Valjean

> "I am going to give you what you deserve. Move to the edge (of the Seine). You don't understand the importance of the law...I am going to spare you from life in prison Jean Valjean. It's a pity that the law does not allow me to be merciful."

As the viewers watch in shock, Javere puts his gun down, takes the chains off of Valjean, puts them on himself and plunges into the Seine. He dies in the place of Valjean.

Of all of the Christ figures in the movie—and there are many—including Valjean—only Javere really portrays Jesus in His role as judicial satisfaction for not only all of the crimes of people like me—but for our identities as celestial criminals. The antagonist of the movie, the harsh unyielding Javere alone understood justice and its power. The Bishop's act of mercy could not set Valjean free. The law marks a person until they die. He understood mercy perhaps, but not law!

All of Valjean's good works didn't remove the guilt, the stigma, the stench of his past, the thief identity. Only death removes us from the relentless authority of the law. At the moment of Javere's death, Valjean is no longer Valjean the thief—he no longer is under the burden of the yellow card. He is now a full card carrying citizen and restored to all rights of citizenry.

Then at last we, the viewers, can see what freedom really looks like—feels like—for Valjean to finally have his sin and the consequences of sin lifted from his shoulders. The dark foreboding Parisian sky lights up with a brilliant sunrise. Valjean's worn façade becomes that of a younger man. There is at last hope in his eyes as he turns his face to the heavens in unbelief and happiness. As he turns, his shoulders are no longer weighed down and drooped, but relaxed. Birds around him break into flight. He is a new man, a new creation. His burdens have been lifted away by the sacrifice of Javere.

Conclusion

For Jesus, only filled cups really have the capacity to forgive. Emptied cups, even debt-free ones, cannot. They can heroically try, but it is a foolish quest doomed to failure. Each of us were once Valjeans, burdened by our sin, yellow-carded felons. But, the death of Jesus paid all of the debt, tore up our yellow card and gave us new identities as sons and daughters of the Great Judge.

As the parable puts it, "[Our] master took pity on [us], canceled the debt and let [us] go."

But the mistake that we Christians so often make is forgetting that though our debt is fully canceled, once for all time, we remain emptied cups until we, by faith, run back to our magnanimous King and get filled over and over again. Emptied cups regularly filled with the *splagchnizomai* of the magnanimous King are powerful.

This ongoing filling changes everything.

Reflection Questions for Individuals or Groups

1) Describe in your own words the moral of Jesus' parable of the foolish unforgiving servant. Based upon what you have learned, how would you counsel someone who has been victimized? How do you think that the counsel would be received? Why?

2) The author suggests that God is very interested in redeeming and healing the Defendant (i.e., the perpetrator). Discuss some of the ways that hurting Plaintiffs may feel toward such a God. In your own words, explain to such Plaintiffs why this might actually be good news for them.

3) Many commentators suggest that the Bishop's actions on Valjean's behalf were redemptive and modeled biblical forgiveness. The author suggests that in the end, the greatest of Christ-figures in Les Miserable—shockingly—was the antagonist, police inspector Javere. Do you agree or disagree? Please explain your point of view.

4) Describe in your own words how Valjean was set free? Why might this be good news to Plaintiffs? To us all?

10

Paul and Forgiveness

Jesus commands that we are to forgive those who hurt us. That's the Law. But then Jesus turns around in the provocative parable of the foolish servant and suggests that even though we have been forgiven so much, we still will fail at forgiving others. Something is amiss.

How do we reconcile the two apparently disparate thoughts? Here's the punch line. Even those of us who are saved, who have had all of our sins forgiven, whose names are permanently ascribed in Heaven's roster, still lack the innate capacity to really forgive.

It matters little that we have seen God's example of great forgiveness, over-the-top forgiveness in our own cases. Sure this does to some degree motivate us to attempt to mimic God's forgiveness. But though we try, try, and try again, we *will* fail.

So what then is Joe to do? The coffee lady? The Amish of Nickel Mines? Am I saying that they should just give up? Absolutely not. God provides His followers the ongoing means and power to forgive others. To access those means and power, we have to first admit our ongoing inability to forgive and second, to run humbly to God to be filled again, and again, and again with His capacity to forgive others.

Paul's Cupology

Go back for a second to Jesus' parable about the foolish servant. Remember the imagery? The over-the-top magnanimous King is portrayed as a huge pitcher hooked up to an endless flowing faucet. So it is always full, always overflowing. In stark contrast, the foolish servant—though in the King's household, was not full, in fact he was a very empty and perhaps a very leaky cup (maybe that is why he owed the King so much). See the contrasts?

The King: innately full and overflowing.
The foolish servant: innately empty and desperately thirsty.

It is the King's nature to forgive—even huge debts.
It is not the nature of the foolish servant to freely forgive—even tiny debts.

Right? This is so important. Though the magnanimous King fully paid the servant's huge debt, the transaction did not change his fool nature. In fact, the servant was not any fuller leaving the King's presence than before he arrived. He was an empty cup when he arrived at the King's throne and an empty cup when he walked out the door.

How do I know? No sooner did the servant leave the King's presence than he turned violently on another cracked cup and demanded filling from them.

The foolish servant was clearly in the right. A debt is a debt. Justice is justice. The servant—unlike the King—did not have a hose that regularly filled him. So in order to be filled—even a little bit—lots of energy was required to get so little justice.

Did the foolish servant have another choice? Of course. He could have run back into the presence of the magnanimous King and begged to be filled from the King's vast supply.

A cup filled with the DNA of the King is also a cup that can forgive.

"Fullness of God" Cupology

Here it is at last. The entire book has been pointing to this. How do Christians forgive? We are invited to run to our magnanimous King and be filled—over, and over, and over again.

Nowhere is this clearer than in Paul's wonderful letter to the vulnerable church plant in Ephesus. We can glean a lot about the struggles that the Ephesians would have. We know that they would have to put up with oppressive forces outside the church (Acts 19)—and from within (Rev 2:1-2). Their mission was to one of the most pagan, international hubs in the 1st century. Their cups would be cracked over and over and drunk dry time and time again.

What direction could Paul possibly give them to deal with the oppression, the attacks, and the betrayals that would happen? He does not tell them to just unilaterally forgive their perpetrators seventy times seven times. He does not say that they need to work really hard to empathize with the betrayers. No, in Ephesians 3, Paul sets out a new path for Christian Plaintiffs to actually be empowered to forgive.

> "I pray that out of his glorious riches he may strengthen you with power through his Spirit in your inner being, so that Christ may dwell in your hearts through faith. And I pray that you, being rooted and established in love, may have power, together with all the saints, to grasp how wide and long and high and deep is the love of Christ, and to know this love that surpasses knowledge — that you may be filled to the measure of all the fullness of God. Now to him who is able to do immeasurably more than all we ask or imagine, according to his power that is at work within us to him be glory in the church and in Christ Jesus throughout all generations, for ever and ever! Amen." (Eph 3:16-21)

I want to point out how important this issue is to Paul. Imagine Paul shaping an important letter in his head. He has very little space to share such important theology to the young fledgling church. What should he prioritize? Well, he goes to great length to pray one thing for the Ephesus church—just one thing. He prays for them that they would have power, an alien power, a power that issues from the being of God Himself.

Power and Forgiveness

Isn't it the nature of victimization to feel powerless to some degree? Someone has taken something from you against your will. You feel powerless. It is the nature of victimization to immediately want to get your power back. You could scramble to get your mojo back. But likely you have discovered that you can't retrieve robbed power from the Defendant.

Good news. Paul offers to Christian Plaintiffs another source of power that has nothing to do with who the Defendant is or what he or she does. Access to this power is also not dependent upon who the Plaintiff is or what he or she has done. This power is freely available to all Jesus-followers now, today, as you are.

The source of the power? Why of course, it is from the infinite supply of the magnanimous King. It comes from his "glorious riches." Emptied cups, why struggle attempting foolishly to gather such glorious riches from other empty cups? Are we such foolish servants?

Paul is clear. This is one of the vast privileges of being a follower of the magnanimous King. No other sacrifices are required other than the one already provided. You don't have to go on a long journey to access such power. Paul says that the King is never far from you. His Spirit is already within your inner being. His DNA, His *splagchnizomai* is readily available by faith to you, 24/7.

I have this image of a child comfortably undisturbed within her mother's womb, being cared for, washed in wonderful life-giving fluids through an umbilical cord. Always connected. Life always flowing.

Paul suggests the opposite. We are not the infant within the mother's womb. It is the Holy Spirit of God who is mysteriously within *our* inner being. The Holy Spirit within us is our source of life.

How do we tap into the life-giving substance of the Spirit? Unlike the infant who passively just receives sustenance, we must regularly ask for filling. Paul models this by interceding on behalf of the Ephesians that God would give them His power by means of the Holy Spirit in them. All you have to do Plaintiff is ask God for that power.

Christian, have you ever actually prayed that God would strengthen you deep within your inner being—down deep where your pain is the greatest, with *His* power?

I was quite surprised that I had missed this section of Paul's teaching. After years of being a Christian, years of flailing around depending heavily upon my own hit-or-miss efforts, particularly failing in the area of forgiving others, I finally saw that I was desperately missing something. Embarrassingly, I had never specifically asked God for His power in my inner being.

Since that time, I have shared this with many individuals and audiences at multiple venues in multiple countries. Normally I ask this same question just to see if I was possibly the only one who didn't understand that I could avail myself of God's healing power. I cannot recall anyone ever saying that they did this at all, much less on a regular basis. We have a spiritual crisis on our hands. Admittedly this is an unscientific survey, but still very telling.

I would suggest that we modern Christians are vast well-meaning *underachievers*, attempting to accomplish on Christ's behalf—by our own very limited capacity and strength—those things that require Christ's power alone to accomplish. Remember the Amish?

According to actual scientific surveys[83], though conservative Protestants rank forgiving others as "very important to us," we still do not forgive measurably more than non-believers. Interesting? It is not that we are not trying. Unfortunately we *are* trying to accomplish something that requires miraculous power.

Good news, beloved redeemed leaky cups, Paul tells us that we have another option. We can access, by faith, God's celestial power deep in our inner being. Right now. What does such power accomplish? Paul defines four goals of God's power in us.

- A palpable present experience of Jesus with you.

- A present experience of God's absolute love and favor toward you and toward others.

- A celestial reframing of the criminal and the crime.

- A present experience of your cup being filled.

A Palpable Present Experience of Jesus With You

One of the first things that you will experience as you drink from God's infinite draught is a palpable sense of Jesus' presence in your life.

"...so that Christ may dwell in your hearts through faith." (Eph 3:17)

Let me point out how provocative Paul is being. Doesn't Paul know that Christ already dwells in the heart of His followers? This is core to his teaching on being born-again. If you have confessed Jesus as Lord, you are not only saved, but you have the Holy Spirit permanently in your inner being. This is Christianity 101 for Paul.

---

[83] Davis, D.E., J. N. Hook, E. Worthington, D.R. Van Tongeren, A.L. Gartner, D. Jennings, and L. Norton, "Relational Spirituality and Dealing With Transgressions: Development of the Relational Engagement of the Sacred for a Transgression (REST) Scale," International Journal for the Psychology of Religion, 20(4) (2010): 288-302.

So why is he saying that the Ephesians need to access an ongoing alien celestial power to have Christ in their hearts? I would suggest that Paul is saying that there is a real difference between experiencing

1) Christ *dwelling* in your inner being and

2) Christ *DWELLING* in your inner being.

Plaintiffs need Christ DWELLING in their hearts. Emptied cups need a radical filling, a radical presence of Jesus. Are you following me, Plaintiff?

Paul knows that victims of great crimes can come to feel so alone in the universe. So abandoned and betrayed. Christian Plaintiffs can even begin to feel that God has abandoned them—or that God Himself is against them, punishing them for some reason. Listen to one of the Psalms penned by the Sons of Korah.

> "My eyes are dim with grief. I call to you, O Lord, every day; I spread out my hands to you... I cry to you for help, O Lord; in the morning my prayer comes before you. Why, O Lord, do you reject me and hide your face from me?" (Psalm 88:9-14)

I have felt such abandonment. Haven't you? How great would it be right now to feel Jesus' vast loving arms around you. The truth is that He never left your presence. His Spirit has been with you always. He did promise (John 14:18, Heb 13:5). But too often we lose the sense of His presence with us. Do you want that sense of His loving honoring presence back?

Ask to be filled with His power until you can hear His Spirit in you crying out "Abba Father!" again (Gal 4:6, Rom 8:15). I have learned that this exercise is not just a one time and done affair. It turns out that I am a very leaky cup. Left unattended my sense of value and worth empties very quickly. I am learning that I need to humbly run to God daily, twice a day (or even more) and plead for His power so that I can feel like I am His adopted son in good standing. My head can tell me all the theological premises involved. But its my heart that wavers—a lot.

God give me your power, now, quickly so that I feel your love for me, so that I won't go looking for love or honor in all the wrong places. Amen.

162

A Present Experience of God's Absolute Love and Favor Toward You and Toward Others

But Paul is not done. This power has other related benefits. Filled presently with such celestial power, you can at last begin to truly
"...grasp how wide and long and high and deep is the love of Christ, and to know this love that surpasses knowledge." (Eph 3:18)

Imagine Plaintiff, right now being able to grab hold of the miraculous love of Christ for *you*. Imagine how that would make you feel? Imagine how that love would wash over your wounds, even heal some. The one who robbed you, betrayed you, or abused you didn't love you (certainly not at the moment of the crime). They treated you as an object unworthy of being loved or honored.

One of the secondary crimes committed against you is that you now wonder if you are an object worthy of being loved. But now as you grab hold of this love, this endless vast love of Christ for you, you remember that you are now, post-Cross, innately lovable. As you are. Drink it in Plaintiff, let its sirenic music reprogram your soul. It is unbelievable, beyond your ability to figure out of course, but it is true.

A Celestial Reframing of the Criminal and the Crime

"...from now on we regard no one from a worldly point of view." (2 Cor 5:16)

Listen very deeply to something else going on deep in your soul. As you access, by faith, this power and have begun to feel the vast incomprehensible love of Jesus for you as you are—you will notice something else critical to your new calling as a new creation in Christ.

You are being filled with the height and length and width and depth of the love of Christ *for the Defendant* as well. No matter who he or she is or what he or she as done, Christ loves them far more than you do. Remember He is the magnanimous King, not you. He is never diminished, never holds grudges, and never needs justice in order to be whole. He is already whole.

In a sense, God's Spirit in you can enable you to "reframe" the Defendant. Reframing techniques are very common in counseling today. Victims of crimes tend to demonize the Defendant. But in fact, Defendants are also very human, so the counselor attempts to assist the victim of the crimes to see the perpetrator through a different lens.

Maybe they had a reason to do what they did.

Maybe it was largely about their upbringing?

Maybe it was drug induced?

Maybe it was truly an accident?

The goal of such reframing is to elicit some inkling of empathy from you for the Defendant as a fellow human being. Any empathy at all can possibly lay seeds that could eventually grow into forgiveness. If the counselor can get you to see the Defendant through a "humanity lens," maybe you might be more ready to choose to forgive. Right?

Christian Defendants, you have something far greater at your access. You can begin to see the Defendant through the "*Christ-lens*," i.e., come to see the Defendant the way that Jesus sees him or her.

Listen to Paul's development of this thought. In 2 Corinthians 5:15-18, Paul speaks of seeing others through a redemptive lens (contrasted to a "worldly point of view").

> "And [Jesus] died for all, that those who live should no longer live for themselves but for him who died for them and was raised again. So from now on we regard no one from a worldly point of view. Though we once regarded Christ in this way, we do so no longer. Therefore, if anyone is in Christ, he is a new creation; the old has gone, the new has come! All this is from God, who reconciled us to himself through Christ and gave us the ministry of reconciliation." (2 Cor 5:15-18)

Plaintiff, you no longer have to regard the Defendant from a worldly point of view. You are a new creation. The old stuff (the way you used to deal with wounds, hurts and emptiness) is gone to you. Filled with new perspectives, you can begin to truly access your real calling. You have been reconciled to God so that you can spend the rest of your life ministering reconciliation to other emptied cups.

In one fell swoop, Paul summarizes the entire ministry of Christians. Bottom line, you are to spend your life reconciling others to God and to each other (2 Cor 5:19). How can you ever accomplish this? You must begin to see things through the new *Christ-lens*. This changes everything.

Let me elaborate. If the Defendant, the one who badly hurt you is indeed a born-again Jesus-follower-gone-awry, your choices are clear. Carefully look at them through the *Christ-lens* and answer this: *When Jesus looks at them, what does He see?*

What does He feel toward him or her *right now*? Of course, the answer is that He loves them, as they are right now.

The Defendant, due to no effort on their own are adopted children of the magnanimous King. Their crimes, their many crimes, including the ones they committed against you are fully and totally paid for by Jesus Himself. Jesus died for even their most vicious and dehumanizing crimes. They, like you, are new creatures in Christ.

Does Jesus take their crimes against you lightly? Oh no. They were so serious that only a death penalty could satisfy justice. Their treatment of you deserved a capital punishment. And so He died on their behalf. Justice smiles and asks no more.

By faith, Plaintiff, you can ask for two things from God. *First*, you can plead with Him to apply that sense of completed justice to your heart until its cries for fairness are realized.

"God cause me to see the Defendant and the crime as you see it. Give me the capacity to see the events through the *Christ-lens*. Make me feel the "It is finished!" the way that you do."

Until that happens, you cannot minister reconciliation to them.

Second, you can access the power of God by faith in order to feel *His* love for the Defendant, the height and length and width and depth of the love of Christ, not just His love for you, but His love for the one who mistreated you so much. Apart from the redemptive work of Jesus, this is mere crazy-talk. But post-Cross, this is real; not just an act of denial or stoicism.

This is not cheap grace. Paul does not deny necessary justice that precedes forgiveness. Jesus took on the sin of the believing Defendant so that you might forgive them and move toward healing the breach in His body—the church (i.e., the ministry of reconciliation).

He Said, She Said

Let me give an example. When I counsel deeply divided Christian couples, who are literally on the brink of separation and divorce, I try to help them see each other through this *Christ-lens*. I typically ask what is wrong with their marriage. The husband usually goes into a list of wrongs committed by the wife. The wife counters with an even larger list of wrongs committed by the husband.

When I think that the moment is right, I ask the wife to leave the office for a bit so that I can speak directly to the husband.

"Whew," I say to him when we are alone. "That is a pretty strong case you are making against your wife. She seems guilty of many things against you. Am I hearing this correctly? Tell me, in light of such dishonor and mistreatment, how do you feel toward her right now?"

It is interesting to see how Christians just hate to see their own ugliness oozing out of their hearts. Typical answers? "I am pretty irritated at her," "I am pretty frustrated," "I am at the end of my rope." So I help them out.

"Well if it were me, and my wife treated me that badly, I would be very angry—in fact, I might even begin to—at moments—actually hate her. Have you ever felt that?"

They usually squirm a bit but finally admit that they had felt that on occasion. I do the same interview with the wife—always with the same ultimate result. When I gather them both in my office, I seriously tell them the bad news.

"So you came to me because of the irreparable damage that your marriage has endured. I get it. It is in very rough shape. But that is not your biggest problem. You are so focused on your marriage that you can't see the real danger each of you is in. Husband, tell me, what does God feel toward your wife right now? How does He see your wife?"

It often takes a bit of time but he eventually gets around to saying that "God loves my wife."

"You mean, the same woman that you have admitted being so angry with, even hating on occasion?"

"Wife, what does God feel toward your husband—right now—as he is right at this moment? How about when he treated you so badly last night? Last week?"

"You see, your biggest problem is not your flagging marriage, or each other. Your biggest and most immediate problem is that each of you is wildly out-of-sync with God. Each of you hates someone that He loves with all of His heart. I wouldn't want to be in your shoes right now. God takes this very seriously. I urge you to get back in line with God first, we can deal with issues in your marriage later."

So almost always I give them this simple assignment. *First* I ask that until our next visit that they speak to each other very sparingly, only if necessary. Their words would only be destructive. *Second*, I instruct them —early in each day—to plead that God would give each of them His love for the other. In the evening, pray the same prayer. Do this morning and evening for ten days.

Do you see what I am hoping to accomplish? Their marriage has huge issues, deep structural problems that may have deeply shattered much of the foundation of their relationship. There is little trust, little positive communication, little love for each other. Their relationship needs a miracle.

I try to get them to put on the *Christ-lens* so that they can see the other in the same way that the Holy Spirit in them does. I ask them to access the power that Paul speaks about, so that they would experience a fresh love toward the other—the height and length and width and depth that He feels for each spouse.

Plaintiff, this is a miraculous transformation that I am asking for. This is a privilege of being a son or daughter of the living God. Son and daughter Plaintiffs can, by faith, see the Defendant (and the crime committed) as Jesus now sees them. They are new creations (2 Cor 5:17), the old things are now gone. Justice has been duly considered and satisfied.

Plaintiff, you can by faith be empowered to reframe the believing Defendant as a redeemed beloved child of God. Their sins no longer counted against them (2 Cor 5:19).

Once you access such a power, such a love for the other, your marriage will have more than a mere hope of surviving. In fact, it could become an example to others of just what God's reconciling power can do.

What About *Unbelieving* Defendants?

Let me say a brief word about God's reconciliatory power and love for *unbelieving* Defendants.

According to the Bible, God promises a trial for all crimes ever committed. There will be a final day in court (real or metaphorical), a final verdict, "Guilty!," and a final act of justice. In the end, all crimes will be fully paid for. All repentant Defendants who throw themselves upon Jesus as their great substitutionary atonement will "have their debt paid and be set free."

But there will be others who high-handedly *refuse* so great a redemption. Some will tragically *refuse* to kiss the hem of the Son (Psalm 2:12), *refuse* to bow to Him as Savior and Lord and so implicitly and explicitly accept the weight of their punishment fully upon their own shoulders. It is truly a sad and tragic choice for image bearers of God.

But nevertheless, justice will be *completely* satisfied. That's the point here, isn't it? Plaintiff, you can ask, by faith, for the Holy Spirit to apply that future *Aaaah! Factor* to your troubled heart right now. Whether your

Defendant is a believer or not, you can immediately experience a *present* foretaste of your *future* perfect promised consolation.

Plaintiff, it changes everything to know above and beyond your comprehension that justice for that crime will indeed be paid—fully.

But what about the debt? What about what the Defendant took from you? What about the hole left by the secondary crimes? Great questions.

A Present Experience of Your Cup Being Filled

Go back to Ephesians 3 for a moment. When you pray to God that He would give you power, there is one last necessary benefit. Paul prays that the Ephesians would have power so that they would be experientially "filled to the measure of all the fullness of God."

Plaintiff, do you see? Paul kindles our imagination to see that ultimately such fullness is from God, not the offender, and not interventions, and not even your own efforts that you can access wholeness again. The emptied-cupped Defendant cannot make you whole. The justice system cannot make you whole.

Lets change the way that we think of this. Paul sees the obvious connection between the death and resurrection of Jesus, the subsequent sending of the Spirit and the invitation to the diminished who are Jesus-followers to come to God—by faith—to be made whole.

So imagine Jesus' parable of the foolish servant again. How would the parable have changed if the wicked cracked cup had run to the Magnanimous King to be made whole from the debt of the other cracked cup? More specifically, lets assume that the King filled up what the other cup owed. Imagine with me how the formerly foolish cracked cup might feel differently toward the other servant? The entire parable would be radically different.

Plaintiff, imagine how you might begin to feel differently toward the one who robbed you, if your cup were refilled in some dynamic equivalence from God's celestial storehouse (Eph 1:18, 3:16: Phil 4:19)? Even if the immediate sensation of the filling is only partial, it still will make a radical difference, right?

Now further imagine that you were also filled up with the capacity to feel toward your Defendant what God feels toward them. That you could finally see them through the *Christ-lens*, instead of your old lens.

This is the theology of Paul. Plaintiffs who run to God as their source of restitution also begin to powerfully feel differently toward the one who hurt them. It is to these that he dares to say,

"Be kind and compassionate to one another, forgiving each other, just as in Christ God forgave you." (Eph 4:32)

"Bear with each other and forgive whatever grievances you may have against one another. Forgive as the Lord forgave you." (Col 3:13)

Filled by the Spirit, Plaintiffs can experience God's compassion toward the offender right now. Lest you fall into the same interpretive error as the well-meaning Amish of Nickel Mines, hear these commands differently. Plaintiff, your heart is not kind, not compassionate. It will not forgive—not really.

Confess your inability to obey and run to God. Be filled with His kindness, His compassion, His forgiveness, and then do what the Spirit leads you to do. Plaintiff, get your empty leaky cup filled again with His fruit and then in one sense, you can go and do what you *want* to do.

In Ephesians, Paul gives us a few stunning examples, just to help us see the miraculous nature of God's fruit working through us by faith. In Eph 5:18, he encapsulates all of Ephesians 3:14-21 passage into just four Greek words: *alla plerousthe en pneumati*. In English it reads, "instead be filled with the Spirit." First, go and get your emptied leaky cup filled with God's power.

What does Paul imagine might just be the evidence of God's miraculous fruit blossoming anew from cracked cups? Well, in v. 22, wives will actually be moved to honor their husbands. This honor is beyond the normal day-to-day stuff. Paul is no doubt speaking of the same substantive honor that Jesus feels toward the Father and toward the Spirit. It is not at all dependent upon the immediate object's (the husband's) worthiness. Not at all. It is an honor that comes from God. Believe me, your husband *will* notice the difference.

Wives then were no doubt much like wives today. Their husbands probably didn't love them to the degree they should have. They probably took them for granted, or worse even used or abused them. Wives then, like today, no doubt had years and years of some form of victimization—some more and some less. But, filled with the Spirit (i.e., accessing by faith the present power of God in their inner being, satisfaction for all injustices committed) they actually begin to see their husband the way God sees him. They now see and begin to respond to Christ's glory in him. This is a miraculous honor, far beyond what the husband is due on his own merits.

But Paul's not yet done. Filled with the same Spirit, husbands will also begin to feel God's love for their spouses—*the height and width and length and depth of Jesus' love* for their wives. Whether she was lovable or not, or whether she had been faithful or not. You can bet, husband, that she will notice this change!

What I am imagining is miraculous, inexplicable by any other way than that God *eucatastrophically* intervened on his or her behalf.

But Paul is not done. I think that the most miraculous of them all is in the first verse of Chapter 6. Filled with such Spirit, children will actually *want* to obey and honor their parents. Whoa!

Can accessing God's Spirit reconcile husbands and wives whose relationship had fallen into great disrepair, dishonor, indifference, years of abuse and use? Of course. Why have we come to the place where we have stopped expecting transformational miracles?

So Plaintiff, first run to the great magnanimous King whose glory overflows and be filled to the full with the fullness of God. Be filled with the fruit of His Spirit and then you will see the believing or unbelieving Defendant differently. You will begin to feel toward them to some degree the same way that God does. You will have new motivations, new direction and a new lens. This opens up a bevy of new options.

Plaintiff, you cannot really forgive apart from the presence of God's Spirit. To put it in modern psychological terms, the injustice gap is too wide to overcome. Therapeutic interventions can be helpful, of course, in many cases. The modern Plaintiff can reframe the offender and the crime and come to some resolution. They can come to a point through significant effort and helpful counseling where they can even to some degree decisionally forgive the perpetrator.

But Paul is not referring to any of these things. He is speaking of the believing Plaintiff, by faith, remembering who you are in Christ, and what Christ specifically did on your behalf. Jesus died, says Paul, so that you would experience horizontal reconciliations that are of the same essence as vertical reconciliation. All forgiveness—horizontal and vertical—ultimately proceeds from God alone. Plaintiff, you can access this by faith.

"All this is from God, who reconciled us to himself through Christ and gave us the ministry of reconciliation: that God was reconciling the world to himself in Christ, not counting men's sins against them. And he has committed to us the message of reconciliation." (2Cor 5:18-19)

Do you now see that your greatest ongoing need as a Christian is power from God right now? Apart from this, you will not really feel like His son or daughter. You will not really feel loved by Christ, and you certainly won't really deeply feel His love for others.

Or to put this in pop-culture terminology, no wonder you have "lost that loving feeling" Christian. Maybe until now, you were ignorant of your need to run to God to have your cup filled today. And the next day...and the next. Maybe you were unaware that the umbilical cord between you and God is your only real source of lasting identity, value, worth, and substance. Maybe now you can see that it has been largely unused.

That would make you a tragic underachiever, largely powerless, and relegated to looking for filling in all the wrong places. The good news is that your upside potential is very high.

The Amish and the *Christ-lens*

Amish, children of the Living God, you have been given the Holy Spirit in your inner being. It is your right and privilege to run to Him in your need, in your pain, and drink freely from the living water until you experience fullness, the fullness of God.

Remember of course, the Great Judge alone knows all aspects of all crimes, alone knows the pains that you humanly have felt. He also loves your murdered children far more than you ever have and God is not limited by death. He does His best and most loving work on things that have perished from this physical life.

As you drink from Him, by faith, through *His* Spirit in your inner being, you will begin to feel a new deep abiding sense of trust in *His* care for your children that were taken into *His* arms so abruptly. You will begin to feel deep healing for the "stripes" of your soul (Isa 53). You will begin to feel *His* great love for you, its stunning height, length, width and depth. You will even begin to feel His love for Roberts.

As mentioned above, if indeed Jesus died for all of the crimes of Roberts, if Roberts was a *Jesus-follower-gone-horribly-awry*, then the justice that your heart has demanded is already perfectly satisfied in the highest of all courts. Plaintiff, assuming that Roberts did confess to Christ, you have every right and privilege to access by faith a present sense of full judicial closure.

In one sense, Robert's trial happened 2000 years ago. On that Cross, through a substitute, Roberts was found absolutely guilty for all of his horrific crimes against God and humanity. The punishment? The only reasonable punishment was death. Jesus (again, *if* Roberts was indeed a *Jesus-follower-gone-horribly-awry*) paid His price in full. As vicious and evil as his crimes against God and humanity were, justice is *still* finished! God is judicially perfectly satisfied by the substitution of Jesus for Roberts. This is unimaginable to our tiny brains and our narrow keyhole view of God's morality and justice. But the Bible proclaims such a great salvation even for vilest of sinners.

Plaintiff, you can by faith, through the Holy Spirit in your inner being, access that present sense of that strange judicial satisfaction. The *Aaaah! factor*. Plaintiff, the Holy Spirit in you already feels such an *Aaaah! factor*.

171

You will feel it perfectly in heaven. But you can request by faith to begin to experience judicial satisfaction right now.

On the other hand, if Roberts went to his grave defiant, unrepentant, unbelieving—a rebel against the Judge, an enemy of God to the end (admittedly this possibility is so much easier for us to imagine)—then Plaintiff, there will be another future trial for Roberts. The verdict will be the same—GUILTY! The punishment will be exactly the same, DEATH! But in this case, Roberts will have no substitute to take his place. He will assume total responsibility for his crime himself. Either way, the *Aaaah! Factor* that your soul cries out for is *still* available for you to experience by faith either way. Justice will be satisfied. Justice will smile and ask no more.

Nickel Mines, you can be assured that your Father in Heaven has not turned away from your plight. He will make all things right again. There must be justice—including an experience of justice in your deepest being—in heaven, or by faith now on earth.

> Imagine if the Amish were filled with such a sense of justice satisfied, of God's love and faithfulness toward their lost children and the survivors.

> Imagine if they would feel a deep filling of their deeply diminished cups.

> Imagine if they were filled with God's powerful love for Roberts and his family?

Their subsequent actions may *look* the same. But, inside of them would be a powerfully different driving force. A new power. A new lens.

The Coffee Lady and the *Christ-lens*

Remember the coffee lady from Chapter 2? She was not a Jesus-follower at all. In fact, she reviled at the possibility of spending eternity with God. "Why would I want to spend even one day with a God who stood by and allowed His son to suffer? Why would I want to spend time with such a child abuser?" What relief might be possible for her?

Imagine with me if she was filled with God's Spirit, deep in her inner being. Imagine if she began to feel human again, God's honor and sense of value and worth displacing all of the years of use and abuse and indifference that she has had to suffer at the hands of so many men.

Imagine that she would begin to feel differently about God as a Good Father—enduring along with His Son a gross necessary evil so that she might feel like a person of glory. Imagine if she began to glean even a small foretaste of satisfied justice for the many, many crimes that she has had to endure? She would arise from her ashes a new creature, all things new and redeemed.

She just might in a new sense of freedom leave the current bad guy and his abuse. She just might blossom—a new powerful life-changing awareness that she is an heir of all the celestial blessings that Jesus bought for her.

> "But when the time had fully come, God sent his Son, born of a woman, born under law, to redeem [the coffee ladies who are] under law, that [she] might receive the full rights of [a daughter]. Because [she is a daughter], God sent the Spirit of his Son into [her heart], the Spirit who calls out, "*Abba*, Father." So [she] is no longer a slave, but a [daughter]; and since [she is a daughter], God has made [her] also an heir." (Gal 4:4-7 *revised*)

Conclusion

Bottom line, Plaintiff, God commands us to forgive. But He is not referring to a unilateral effort by you that forsakes justice—nor one that dishonors you further. In His forgiveness, you are not required to first be empathetic toward the person who treated you so badly. Never. His process of forgiveness begins with you running to Him to be made whole. By faith, access judicial satisfaction for all crimes committed against you by the Defendant. And then, filled with His Spirit, you will begin to see the Defendant and the crime through a new *Christ-lens*. You now know that you are *not* an eternal victim. You are victorious in Christ.

Reflection Questions for Individuals or Groups

1)   What do you think is the difference between modern socio-psychological reframing techniques and the "celestial reframing" proposed in this chapter? While there are some similarities, specifically what are the huge differences between seeing the perpetrator through "lens of *empathy*" and the "Christ-lens?"

2)   The author argues that there is a real difference between the Spirit dwelling in you and the Spirit DWELLING in you. What do you think that he is referring to? Can you think of a time when the Spirit was DWELLING in you? What difference did it make in the way that you dealt with others? The way you forgave others?

3)   Do you regularly ask God for power to be able to love others and to be loved by others? Why or why not? A typical response to Paul's prayer is that it seems "too easy." What are your thoughts?

PART FOUR

Next Steps for Filled Cups

11

Next Steps

Now What?

Former Plaintiff, the Cross accomplished two things for Jesus-followers:

First, your debt has been paid. *Second*, you can, by faith, access the *splagchnizomai* filling of the outrageously magnanimous King over and over and over. Then out of that fullness you will actually begin to *want* to fill others—to pay the debt of others, seventy times seven times. You may even for the sake of others strategically choose to turn the other cheek—but this after your cup has been filled to all the fullness of God (per Paul in Eph 3:14-21).

Until you experience by faith such a *eucatastrophic* intervention by God, your empty heart will do what it has always done.

Your Empty Heart's Go-To Strategies

Your emptied heart's natural strategies normally include some or all of the following: complaining, gossiping, withdrawing, tragically taking on the actual identity of a victim, pursuing retaliation and/or working even harder to forgive on your own strength.

Complaining

Don't we all do this? You have been hurt so you privately or publicly complain against the perpetrator. It feels pretty good if the truth were known—but it does nothing to really fill your cup. This complaining is not really constructive. It is designed to tear down the persons or institutions that you imagine were somehow involved.

Gossiping

The great American pastime. It is another form of passing on information in a way that makes you feel better about yourself. In Christian circles, gossip is often draped over with the sacred robe of prayer. Like complaining, it feels good in the short run, but it does not bring about reconciliation. It is not designed to. It is largely self-focused.

Withdrawal

This is my personal weapon of choice. You can justify withdrawing and setting up boundaries easily, of course. Sometimes it is even wise to do so. You can withdraw your friendship, change the locks on the doors, or even de-friend them on Facebook. But if you were honest, this is also a very self-centered act. It feels like a good short-term solution, but it cannot fill your cup. It is the opposite of Miroslav Volf's critical component of forgiveness and reconciliation: that "vital desire to embrace."[84]

Taking on the Identity of a Victim

How many times have we done this? You may choose to actually take on the identity of a victim in order to appeal for others' sympathy and compassion. No real healing here. There is a vast difference from being a victim of a crime—and being a victim. The former is still a person—who at their core is still aware of their great value and worth. The crime has diminished them, but has not changed their DNA. The latter is on a tailspin of becoming a functional object—whose value is a function of their utility to the stories of others. *Cupology 101's* principle message for both is to run to their Creator God who alone ultimately knows their true worth and be filled to all of His fullness (Eph 3:19-21).

---

[84] M. Volf, *Exclusion and Embrace* (Nashville, Tn.: Abingdon Press, 1996).

Pursuing Vengeance

Even though we know deep down at a certain level that vengeance doesn't work, it is historically humanity's knee-jerk reaction. It seems so just doesn't it? They hurt you, you hurt them. Eye for an eye, right?

No vengeance reflects real objective moral justice. All vengeance is flawed. All flawed justice creates new injustices. To the degree that the justice is not objective and "right," new offenses are created; beginning a new cycle of offenses that require forgiveness. The events spiral *ad infinitum.*

"Any action we undertake now is inescapably ambiguous, at best partially just and therefore partially unjust. No peace is possible within the overarching framework of strict justice for the simple reason that no strict justice is possible."[85]

You Try Really Hard to *Decisionally* Forgive

Remember Nickel Mines?

Perhaps, Jesus was referring to the consequences of these typical human responses to crimes against us when he says,
"This is how my heavenly Father will treat each of you unless you forgive your brother from your heart." (Matt 18:35)

I suggest that what Jesus is saying rhetorically is:
"If you aren't feeling forgiveness for others, it is a red flag that even though your outrageous debt against the King has been fully paid once for all times, you are still tragically acting *on your own* and not full of the *splagchnizomai* of the outrageously magnanimous King. Since you are acting as if you are alone in the universe, your orphan heart will naturally need *others* to fill *your* cup. If you stay on this path, you will likely begin to feel even more alienated from God. You will likely begin to feel unforgiven, ashamed, and even guilty. If you go down the self-effort path, you might even come to the point where you begin to even doubt your own salvation. Unabated, the destructive cycle will continue. You will grow more cynical, angrier with God and His church, and possibly even angrier at yourself too. In Cupology terms, your cup will begin to feel *really* empty. You will be miserable."

---

85 Volf, *Exclusion and Embrace,* 39.

The King's Heart's 7 Top Go-To Fruit

On the other hand, if you are filled with the heart of the abundantly full King seventy times seven times, something else rises up that will surprise everyone:

A Deep alien *splagchnizomai* for the Defendant

If your cup is filled with the King's heart-stuff, you will necessarily begin to notice the unexpected outlandish compassion that the King feels toward the one who hurt you.

Paul urges the Philippians to have the same attitude—the deep motivation in the heart of Christ that moved Him to die for them.

What would that look like, if that attitude was driving your thoughts, words and deeds? Paul tells us some of the fruit of the mind of Christ:

"Do nothing out of selfish ambition or vain conceit, but in humility consider others better than yourselves. Each of you should look not only to your own interests, but also to the interests of others." (Phil 2:3-4)

As one pastor put it, you will feel a new divine *selflessness* irrupting from your inner-being; not a thinking less of yourself, but a profound thinking of yourself less. Filled cups do this.

Filled with God's fullness, you will begin to be newly motivated and empowered to see the perpetrator as a fractured image bearer—very much like you. This is in no way minimizing the violation, or giving up any justice whatsoever. You will begin to feel concerned for the healing and restoration of the perpetrator.

A Profound Awareness of Your Own Sin

The Spirit in your inner being has the capacity to point out harmful and hurtful ways. These are those harmful bents of your heart that get in the way of your experiencing the present love of God.

"Search me, O God, and know my heart; test me and know my anxious thoughts. See if there is any offensive way in me, and lead me in the way everlasting. " (Ps 139:23-24)

Emptied cups can by nature be very guarded and have little interest in being exposed. But filled with the boldness of the King, you are much more free to really do severe heart-searching. You are also far more willing to invite the Holy Spirit to expose and illuminate the painful space, to consider your crimes against *other* people.

A New and Improved Story

The nature of God's *eucatastrophe* is that it changes the trajectory of your narrative from a path of meaningless smoldering suffering into a new path of meaningful life-giving suffering. God is big enough to speak light into the worst darkness. Paul seems to have this in mind in Rom 8:28:

> "And we know that in all things God works for the good of those who love him, who have been called according to his purpose."

God can write a surprisingly happy ending into the most horrific narrative. God is that big. If you have any remaining doubts, just consider the Cross. Such injustice resulting in great glory.

Now former Plaintiff, you should be able to at least begin to imagine how your narrative is being rewritten. Your story *will* end, "and they all lived happily ever after."

A New Outrageous Testimony of God's Faithfulness

Now you have an even greater testimony than you had before. To tell you the truth, it is even *interesting*. You might even feel a new freedom—and a new motivation to tell other sufferers the good news of what has happened to you. Telling others about God's *eucatastrophic* intervention is a great privilege. It is one of the most impressive gospel presentations around.

Wisdom of the King for the Next Steps

Wisdom comes from God. What is the right next step for you? That is a *wisdom* question.

Former Plaintiff, even full cups must choose between a myriad of options of possible next steps. For the sake of the community, for the sake of the gospel, you *can* pursue justice or discipline. You *can* go to the perpetrator per Matt 18 for the sake of reconciliation. You *can* flee. You *can* hide. You *can* even turn the other cheek if it would further the overall community of God—but the landscape of possible next steps looks and feels very different to *filled* cups.

Important Biblical Next Step: Wise Confrontation

Plaintiff,

Assuming that you have run to God and have been filled to all of His fullness.

Assuming that you now can see the Defendant through *Christ-lens*.

Assuming that you concur with Paul that your key role—and surprisingly your deepest desire is reconciliation, for the sake of the Defendant and the Body of Christ as a whole.

Now what? In one sense, since you are filled with *His* powerful Spirit and *His* wisdom, you can do what you want to do.

God has given you new desires, new power to accomplish *His* goal of reconciliation. God has given you *His* desires.

One of God's desires, as noted in both Testaments, Old and New, is for you to wisely and safely confront your perpetrator. In the Old Testament, the offended parties were charged to confront the perpetrators by bringing the legal case before the God-ordained judicial institutions in His presence. The New Testament concurs.

Initiate God's Forgiveness Process Through the Established Courts

Jesus was very explicit really in Matt 18. Listen.

"If your brother sins against you, go and show him his fault, just between the two of you. If he listens to you, you have won your brother over. But if he will not listen, take one or two others along, so that 'every matter may be established by the testimony of two or three witnesses.' If he refuses to listen to them, tell it to the church; and if he refuses to listen even to the church, treat him as you would a pagan or a tax collector. I tell you the truth, whatever you bind on earth will be bound in heaven, and whatever you loose on earth will be loosed in heaven." (Matt 18:15-18)

Former Plaintiff, the goal of such a confrontation is not punishment, not revenge, and not to somehow get your own cup filled. Remember these are instructions to Plaintiff cups *who have already run to God to be filled to the full.*

The question before you now is what do *filled-cup* Plaintiffs do? You can now—and likely will even really want to—boldly pursue an *eucatastrophic* reconciliation with the hurtful brother or sister. This is the way of God in both Testaments.

I would quickly point out that in *no* way is Jesus requiring that you put your self in harm's way as you pursue such a reconciliation. Use wisdom of course. There are situations where such a confrontation is highly inappropriate and unsafe. Seek guidance from leaders you trust before proceeding.

Assuming that it does not put you in a dangerous or compromising situation, Plaintiff, you are commanded by Jesus Himself to go and personally confront the Defendant in hopes that he or she will repent, be remorseful, and run into the presence of the magnanimous King to also be filled to all His fullness.

The goal of such intervention is always reconciliation. By faith, *you* have already experienced a restoration of what the Defendant took from you (at least in part). To say it in a more direct way, by His work on the Cross, Jesus has already paid you back for what the Defendant took. So then, your goal is *no* longer *Retributive Justice.*

The Spirit in you wants a just reconciliation. You are now called to be a *missionary* to an unreachable people group (your offender)—*once again, where it is safe and wise to do so.*

If the Defendant remains unremorseful about what they did, and refuses to repent, Jesus commands that another objective and credible person be brought to witness the confrontation.

If the Defendant is *still* unremorseful, then you are to bring your case to the church. In the Old Testament, the God-appointed judges were the elders who held court at the city gates. In this modern era, that responsibility is committed largely to the church, specifically the officers of the church.

The Book of Discipline (Reconciliation)

My particular denomination[86] provides very helpful guidelines to use when one of the church body allegedly hurts another. The guidelines are in a section of our *Book of Order*, titled, the *Book of Discipline*. I think that the title is badly dated and imprecise, for the heart of the *Book of Discipline* is reconciliation. I would prefer to change the title to *Book of Reconciliation.*

"Discipline is the exercise of authority given the church by the Lord Jesus Christ to instruct and guide its members and their children to promote its purity and welfare...The purpose of the discipline is to

---

83 The Evangelical Presbyterian Church (www.epc.org)

maintain the honor of God, to restore the sinner, and to remove offense from the church."[87]

Here's the point. You are to confront the alleged Defendant in hopes of furthering a real reconciliation. If your "confrontation" is rejected, then you are to—according to Matt 18—take another with you to witness the accusation. And then if there is still no satisfaction, you are invited to bring the issue to the officers of the church for an "ecclesiastical judicial procedure" whose goal is a miraculous consolation in the presence of God.

In my particular faith community, the Session (made up of elders elected and ordained by the church body) will then call an official ecclesiastical trial, complete with indictments, summons, testimonies, opening and closing arguments, and of course, a verdict.

Some of the tools at the Session's disposal? The Session can formally admonish either or both of the litigants—i.e., warn the litigants that they are dangerously out-of-sync with the Living God and to urge them to run to Him to be filled with His power and His love for the other.

If the parties are *still* unrepentant, the Session can officially withhold participation in the Lord's Table.

Or if *still* high-handed and unrepentant, the Session can move to "excommunicate" the *unrepentant* guilty party.

Neither of the latter actions assumes in any way that the Session has any authority at all to change the person's status as an adopted child of God of course. Salvation is in the hands of God alone. All judicial actions are meant to cause the *unrepentant* see that the consequences of his or her actions (shame, guilt) have emotionally and spiritually disenfranchised them from their once glorious experience of adoption as a child of God. His or her choices and actions have resulted in a breach in the unity of the Body of Christ. This is a very serious offense. Jesus died so that His Body could be whole.

Maybe it is helpful to see the interventions as spiritual shock therapy— tough love to help him or her see that they need to run to God and be filled to all the fullness of God. If they hear and obey, the rest is pretty easy really.

The Session—acting as an official ecclesiastical court—understands that nothing is going to happen until the *unrepentant* cup runs to the magnanimous King and is filled. If and when that occurs, he or she will also be filled with God's compassion for the person they hurt. This changes things.

---

[87] The Book of Order (Evangelical Presbyterian Church, 2009-2010).

I have seen such "discipline" work brilliantly. Its goal is a miraculous *eucatastrophic* intervention of God that changes the trajectory of the narrative from destruction to "and they all lived happily ever after."

Should You Ever Call the Police?

Am I saying that Christians should not ever use the secular judicial instruments? *Not at all.* There are *many* occasions where the first appropriate action is to call the police, particularly in cases where there has been, or there is the high possibility of physical or emotional harm. In those cases, the right first step is to quickly involve the human justice system. The Apostle Paul understood that the state maintains a very important role.

> "Everyone must submit himself to the governing authorities, for there is no authority except that which God has established. Consequently, he who rebels against the authority is rebelling against what God has instituted, and those who do so will bring judgment on themselves...if you do wrong, be afraid, for [the authority] does not bear the sword for nothing. He is God's servant, an agent of wrath to bring punishment on the wrongdoer." (Rom 13:1-5)

I have been involved in a number of cases where the Session continued its reconciliation efforts long after the Defendant had been arrested, found guilty in the secular court of law, and was behind bars.

The gospel can reach into the jails. An incarcerated Defendant can still access a powerful transformation and cup-filling even if they rightly are in jail for the crime they committed. The gospel of Jesus Christ redeems sinners—even incarcerated ones. That is what it does.

Let me put this in perspective. Do you remember from a previous chapter that the modern justice system is designed to accomplish *Retributive Justice* alone? Meaning, that its goal is to determine the appropriate punishment for the guilty Defendant.

It is not designed to point the parties to God for a miraculous healing and reconciliation.

It is *not* designed to fill the Plaintiff's cup.

It is not designed to transform the Defendant.

That does not make it evil. It does what it is designed to do.

Here is the point. God working powerfully by means of His Spirit through the auspices of His Church can bear vastly more reconciliation fruit than even the best of the best of human courts. In God's presence, we actually by faith *expect* a remarkable *eucatastrophic* intervention that can lead to a miraculous reconciliation. God's justice can result in inexplicable transformation that is beyond our comprehension.

Both judicial *systems* have their purpose and designed roles in our modern contexts. This book is primarily about only one of the systems: God's *eucatastrophic* consolation available by faith to all believers.

All things equal, why wouldn't you pursue this path—perhaps in addition to secular legal venues, but definitely pursue God's reconciliation?

Paul sarcastically mocks the Corinthians for despising God's *eucatastrophic* justice. Listen to 1 Corinthians 5:1-6 from the creative interpretive vantage point of *The Message*:

"And how dare you take each other to court! When you think you have been wronged, does it make any sense to go before a court that knows nothing of God's ways instead of a family of Christians? The day is coming when the world is going to stand before a jury made up of followers of Jesus. If someday you are going to rule on the world's fate, wouldn't it be a good idea to practice on some of these smaller cases? Why, we're even going to judge angels! So why not these everyday affairs? As these disagreements and wrongs surface, why would you ever entrust them to the judgment of people you don't trust in any other way? I say this as bluntly as I can to wake you up to the stupidity of what you're doing. Is it possible that there isn't one levelheaded person among you who can make fair decisions when disagreements and disputes come up? I don't believe it. And here you are taking each other to court before people who don't even believe in God! How can they render justice if they don't believe in the *God* of justice?" (1 Cor 6:1-8)

This is a great example of 1st century Jewish rhetoric—and likely quite sarcastic. "Look," says Paul, "I would prefer to put my case before even the least in the body of Christ versus putting my hope in what even the greatest secular Judge might decide. Why? I need a miraculous reconciliation!"

The Corinthians had stopped believing that God really does impose a *eucatastrophic* intervention in the day-to-day affairs of mankind. This is *unbelief* of the highest order. So they relegated themselves to the minimal outcomes that can possibly come from *Retributive Justice*. All secular courts can do is to fine, punish, reprimand, order community service or jail time, etc., for the guilty Defendant. *God is not so limited.*

God can bring *miraculous* consolation and restoration to those involved. He can give the Defendant a new heart with a new love for the Plaintiff—and vice versa.

What do you expect from a secular magistrate? They cannot change the heart of the Defendant or the Plaintiff. God can usher in a miraculous lasting reconciliation. Can the courts that you are going to do that?

Conclusion

Plaintiff, you can't forgive—not at the level that God requires—certainly not at the level that God forgives. God's forgiveness involves perfect two-fold consolation: a purging of evil, a punishment for *unrepentant*, redemption and restoration for the repentant, and a restoration of the diminished party to wholeness. Then and only then will God release the debt owed—i.e., forgive. Only then is there *any* possibility of a Tolkien-esque ending, "And they all lived happily ever after."

You Foolish Galatians (Gal 3:1)

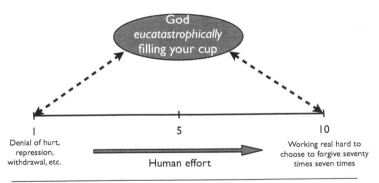

Figure 10- "Observing the Law" Forgiveness Spectrum (Galatians 3:1-5) Post-Cross

Back in Chapter 4, I discussed Paul's two choices for Christian Plaintiffs. Consider Galatians 3:1-5 revised slightly to specifically speak to forgiveness:

"You foolish Galatians! Who has bewitched you? Before your very eyes Jesus Christ was clearly portrayed as crucified. I would like to learn just one thing from you: Did you receive the Spirit by observing the law, or by believing what you heard? Are you so foolish? After [experiencing a vast miraculous forgiveness by the power of the] Spirit, are you now trying to [forgive] by human effort? Have you suffered so much for nothing—if it really was for nothing? Does God give you his Spirit and work miracles among you because you [work hard to forgive on your own], or because you believe what you heard?" (Gal 3:1-5 *revised*)

Your options in Christ are vastly expanded. Apart from the Spirit in you, you can choose to either do nothing (left hand-side of the horizontal spectrum) or work really hard to choose to forgive the crime (the right hand-side of the horizontal spectrum). But that would be so foolish, wouldn't it?

Or, you can run to the Magnanimous King and have your emptied cup filled. *God can work a miracle in you, Plaintiff.* This miracle in you can also end up in a miracle in the whole community: reconciliation. God can *do* this. By faith, run to Him and be filled.

Cupology-Adjusted Modern Path of Forgiveness

Then, once your cup is filled to all the fullness of God, new options will open for you. You may even find that forgiveness counseling will bear striking new fruit in you. It is a matter of order really. Access the Cupology 101 principles first. As illustrated in the figure below, full cups can benefit greatly from skilled modern counselors and modern forgiveness interventions.

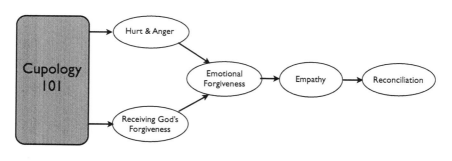

Figure 11- Proposed Path of Forgiveness and Reconciliation (adapted from Walker and Gorsuch 2004)

Do these principles actually work? Can they really help Plaintiffs forgive? Absolutely. The next chapter discusses a practical example of how these principles can be "fleshed out."

Reflection Questions for Individuals or Groups

1)   The author argues that wise confrontation of the perpetrator (i.e., where it is wise and safe) should only happen *after* the Plaintiff has experienced God's *eucatastrophic* intervention of consolation. Why would he argue for this order?

2)   Speaking of possible "next steps" Dr. Senyard says, "Now what? In one sense, since you are filled with *His* powerful Spirit and wisdom, you can do what you want to do."

Do you agree or disagree? Why?

3)   How has this book changed the way that you look at forgiveness? Write out a two-sentence definition of biblical forgiveness in your own words. How would you counsel a victimized person to forgive a crime committed against them?

4)   The Apostle Paul sums up the entire work of the Church as a ministry of reconciliation. Listen:
> "All this is from God, who reconciled us to himself through Christ and gave us the ministry of reconciliation: that God was reconciling the world to himself in Christ, not counting men's sins against them. And he has committed to us the message of reconciliation." (2 Cor 5:18-19)

The author strongly suggests that this "reconciliation" is as much horizontal as it is vertical. Do you agree? Why or why not? Assuming that you agree, how are we Jesus-followers to better minister reconciliation to both the perpetrators and the offended in our circle of influence? What are the barriers to our success?

Postscript: The *Forgiveness Labyrinth*

So, does this stuff really work? You would be surprised.

The *Forgiveness Labyrinth*

For my doctoral thesis, I designed a physical "labyrinth:" a structured, self-guided nine-station process built upon the principles taught in this book.

In 2009, we set up the first crude *Forgiveness Labyrinth* at a men's retreat as part of a lecture series on the power of the gospel to shape our hearts and relationships. Thirty men went through the one-and-a-half-hour *Labyrinth*. The results were very surprising. Many of the men were in tears as they finished their journey. Miracles happened beyond what any of us were expecting from the crudely designed stations. Many commented that they had actually been empowered to forgive a crime that they had never been able to forgive before.

In 2010, the *Labyrinth* was set up at my church as a part of a seven-week sermon series on Biblical forgiveness. Once again, the results were very positive. In answer to the question "Did you receive some forgiveness for the crime you carried into the *Labyrinth*?," 62% said that they had experienced significant or total forgiveness for the offender; 19% testified

191

that they had experienced some forgiveness. A total of 81% actually experienced a *eucatastrophic* intervention by God Himself.

Many testified of feeling "new hope," "relieved," a "new sense of mercy for the Defendant," "ready to dance," and "free now to move forward." One participant wrote,

"[I am] excited, thankful, so grateful. I didn't even know I was so wounded—but I see how it colored my 'view' of the world. Already I have noticed a different view of myself. I see God's restoration and healing. I see that I have been healed of a very deep crime."

Another agreed,

"[I] was surprised when I asked the Lord who I should be bringing to trial—[I] thought I was all done with that—[I] experienced healing and release."

And again,

"I mostly feel relieved that some of the guilt I have been internalizing has been lifted. I feel worthy... I should not feel like it is all my fault that I was unloved."

As well,

"This [crime] does not have to own me anymore. I do not have to define myself by another's (abusive) behavior."

In January 2011, another church from a different denomination took the *Labyrinth* and set it up in their facilities. Forty-one participants, none of whom had been exposed to my sermon series on forgiveness, went through the *Labyrinth* in one weekend. Over two thirds (68%) said that they had experienced at least some forgiveness.

What were the participants required to do to achieve such surprising results? All we required was that they come to the *Labyrinth* with a single unresolved crime for which they needed healing—that needed forgiveness. Each station was designed using audio instructions, creative visuals, and a variety of activities to bring home key forgiveness principles. The entire process only took about an hour and a half. It required no specialist present, no trained therapist. It can be set up in almost any large room.

My 2012 doctoral dissertation[88] calculated the success of the *Labyrinth* to facilitate forgiveness according to TRIM-18, an industry standard measurement device. Remarkably, test participants experienced 20%

[88] W.H. Senyard, "Evaluation of the Forgiveness Labyrinth as a Stand-Alone Device to Facilitate Forgiveness Between Christians" (DMin dissertation, Biblical Theological Seminary, 2012)

reduction in their desire to avoid their perpetrator, a 20% increase in their feelings of benevolence toward the perpetrator, and an almost 30% reduction in their desire to seek revenge.[89]

The dissertation also measured the participant's sense of experienced justice. We asked the participants before and after the *Labyrinth* "Have you experienced justice for the crime committed against you?" Those that went through the *Labyrinth* reported a positive improvement of over 70%. Meaning, that in a mere 90 minutes, the participants had experienced a deep sense of real justice for the crime that they had been carrying, some for a very long time.

What made the difference? I would suggest that the *Forgiveness Labyrinth* is ultimately a nine-fold very-relevant presentation of the gospel to the Plaintiff. The result? Miraculously, emptied cups began to feel just a little bit of fullness.

By the way, compared to twenty-five other published secular and Christian forgiveness interventions, the *Forgiveness Labyrinth* ranked #2. The only intervention that proved to be more successful required six times more time and the oversight of expensive trained professionals. These principles work.

Listen to one person's story of how God moved them powerfully through their participation in the physical *Forgiveness Labyrinth*. The gospel can do this.

Rick's Story[90]

"I'm okay with my dad now. It wasn't always that way. The crimes he committed against me are certainly not as big as the crimes others have endured, but they hurt me. Deeply. People would tell me "He did the best he could." But he didn't. He did *not* do the best he could.

At 3 am, I would lie awake angry then I'd pound the pillow with my fist. Even after he died I held this bitterly against him. But I didn't want to hold it against him. I knew that he was just a man and that I too was making mistakes, many of them significant. I couldn't shake it. Even when I really wanted to I just couldn't forgive him.

Then as he developed Alzheimers I stayed angry with him. I felt bad for him getting this disease but I often saw that the only difference now was

---

[89] Results were based upon a one-way t-test for correlated samples statistically significant at the 0.005 level. The actual reduction on the TRIM-18 *Avoidance* scale was 22.54% (n=13, SD=5.06), reduction of *Revenge* scale was 29.37% (n=13, SD=2.94), and the increase of *Benevolence* scale was 19.43% (n=13, SD=2.94). The increase in the experience of Justice as measured by FLDS was 71.43% (n=13, SD=1.05).

[90] Not his real name.

that his same long-standing behaviors were beyond his present control. He was officially not responsible for the same things that he didn't take responsibility for in the past. He had actually been given the excuse for his behavior that he'd always granted to himself as a perk.

His behavior had been difficult for decades. He had disrespected my mother for decades. And I just couldn't forgive him. And everyone suffered because of it.

I listened to Dr. Senyard's sermon series on forgiveness. I heard about forgiveness in a way that made sense to me for the first time. The crimes against me were real. The injury was real. My craving for justice was right, not wrong—and that these feelings reflected strength not weakness.

I accepted the invitation to the *Forgiveness Labyrinth*. I was asked to name a specific crime. I couldn't think of one small enough to test the premise. I decided not to do a trial run but rather to choose the hardest one, my dad and his crimes against me and in turn my failure to forgive him.

In that hour and over the following weeks my life changed. I got my hearing. I got my day in court. I didn't have to minimize my pain and anger. I got the justice I longed to have. In the *Labyrinth* I learned why I couldn't give it to God in the past. It wasn't mine to give. I was no longer engaged only by the theoretical forgiveness of Jesus. But at most I hoped for some relief of the burden. I simply didn't expect the incredible and joyful forgiveness of Jesus.

My shackles have been removed and I have great sympathy for my father and his brokenness secure in the knowledge that Christ loves him and cares for him and wants him desperately. And me.

I learned what it truly meant that the judgment belongs to God. He will handle things with my dad. And I do not need to.

And for me, I will stand my own trial where my own crimes will be judged and those who suffer from my shortcomings will be able to have their day in court. And I will be judged guilty and I am guilty. And the sentence, the harsh sentence I deserve, will be pronounced. It will be death. And it will be paid. But I will not die. I will have everlasting life because my penalty has been paid by Christ on the cross.

So even though my dad was dead when I went through the labyrinth, he and I walked out together with our arms around each other in tears. Eventually I would laugh with my dad about the good times.

This freedom has been present for over two years. The worst feelings I get recalling all those bad years is some frustration. No anger.

I feel free to enjoy my dad's love not be burdened by his actions. God truly changed my heart. Changed it. He did not suppress it or make me consume a meal of denial. He brought justice and then He brought me a new heart. I walk in peace with my father. Not out of his perfection or mine. But in the perfection and sacrifice of Jesus.

And the nature of forgiveness has changed in me completely. I could succeed at times in the past but it used to be mostly a burden and with my dad, only a burden.

I think the common advice to forgive and forget diminishes our humanity. Our God given nature cries for justice, just as the God in whose image we are made, demands justice. I know now that forgiveness is as essential as I was always taught it to be. It is essential to our faith, our friendships, our relationships. And rather than being hard, it is now easy. It is surrender but not to the one who hurt us but to the one who made us.

I walk each day, more than ever, a child of God."

Read on for an excerpt from *Cupology 101: A Biblical Theology of Forgiveness'* companion book, *The Forgiveness Labyrinth.*

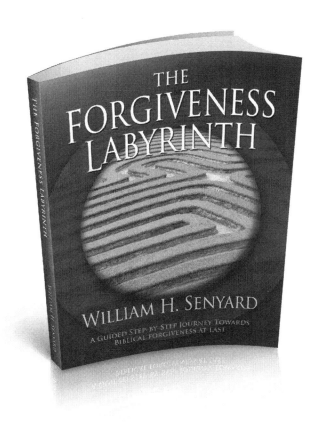

The Forgiveness Labyrinth available online
at www.drbillministries.com, Amazon, Kindle and Nook.

Also check out the ongoing dialogue on
www.facebook.com/cantforgive.com.

The Seven Propositions of the Labyrinth

This *Forgiveness Labyrinth* is built on seven fundamental propositions related to real lasting forgiveness.

Proposition 1 - All Violations Cause Debts.

Someone has committed a disrespectful act against you, depriving you of something that was rightfully yours. It could be your sense of security, love, appreciation, comfort, safety; perhaps something material, your dreams, your purity, or your childhood. This act diminished you—robbed you, your self-esteem and your self-image. The experience of the diminishment is perceived as larger if:

- It involved someone close to you (the normal expectation of the heart is that you should expect honor from those close to you).
- The crime was public.
- The crime was premeditated.
- The violation was an accident. If you are anything like me, it could still feel like a great violation if you think the accident was obviously foreseeable.
- The lingering debt is exacerbated depending upon the nature or absence of any apology or attempt at restitution—the classic "I'm sorry *if* I hurt you."
- The injured person has no freedom or platform to voice pain and anger to an objective, listening, compassionate authority figure.

The bottom line is that *every violation incurs a debt*. Every situation is unique, every temperament is unique, every crime is complex, and everyone copes differently; but this can always be said. Your heart has measured the event and its consequence and weighed a debt. The scales of your heart are tipped, and unbalanced. It is not only that someone did something *to* you; they also took something *from* you. This truth will require some sort of emotional reprogramming on our part to fully understand.[91]

---

[91] Dale T. Miller, "Disrespect and the Experience of Injustice," *Annual Review of Psychology*, Annual (2001): 19.

Proposition 2 - There Can Be No Forgiveness Until the Entire Debt Has Been Experienced as Paid.

Your efforts to date have generally failed because you are fighting against your heart which, at least to some degree, rightly demands full compensation for the crimes against it. Your soul demands that the scales get balanced by some means. Perhaps you are largely guilty of ignoring its cries.

Well-meaning, nice people and many Christians will want to push back at this point and argue: "This seems a bit petty, or a bit unlike Jesus, right? Aren't we just supposed to make a decision to be merciful, to absorb the loss?"

We must hear again: *God never forgives anyone until there has been full justice paid.* God never, ever surrenders the right to get even. He never cancels expectations. He never just releases the person from the debt that is owed. Isn't that great news? God, the Great Celestial Judge, requires absolute payment for all crimes—*all* crimes. When Moses asked about God's core character, "What is your name?" God answered him by moving before him and proclaiming:

> "The Lord, the Lord, the compassionate and gracious God, slow to anger, abounding in love and faithfulness, maintaining love to thousands, and forgiving wickedness, rebellion and sin. Yet he does not leave the guilty unpunished." (Ex. 34:6-7)

Remember the Bible teaches that God is both abounding in love and forgiveness, yet still perfectly requiring judgment. How do we reconcile the apparent conflict? He forgives wickedness, rebellion, and sin, yet He does not leave the guilty unpunished. What is this forgiveness that also requires complete and perfect justice? In our language, we pit the two against each other. Either we forgive or we pursue justice—one or the other.

But there is no conflict between the two in God's character. God's forgiveness is a function of perfect justice.

Let me put it another way, though it will initially sound strange to our western, modern ears. Once *all* crimes are fully paid for, only then does God forgive. God's forgiveness does not in any way get criminals off any hook. Isn't this wonderful news? Since the Bible is accurate and true, then we will all experience a final, huge trial where:

> "God will bring every deed into judgment, including every hidden thing, whether it is good or evil." (Ecc. 12:14)

Even if you don't know that God is real or not, don't you honestly hope that something like this goes down? Bottom-line, for the crime against you, someone needs to pay so that you will be whole again—before forgiveness is truly forgiveness.

Ironically, many of our acts of forgiveness have ultimately been destructive works against our own flesh. This may sound pretty harsh, yet listen to the cries of your heart. Imagine what you might feel if someone who really hurt you came to you and just said, "Sorry. My bad." There may be a part of you that thinks that now you have to take the high road and accept this. It would be the peacekeeping thing to do—the "Jesus thing."

At another level, you could be choosing to absorb the loss yourself, to violently depreciate yourself, and write a very costly check yourself to pay for the damages caused by the one who has hurt you so much. While it sounds so Christ-line, in fact it is another form of self-deprecation, a subtle form of self-victimization. Your heart will fight against you ten times out of ten.

There will come a time in the forgiveness process where such a sacrifice may be appropriate, but not until you have first experienced a re-filling of your substance from the hand of God Himself. Emptied cups have nothing to give.

Have you come to suspect that perhaps as much as 99.9% of your forgiveness efforts have been only heroic works of the flesh—child-like, well-meaning mimicry of the real thing?

Any supposed "forgiveness" that may be forthcoming apart from perfect justice is wildly incomplete. Ironically it is a further offense to you, and a denial of the immense moral cost of the offense.

According to justice expert Cynthia Ozick, such a forgiveness actually "re-brutalizes" the offended party.[92] It blurs your suffering. Culturally and relationally it cultivates sensitiveness toward the offender at the price of insensitiveness toward you. Keep doing that and you will lose moral authority in your life. Does this ring true?

No matter who you are, what you have done, or what has been done to you, you carry the debt of your losses due to the crime(s) against you.

This proposition isn't very different if you don't recognize your DNA is fundamentally the same as mine in this area. If it were not, such violations wouldn't affect you at all. You would just get up from the ground and get on with your life.

But your inner sense of the need for balance will not remain silent. One of the first sentences that children learn is "But that's not fair!" Exactly. You had a value and it has been diminished without your

---

[92] See L. Gregory Jones, *Embodying Forgiveness: A Theological Analysis*, (Grand Rapids: Eerdmans, 2003) : 285.

permission. If you didn't see yourself as valuable, you would expect to be treated like garbage.

Proposition 3- You are a Person of Great Worth

In this *Forgiveness Labyrinth* you must hear the truth. No matter how badly you have been mistreated, dishonored, treated lightly, used, abused, betrayed or rejected, you are yet a masterpiece—made in the image of God. Compared to your intrinsic value and worth, the Mona Lisa is a mere stick figure drawing. *Just hear that.* Allow the truth to splash against the doubt and cynicism of your beat-up heart. You are innately a masterpiece.

The Bible tells us that all of us—no matter who you are, what you have or have not done, what you believe or don't believe—are made in the image of God Himself.

"Then God said, "Let us make man in our image, in our likeness, and let them rule over the fish of the sea and the birds of the air, over the livestock, over all the earth, and over all the creatures that move along the ground." So God created man in his own image, in the image of God he created him; male and female he created them." (Genesis 1:26-27)

It is a complicated, mysterious and highly discussed passage. What could it really mean *for you* to reflect the very image of God? Minimally it means that you—no matter who you are, where you were born, what you have done, what has been done to you, what you believe or don't believe, you are called to be an official ambassador of God to the world.

Ambassadorships are very important appointments. To be an ambassador means that your people, your government, and your country trust you to represent them to another country. When you travel to other countries as an official ambassador, you are treated with great honor—the honor that your entire people deserve.

So Traveler, you are the ambassador of the singular Creator God. You are here as the representative of the Triune God of the Celestials: the Father, Son and Spirit. Whether you are good or incompetent ambassador based upon your choices and actions, you are still to be treated with due honor in accord to your high office alone.

We have a glimpse of how God sees our value in the Abraham narrative. Long before Abraham becomes a patriarch of Israel, he is merely Abram, an unknown Chaldean pagan. God breaks on to his radar with an appointment to official ambassadorship.

"The Lord had said to Abram, "Leave your country, your people and your father's household and go to the land I will show you. I will make you into a great nation and I will bless you; I will make your name great, and you will be a blessing. I will bless those who bless you, and whoever curses (Heb.-*qll*) you I will curse (Heb.- *'arar*); and all peoples on earth will be blessed through you." (Gen. 12:1-3)

This is more than a Hallmark feel-good statement. God is telling Abraham a great deal about what it means that He is with him. In essence, God says, "Whoever treats you lightly (Heb.- *qll*), or doesn't bow when you enter the room out of respect, I will curse (Heb.- *'arar*)!"

The Hebrew word *'arar* carries the severe connotation "to bind (with a spell), hem in with obstacles, render powerless to resist."[93] It's as though God is saying, "Abraham, if they mess with you in the least, they will feel the full weight of my anger."

We don't know who or what Abram was before God chose him. He may have been a local dignitary, a wealthy sheep magnate, or he could have been literally a nobody in his homeland. Yet when God introduces Himself, the clear message to Abram is that in God's eyes, he has true worth and value. If anyone treats him lightly, they will learn quickly that they misjudged his status.

The person that treated you lightly totally underestimated your value and social position. You are an ambassador of God.

Proposition 4 - There Will Be a Perfect Trial and Objective Verdict For All Crimes Against You

This could take some reprogramming for you to hear. Based upon Proposition 3, you are a masterpiece. You were pre-crime—and you remain so now. God says so. Your DNA says so. God is the ultimate determiner of value. He protects that value.

How? There will be a trial. Every diminishment of your glory, every time anyone even thought of treating you as less than God's ambassador, every time they didn't honor you or stand up when you entered the room. You get the idea. There will be a perfectly objective trial by the perfectly objective Judge, the Judge who sees the calamity of both the offended and perpetrators.

There will be a trial for you. There will come a time when all of the crimes against you—every single one—will be fully and perfectly dealt with

---

[93] Victor P. Hamilton, "*'ârar*" in R. *Laird Harris, Gleason L. Archer and Bruce K. Waltke, Theological Wordbook of the Old Testament* (Chicago: Moody Press, 1990), Vol 1, 75.

by the Holy, Holy, Holy Judge over all creation to the satisfaction of all of the celestials—including, of course, you.

This implicit promise is made by the Creator God to all of His image bearers. It does not apply just to believers, but to all. The promise of a final trial—which includes restoration from all crimes against them—must also extend to Hindus, Buddhists, Muslims, Mormons, Jews, Catholics, Protestants, Agnostics and Atheists. All who have been victimized—and we have all been victimized—will have his glorious day in court for all crimes against him. It doesn't matter what you have done, or what has been done to you.

Proposition 5 – There Will Be Perfect Punishment and Payment

"I will repay you for the years the locusts have eaten." (Joel 2:25)

We need restoration of our loss in some dynamic equivalence before there can be real forgiveness or real restored relationship, much less intimacy. I would prefer that the bad guy pay back what he took: plus interest, plus apology and plus pain. But my heart is very happy to have *anyone*, including God, fill the hole.

Two-Fold Consolation

Per the Bible, God Himself promises that we *will experience* full, two-fold consolation. *First*, there will be perfect and objective *punishment* for all of the violations against us.

Second, we will experience full *restoration* in the place of our deepest pain and greatest loss. There will be a time and a place where there will be no more tears and no more pain (Rev 7:17). What was taken from us, including self-esteem, joy, peace, fullness of life, and freedom will be restored. We *will* experience *shalom*.

Even if you do not consider yourself a Jesus-follower, these first five propositions ought still very much resonate with your DNA and begin to explain why your efforts at forgiveness have been failures.

The last two propositions are part of the infinite store of benefits *specific* to Christians-who-have-been-victimized. Non-Jesus followers, this is in no way saying that Christ-followers are any better than you—or more moral—or deserve justice any more. They have just thrown their victimhood to some degree or another upon God's shoulders. That makes a world of difference.

Does trial language bother you? Check out Revelation 6:10. Here we get a poetic colorful glimpse into the thoughts and desires of dead martyrs—post-death and post-"glorification." This image is definitely on point in our discussion. Whatever these dead-and-yet-still-alive saints think or say is by definition "godly" (i.e., objectively "right"). They are above pettiness, human vengeance, grudges, etc. I love this:

> "They called out in a loud voice, "How long, Sovereign Lord, holy and true, until you judge the inhabitants of the earth and avenge our blood?" (Rev. 6:10)

Do you hear it? Their concern is for all of the injustices done to them to be resolved. They feel the chaos of injustice and long for its settlement. There is a sense that the cosmos is out of whack until all things get restored. Justice is a good thing. Unresolved justice leaves a nagging tinnitus ringing that affects us all unaware.

Proposition 6 - The Beginning of Consolation Can Be Accessed by Faith Through the Holy Spirit Now

Christian traveler, in Heaven or in Hell there will be lots of things, but there will *not* be unresolved issues between you and God, or you and others.

In Heaven there will be no more tears. The tears will be acknowledged and proactively washed away (Rev 7:17). You and I will be made whole, for that is the nature of God's justice. So Heaven will be filled with beat-up people made whole, and Hell will be made up of beat-up people made whole.

Biblically the difference between the two camps is that the latter camp is made up of people who have elected to pay for their *own* crimes against God, creation, and humanity.

Justice requires payment for all crimes. Somebody has to pay. It is a moral universe. There can be no system of judicial balance unless there is full payment of *all* guilty verdicts.

Yet you may say, "Aren't we are all guilty?" What about the first camp, the Heaven-bound? They were absolutely as guilty as the rest, but they did something remarkable. They threw themselves on the only other legal option for whole people. They agreed to name Jesus, the historical sovereign Son of God, as their legal substitute. In an Old Testament sense, they laid their grimy, busted, guilty hands upon *His* head and transferred legal responsibility upon *Him*—by faith. All of this transaction mysteriously *took place 2000 years ago* but was experienced *in their own lifetime.*

This is the judicial basis for what we refer to as "salvation," being "reborn," etc. The idea is that legally filthy, vile, hypocritical, celestial rebels and criminals, "guilty as sin," throw themselves not on the court's *mercy* but its *justice*. The Judge requires *all* payment for *all* charges from the only volunteer who is capable: the Judge's very own Son. The prophet Isaiah gives us a prophetic image of the substitutionary payment by another.

"Surely he took up our infirmities and carried our sorrows, yet we considered him stricken by God, smitten by him, and afflicted. But he was pierced for our transgressions, he was crushed for our iniquities; the punishment that brought us peace was upon him, and by his wounds we are healed. We all, like sheep, have gone astray, each of us has turned to his own way; and the Lord has laid on him the iniquity of us all. He was oppressed and afflicted, yet he did not open his mouth; he was led like a lamb to the slaughter, and as a sheep before her shearers is silent, so he did not open his mouth." (Isa 53:4-7)

Then it is finished. By faith alone, we get it. We who are now Jesus-followers are washed from our guilt. It *was* indeed our guilt, but now we are free. We do not ever need to fear another trial. It is finished. We are free indeed.

Here is the point. These people, by faith, can actually experience that forensic legal cleansing and the renewed life and identity that necessarily flows from it. It is part of the present value of the blood of Christ.

"So...we were in slavery under the basic principles of the world. But when the time had fully come, God sent his Son, born of a woman, born under law, to redeem those under law, that we might receive the full rights of sons. Because you are sons, God sent the Spirit of his Son into our hearts, the Spirit who calls out, "Abba, Father." So you are no longer a slave, but a son; and since you are a son, God has made you also an heir." (Galatians 4:3-7)

The Victimized Made Whole Again

So—follow me—if it is reasonable to us that we can by faith experience the judicial satisfaction due our crimes today, isn't it equally reasonable that we can also by faith run to the Judge for a powerful and noticeable foretaste of the ultimate *being made whole*?

By faith, through the Holy Spirit's testimony and power in you, you can experientially begin to get foretastes of the future perfect repayment of the years that the locusts have eaten (Joel 2:25).

You can viscerally enjoy a foretaste of the stunningly, life-changing, future glorification *now*. The Apostle Paul speaks of such a present value of the blood of Christ in his letter to the Ephesians:

"I pray that out of his glorious riches he may strengthen you with power through his Spirit in your inner being . . . so that . . . you may be filled to the measure of all the fullness of God. Now to him who is able to do immeasurably more than all we ask or imagine, according to his power that is at work within us." (Eph. 3:16-21)

I do not think that this power can happen within us without our knowledge. I do not think that your experience of this accessible-by-faith power can only happen once, or a couple of times. Christian, by faith through the Holy Spirit in you, you can begin to personally experience a powerful foretaste of this two-fold trial and subsequent *shalom* today, tomorrow—the next day after that.

You can right now—by faith—access the present value of the blood of Christ to you. You *cannot* truly forgive any crime against you, no matter how small, until the debt is largely experienced for you as paid—until the pre-crime shalom is largely restored.

Remember, the crime was huge because you are a masterpiece. This is how we are made as image bearers of God. We require objective justice and consolation. Only people who experience, by faith, the present fullness of God's mysterious filling the hole left by the crime(s) against them—can truly offer forgiveness to others. *First things first.*

Proposition 7 – After You Have Experienced Consolation, Real Forgiveness is Actually Very Possible

After consolation has been experienced, Christian Plaintiff, you are then free to go to the objective Judge and ask for specific wisdom for the next steps. Too often, beat-up people want to skip the early difficult steps in forgiveness and quickly scurry to resolving the conflict. I understand— there is a strong desire to get things fixed quickly. How has that approach worked for you thus far? Remember, *first things first.*

Once consolation has miraculously happened (or begun to happen experientially), you will also necessarily begin to feel the Spirit's powerful urge toward reconciliation.[94] You will realize that this urging is far different than your previous shallow peacekeeping flailings. Now you can act, not as

---

[94] Of course there are times and situations where wisdom might strongly not encourage actual restoration of relations as part of reconciliation; particularly when it would be physically dangerous to do so. This requires wisdom and often counsel from wise friends.

a fractured victim, but as a restored free agent. Now you can boldly move toward the "other" not needing them to do anything in response.

The key concept is that now—post-consolation, you do not *need* the perpetrator to respond in anyway. Post-trial, you are free. My issue with most modern forgiveness approaches is that a large portion of the path— the part with the necessary trial on it—is missing. The part with the necessary distribution of justice is missing. The part with the necessary experience of restoration is missing. *First things first.*

Forgiveness vs. *Works* of Forgiveness

In the *Forgiveness Labyrinth*, the notion of "forgiveness" has purposely been separated from "works related to forgiveness." The immediate goal of this journey is for you to experience forgiveness for the crime committed against you. One that has occurred, the other critical questions can be addressed in a whole new light.

Imagine with me, how different the next steps would be if the massive debt in your soul has been experienced as at last *paid*, and you are aware of how valuable you truly are—*as you are*—to the Creator God. It is in this new spirit alone that you can actually truly *love* the offender, turn the other cheek, have the person arrested, etc. There are a myriad of opportunities for you once you have begun to experience real consolation for the deep hurts. The next steps require wisdom. Wisdom—the wisdom you and I need—comes from God.

God has very bad PR. In general this is true whether you believe there is a God or not. Biblically, God looks a lot different than His press clippings. God is moved, is very concerned by all the chaos in our world and His creation—the disorder and the mistreatment of His image bearers. God describes Himself to us as a Good Judge, the Weeping Judge who sees the calamity of perpetrators and those victimized.

His desire is not just punishment (that is, to punish, to vent, to wreak vengeance) but rather the healing of individuals, communities, and families; the end of crimes, wounds, and oppression. He proclaims freedom for us, and He actually has the power to pull it off. If that is not the case, we should all run away from Christianity. And if that is not the case, where else would we turn? What else have we got?

Welcome to the *Forgiveness Labyrinth*. All I ask is that you come ready for business. This is not like the other paths that you have been on. You are preparing for your day in court before the Lord of the Universe for the crime committed against you. All you need to do is to bring *one* crime that you have not been able to forgive. Just *one*. Can you do that?

Why "Labyrinth?"

The construct of "labyrinth" was chosen over other options such as "path" or "journey" for a couple of important reasons. The labyrinth in ancient lore imagines a *spiritual healing pathway* and journey. For the frantic soul, labyrinths have been places off the beaten path of life that have invited thoughtful meditation—offering time, space, gentle guidance, probing questions, provocative truth, rest and hope for weary overburdened travelers.

It is not just another path to walk, but more of a healing journey that offers a re-creation of what was taken from you including your wholeness, identity, worth and value.

Of course, it is just a participative metaphor. There is nothing intrinsically powerful in the bare paths of the labyrinth alone. It is only a tool. And yet, as you enter the labyrinth, you enter the realm of the miraculous "Other." God dwells here in power, by faith. This power is not only good, it's essential.

To forgive someone who has hurt you, you need something external to your hearts. You need an external power—something fresh—above and beyond your personal capacity. Paul says in Romans that the gospel of Christ is an actual "power" to salvation (Rom 1:16). Yet it is *more powerful than that.* Not only does the gospel have the power to regenerate lost souls, it also has the ongoing power to set your beat-up soul free!

As you walk the path of this *Forgiveness Labyrinth*, you will encounter the promises made by the Creator God Himself. As you journey to the center, you will be invited to walk with and dine with the Triune Creator God—to be embraced, to be loved, to be re-created. Then, hopefully you will return to your everyday life not only refreshed, but in some way transformed—recreated and reminded of who you are and why you are on the path in the first place.

It's important to point out that labyrinths are not mazes. Mazes require great energy and intuitive effort. In a maze, you choose your route and direction with significant risk of being lost, or even devoured by wild minotaurs.

Labyrinths, on the other hand, have only one path. They are unicursal. There are no blind alleys, no tricks and no secret passageways. *The way in is also the way out.* The singular path leads you on a single gently circuitous path to the heart of the gospel and out again to the everyday life. There is no risk of being lost, only a risk of being found.

Labyrinths are not just something to be experienced once, but something to be experienced again and again. You may indeed be one whose journey has been crushing and demeaning. You may need to come often and dwell long, eating of the truth inside the labyrinth, resting in it and submitting to the transformation of it.

For those of you have been *greatly* diminished, becoming whole again may take much perseverance. Like the woman in Jesus' parable, sometimes results require much knocking. Look at Luke 18:2-8. Jesus said,

> "In a certain town there was a judge who neither feared God nor cared about men. And there was a widow in that town who kept coming to him with the plea, 'Grant me justice against my adversary.' For some time he refused. But finally he said to himself, 'Even though I don't fear God or care about men, yet because this widow keeps bothering me, I will see that she gets justice, so that she won't eventually wear me out with her coming!' And the Lord said, 'Listen to what the unjust judge says. And will not God bring about justice for his chosen ones, who cry out to him day and night? Will he keep putting them off? I tell you, he will see that they get justice, and quickly. However, when the Son of Man comes, will he find faith on the earth?'" (Luke 18:2-8)

The idea here is that if an indifferent Judge is moved by urgency and perseverance, God, the empathetic Judge, who loves you more than anyone has ever loved you, will certainly be moved to respond. *He will see that you get justice.* Sometimes you will come to the *Forgiveness Labyrinth* the first time and the second time and even the third, with hardened cynicism, deep unbelief, debilitating fears, doubts, massive blind spots, and denial. Still, you are welcomed on this path worn down by many cynics before you. It is for you that the *Forgiveness Labyrinth* is here and remains here. Cynics are its special guests of honor.

Come as you are. Stay as long as you like. Come as often as you desire.

The Journey Ahead

Labyrinths are typically laid out on flat ground. The *Forgiveness Labyrinth* is best imagined as a path dotted with rest stations carved into a mountain. It's a meandering, circuitous path encircling and ascending a slope. It's like Moses going up Mount Sinai to meet with God and then coming back down the mountain.

Along the tranquil ascent, you will be invited to stop and linger at six stations. Instruction will be offered at each. None of the six stations are the goal of the journey, but each in its own way points to the pinnacle of the mountain—Stations 7 & 8: the trial for crimes against you. There is justice for you there; it's the kind of justice for which you've longed. You can stay there and rest. Its fruit is Sabbath.

Remember the *Forgiveness Labyrinth* is always there for the willing Traveler, whenever needed. No matter where you may be, you can just step into the first station to begin to find Shabbat—today, ten days from now, ten years from now. The author of Hebrews echoes this call.

> "There remains, then, a Sabbath-rest for the people of God; for anyone who enters God's rest also rests from his own work, just as God did from his. Let us, therefore, make every effort to enter that rest." (Heb 4:9-10).

Are you ready?

Glossary of Key Terms

Consolation- Term coined by J.R.R. Tolkien. Consolation requires that the right order of the world be restored. This would include the appropriate punishment to the evildoer, and a restoration of all who have been victimized. Consolation is required for any story to have a happy ending.

Distributive Justice- One of the four aspects of full-orbed justice referred to in this book. Distributive justice attempts to involve all participants in a dispute to define an ultimate resolution is fair and equitable to all involved.

Dyscatastrophe- Literally it is a "bad catastrophe." It is a word coined by Tolkien to describe the conflict in a tale that would inevitably lead to a tragedy apart from some change in direction or a resolution of said conflict.

Empathy- In socio-psychological circles, empathy is a fresh feeling of compassion on the part of the one victimized toward the one who hurt them. Modern counseling utilizes significant cognitive therapeutic tools to guide the victimized to reframe the criminal and crime; hopefully to begin to see the events from the perpetrator's point of view. Such empathy creates a powerful positive emotional identification with the perpetrator and ideally leads to some level of forgiveness.

Evangelium- Good news

Eucatastrophe- Literally it is a "good catastrophe." It is a word coined by Tolkien to describe an external event that breaks into a fairy tale or narrative ultimately changing the direction of the narrative from a tragedy to a happy ending. The opposite of dyscatastrophe.

Primary Crimes- Primary crimes refers to the objective answer to the question, "What happened to you?"

Procedural Justice- One of the four aspects of full-orbed justice referred to in this book. Procedural justice's emphasis is on the fairness of the methods, mechanisms, and processes used to determine outcomes as opposed to the fairness of the outcomes themselves.

Restorative Justice - One of the four aspects of full-orbed justice referred to in this book. Restorative justice attempts to find equitable and just solutions that likely include remorse, repentance, a plan of restitution from the offender (where appropriate), and forgiveness from the Plaintiff. The Plaintiff, offender and the affected community are all active in discussions regarding what "justice" is to entail.

Retributive Justice- One of the four aspects of full-orbed justice referred to in this book. Retributive justice focuses upon determining what punishment would be the best response for any give crime.

Sanctification- Per the Westminster Shorter Catechism of Faith, sanctification is the work of God's free grace, whereby we are renewed in the whole man, after the image of God, and are enabled more and more to die unto sin, and live unto righteousness. In Cupology terms, it is the process of having our emptied cups filled time and again with the fullness of God (Eph 3:19-21).

Secondary Crimes- Where Primary crimes refer to the objective answer to the question, "What happened to you?," Secondary crimes relate to the subsequent consequences of said primary crime. "What did the crime *take* from you?" "What effect did the primary crime have on your identity, emotions, relationships, sense of value, and worldview?"

BIBLIOGRAPHY

Abu-Nimer, M. "Conflict Resolution Between Arabs and Jews in Israel: A Study of Six Intervention Models." PhD Diss., George Mason University, VA., 1993.

Aquino, K., T. Tripp, & R. Bies. "Getting Even of Moving On? Power, Procedural Justice, and Types of Offense as Predictors of Revenge, Forgiveness, Reconciliation, and Avoidance in Organizations." *Journal of Applied Psychology* 91(3) (2008): 653-668.

Alcorn, R. *If God is Good: Faith in the Midst of Suffering and Evil.* Colorado Springs: Multnomah Books, 2009.

Amstutz, M. *The Healing of Nations: The Promise and Limits of Political Forgiveness.* Lanham, Md.: Rowman & Littlefield, 2005.

Anderson, G. *Sin: A History.* New Haven: Yale University Press, 2009.

Bass, E., & L. Davis. *The Courage to Heal* (3rd ed.). New York: Harper and Row, 1994.

Belicki, K. J. Rourke, & M. McCarthy. "Potential Dangers of Empathy and Related Conundrums." In *Women's Reflections on the Complexities of Forgiveness,* edited by W. Malcolm, N. DeCourville & K. Belicki. 165-185. New York: Routledge/Taylor & Francis Group, 2008.

Ben Avraham, Y. *The Gates of Repentance.* New York: Feldheim. 1967.

Bettelheim, B. *The Uses of Enchantment: The Meaning and Importance of Fairy Tales.* New York: Vintage Books, 1977.

Blader, S., & T. Tyler. "A Four-component Model of Procedural Justice: Defining the Meaning of a 'Fair' Process," *Personality and Social Psychology Bulletin (2003): 29*(6), 747-758.

Bloch, A. P. *The Biblical and Historical Background of Jewish Customs and Ceremonies.* New York: KTAV Publishing House, 1980..

Boller, P. F. Jr. *Hollywood Anecdotes.* New York Ballentine Books, 1987.

Bono, G. *"Commonplace Forgiveness Among and Between Groups and the Cross-Cultural Perception of Transgressors and Transgressions."* PhD diss., Claremont Graduate University, 2003.

Borain, A. *A Country Unmasked: Inside South Africa's Trut and Reconciliation Commission.* Cape Town: Oxford University Press, 2000.

Christie, K. *The South African Truth Commission.* New York: St. Martin's Press, 2000.

Cobban, H. *Amnesty After Atrocity.* Boulder Co.: Paradigm, 2007.

Cohn-Sherbok, D. *The Vision of Judaism: Wrestling with God.* St Paul: Paragon House, 2004.

Cose, Ellis. *Bone to Pick: Of Forgiveness, Reconciliation, Reparation and Revenge.* New York: Atria Books. 2004.

Coyle, C., and R. Enright. "Forgiveness Intervention with Post-abortion Men." *Journal of Consulting and Clinical Psychology (1997): 65*(6) 1042-1046.

Darby, B., and B. Schlenker, "Children's Reactions to Apologies." *Journal of Personality and Social Psychology (1982 October): 43*(4), 742-753.

Davenport, D. "The Functions of Anger and Forgiveness: Guidelines for Psychotherapy with Victims." *Psychotherapy: Theory, Research, Practice, Training (1991 March):* 28(1), 140-144.

Davis, D.E., J. N. Hook, E. Worthington, D.R. Van Tongeren, A.L. Gartner, D. Jennings, & L. Norton. "Relational Spirituality and Dealing With Transgressions: Development of the Relational Engagement of the Sacred for a Transgression (REST) Scale." *International Journal for the Psychology of Religion* (2010); 20(4), 288-302.

DiBlasio, D. "Decision-based Forgiveness Treatment in Cases of Marital Infidelity. *Psychotherapy: Theory, Research, Practice, Training (2000): 37*(2), 149-158.

Dorff, E. "Individual and Communal Forgiveness," in *Autonomy and Judaism: The Individual and the Community in Jewish Philosophical Thought,* edited by D. Frank, 193-218. New York: State University of New York Press, 1992.

Dorff, E. "Elements of Forgiveness: A Jewish Approach," in *Dimensions of Forgiveness,* edited by E Worthington, 29-58. Philadelphia, Pa: Templeton Foundation Press, 1998.

Dorff, E. N. *Love Your Neighbor and Yourself: a Jewish Approach to Modern Personal Ethics.* Philadelphia: The Jewish Publication Society, 2003.

Dorff, E. N., and A. Rosett. *A Living Tree: the Roots and Growth of Jewish Law.* Albany: State University of New York Press. 1988.

Bibliography

Engel, B. *The Right to Innocence: Healing the Trauma of Childhood Sexual Abuse*. Los Angeles: Jeremy P. Tarcher, 1989.

Enright, R., and C. Coyle. "Researching the Process Model of Forgiveness Within Psychological Interventions," in *Dimensions of Forgiveness*, edited by In E. Worthington, 139-152. Philadelphia, Pa: Templeton Foundation Press, 1998.

Enright, R., S. Freedman, and J. Rique. J. "The Psychology of Interpersonal Forgiveness," in *Exploring forgiveness*, edited by R. D. Enright and J. North, 46-63. Madison: University of Wisconsin Press, 1998.

Enright R. and J. North. *Exploring Forgiveness*. Madison: University of Wisconsin Press, 2003.

Enright, R. *Forgiveness is a Choice: A Step by Step Process for Resolving Anger and Restoring Hope*. Washington: American Psychological Association, 2001.

Exline, J. "Beliefs about God and Forgiveness in a Baptist Church Sample." *Journal of Psychology and Christianity, 27*(2) (2008): 131-139.

Exline, J., B. Bushman, R. Baumeister, K. Campbell, and E. Finkel. "Too Proud to Let Go: Narcissistic Entitlement as a Barrier to Forgiveness," *Journal of Personality and Social Psychology. 87*(6) (2004): 894-912.

Exline, J., E. Worthington, P. Hill, and M. McCullough. "Forgiveness and Justice: A Research Agenda for Social and Personality Psychology," *Personality and Social Psychology Review, 7*(4) (2003): 337-348.

Fagenson, E. & J. Cooper. "When Push Comes to Power: A Test of Power Restoration's Theory's Explanation for Aggressive Conflict Escalation." *Basic and Applied Social Psychology*, 8(4)(2008): 274-293.

Falk, Z. W. *Hebrew Law in Biblical Times: An Introduction* (2nd ed.). Provo, Utah: Brigham Young University Press, 2001.

Fincham, F. "Forgiveness: Integral to Close Relationships and Inimical to Justice?" *Virginia Journal of Social Policy & the Law. 16*(2), (2009): 357-384.

Fitzgerald, H. *The Mourning Handbook*. New York: Fireside. 1994.

Flanigan, B. *Forgiving the Unforgivable*. New York: MacMillan, 1992.

Folger, F., and J. Greenberg. "Procedural Justice: An Interpretive Analysis of Personnel Systems." In *Research in Personnel and Human Resources Management*, 3, (1985): 141-183.

Freedman, S., & Enright, R. "Forgiveness as an Intervention Goal With Incest Survivors." *Journal of Consulting and Clinical Psychology*, 64(5) (1996): 983-992.

Frost, B. *The Politics of Peace*. London: Darton, Longman and Todd, 1991.

Gordon, K., D. Baucom, and D. Snyder. "The Use of Forgiveness in Marital Therapy," in *Forgiveness: Theory, Research and Practice*. edited by McCullough, M., K. Pergament, and C. E. Thoresen, 203-227. New York: Guilford, 2000.

Gorsuch, R., and J. Hao. "Forgiveness: An Exploratory Factor Analysis and its Relationships to Religious Variables," *Review of Religious Research*, *34*(4), (1993, June): 333-347.

Haber, J. *Forgiveness*. Savage, MD: Rowman & Littlefield, 1991.

Hamilton, V. "*'ârar'* in Theological Wordbook of the Old Testament, ed. Harris, R., G. Archer, and B. Waltke. (Chicago: Moody Press, 2003).

Hammer, R. *Entering the High Holy Days: A Guide to the Origins, Themes, and Prayers*. Philadelphia: The Jewish Publication Society, 1998.

Hargrave, T. *Families and Forgiveness: Healing Wounds in the Intergenerational Family*. New York: Brunner/Mazel. 1994.

Hargrave, T.D., and J. Sells. "The Development of a Forgiveness Scale." *Journal of Marital and Family Therapy*. 23 (1997): 41-63.

Harris, R., A. Laird, & B. Waltke. *Theological Wordbook of the Old Testament*. Chicago: Moody. 1990.

Harris, S. *Letter to a Christian Nation*. New York: Borzoi Books. 2006.

Hartley, J. *The Book of Job*. Grand Rapids: Eerdmans Publishing, 1988.

Henderson, M. *Forgiveness: Breaking the Chain of Hate*. Wilsonville, Book Partners, 1999.

Hiebert, F. F. "The Atonement in Anabaptist Theology," *Direction*, Vol 30 No. 2 (Fall 2001): 122-138.

Hill, P., J. Exline, and A. Cohen. "The Social Psychology of Justice and Forgiveness in Civil and Organizational Settings." In *Handbook of Forgiveness*, edited by E. Worthington, Jr., 477-490. New York: Routledge, 2005.

Bibliography

Hodin, J. P. *Edvard Munch*. Thames and Hudson, 1972.

Hoffman, L. A. *The Canonization of the Synagogue Service*. Notre Dame, Ind.: University of Notre Dame Press, 1979.

Howieson, J. "Perceptions of Procedural Justice and Legitimacy in Local Court Mediation." *Murdoch University Electronic Journal of Law. 9*(2) (2002).

Irani, G., and N. Funk. "Rituals of Reconciliation: Arab-Islamic Perspectives." Paper presented at the Kroc Institute Occasional Paper #19:OP:2, August 2000).

Jones, L. *Embodying Forgiveness: A Theological Analysis*. Grand Rapids: Eerdmans Publishing, 1995.

Kafka, F. *The Trial*. New York: Schocken Books, 1998.

Karen, R. *The Forgiving Self: The Road From Resentment to Connection*. New York: Anchor Books, 2003.

Keil, C. and F. Delitzsch, Commentary on the Old Testament in Ten Volumes. Grand Rapids: William B Eerdmans, 1978.

Koehler, L. and W. Baumgartner. *The Hebrew and Aramaic Lexicon of the Old Testament (HALOT)*. New York: E.J. Brill, 1996.

Kraybill, D., S. Nolt, and D. Weaver-Zercher. *Amish Grace: How Forgiveness Transcends Tragedy*. San Francisco: Jossey Bass, 2007.

Kselman, J. "Forgiveness (OT)." in *Anchor Bible Dictionary*. (II 831-833). New York: Doubleday, 1992.

Kushner, H. When Bad Things Happen to Good People. New York: Avon, 1983.

Lauritzen, P. "Forgiveness: Moral Imperative of Religious Duty?" *Journal of Religious Ethics*, 15 (1987): 141-150.

Legaree, T., J. Turner, and S. Lollis. (2007). "Forgiveness and Therapy: A Critical Review of Conceptualizations, Practices and Values Found in the Literature." *Journal of Marital and Family Therapy, 33*(2) (2007):192-213.

Levine, B. *Leviticus: the Traditional Hebrew Text with the New JPS Translation*. Jewish Publication Society, 1989.

Lewis, C. S. *The Lion, the Witch and the Wardrobe*. Harper Trophy, 1994.

Lovelace, R. *Dynamics of Spiritual Life: An Evangelical Theology of Renewal.* Downers Grove: InterVarsity Press. 1979.

Luskin, Fred. *Forgive for Good: A Proven Prescription for Health and Happiness*, San Francisco, HarperSanFrancisco. 2002.

Malcolm, W. and L. Greenberg. "Forgiveness as a Process of Change in Individual Psychotherapy," in *Forgiveness: Theory, Research and Practice,* edited by McCullough, M., K. Pergament, and C. E. Thoresen, 179-202. New York: Guilford, 2000.

McCullough, M. E., G. Bono, G., and L. Root. "Religion and Forgiveness," in *Handbook of the Psychology of Religion and Spirituality*, 394-411. New York: Guilford, 2005.

McCullough, M., L. Root, and A. Cohen. "Writing about the Benefits of an Interpersonal Transgression Facilitates Forgiveness." *Journal of Consulting and Clinical Psychology, 74*(5) (2006): 887-897.

McCullough, M., F. Fincham, and J. Tsang. "Forgiveness, Forbearance, and Time: The Temporal Unfolding of Transgression-Related Interpersonal Motivations." *Journal of Personality and Social Psychology, 84 (*2003*):* 540-557.

McCullough, M., K. I. Pergament, and C.E. Thoresen. *Forgiveness: Theory, Research and Practice.* New York: Guilford, 2000.

McCullough, M., K. I. Pergament, and C. E. Thoresen. "The Psychology of Forgiveness," in *Forgiveness: Theory, Research and Practice,* edited by McCullough, M., K. Pergament, and C. E. Thoresen, 1-14. New York: Guilford, 2000.

McCullough, M., W. Hoyt, and C. Rachal. "What We Know (and Need to Know) About Assessing Forgiveness Constructs," in *Forgiveness: Theory, Research and Practice,* edited by McCullough, M., K. Pergament, and C. E. Thoresen, 65-88. New York: Guilford, 2000.

McCullough, M., C. Rachal, S. Sandage, E. Worthington, S. Brown, and T. Hight. (1998). "Interpersonal Forgiving in Close Relationships: II. Theoretical Elaboration and Measurement." *Journal of Personality and Social Psychology, 75*(6) (1998): 1586-1602.

McCullough, M. and E. Worthington. "Religion and the Forgiving Personality," *Journal of Personality and Social Psychology, 67* (1999): 1141-1164.

McCullough, M., E. Worthington, and K. Rachal. "Interpersonal Forgiving in Close Relationships," *Journal of Personality and Social Psychology, 73*(2) (1997): 321-336.

McCullough, M., & E. Worthington, E. (1994). "Encouraging Clients to Forgive People in Close Relationships." *Journal of Psychology and Theology, 22,* 3-20 (1994).

Milgrom, J. *Leviticus.* Minneapolis: Fortress Press, 2004.

Miller, D. "Disrespect and the Experience of Injustice." *Annual Review of Psychology, 52,* (2001): 527-553.

Minow, M. (1998). *Between Vengeance andForgiveness: Facing History After Genocide and Mass Violence.* Boston: Beacon Press. 1998.

Muller-Fahrenholz, G. *The Art of Forgiveness: Theological Reflections on Healing and Reconciliation.* Geneva: World Council of Churches. 1997.

Mullet, E., and F. Azar. "Apologies, Repentance, and Forgiveness: A Muslim-Christian Comparison." *International Journal for the Psychology of Religion, 19,* (2009): 275-285.

Mullet, E. and M. Girard. "Developmental and Cognitive Points of View on Forgiveness," in *Forgiveness: Theory, Research and Practice,* edited by McCullough, M., K. Pergament, and C. E. Thoresen, 111-132. New York: Guilford, 2000.

Murphy, J. "Forgiveness in Counseling: A Philosophical Perspective," in *Before Forgiving: Cautionary Views of Forgiveness in Psychotherapy,* edited by S. Lamb and J. Murphy 41-53. New York: Oxford University Press, 2002.

Newberg, A., E. d'Aquili, S. Newberg, and deMarici. "The Neuropsychological Correlates of Forgiveness," in *Forgiveness: Theory, Research and Practice,* edited by McCullough, M., K. Pergament, and C. E. Thoresen, 91-110. New York: Guilford, 2000.

Newton, J. *The Works of The Rev. John Newton. 2*(III). New Haven, CT: Nathan Whiting, 1826.

Nussbaum, C. *The Essence of Teshuvah: a Path to Repentance.* Northvale, N.J.: Jason Aronson Inc, 1993.

O'Malley, M., and J. Greenberg. "Sex Differences in Restoring Justice: The Down Payment Effect." *Journal of Research in Personality, 17*(2), (1983, June): 174-185.

Oyserman, D. "The Lens of Personhood: Viewing the Self and Others in a Multicultural Society." *Journal of Personality and Social Psychology, 65*(5), (1993): 993-1009.

219

Ozick, C. "Notes Toward a Meditation on 'Forgiveness'." in *The Sunflower: On the Possibilities and Limits of Forgiveness*. edited by S. Wiesenthal 213-220. New York: Schocken Books, 1997.

Rawls, J. *A Theory of Justice*. Cambridge: Harvard University Press, 1971.

Reed, G., and R. Enright. "The Effects of Forgiveness Therapy On Depression, Anxiety, and Posttraumatic Stress for Women after Spousal Emotional Abuse." *Journal of Consulting and Clinical Psychology*, *74*(5), (2006, October): 920-929.

Risen, J., and T. Gilovich. "Target and Observer Differences in the Acceptance of Questionable Apologies." *Journal of Personality and Social Psychology*, *92*(3), (2007, March): 418-433.

Rokeach, M., *The Nature of Human Values*. New York: Free Press, 1973.

Rosenak, C. M., and G. M. Harnden, G. M. "Forgiveness in the Psychotherapeutic Process: Clinical Applications." *Journal of Psychology and Christianity*, *11*, (1992): 188-197.

Rusbult, C., P. Hannon, S. Stocker, and E. Finkel. "Forgiveness and Relational Repair." In *Handbook of Forgiveness*, edited by E. Worthington, Jr., 185-205. New York: Routledge, 2005.

Rye, M. S., K. I. Pergament, M. Ali, G. L. Beck, E. N. Dorff, C. Hallisey, V. Narayanan, and J. G. Williams. "Religious Perspectives on Forgiveness." In *Forgiveness: Theory, Research and Practice*, edited by McCullough, M., K. Pergament, and C. E. Thoresen, 17-40. New York: Guilford, 2000.

Schierse, L. *The Wounded Woman: Healing the Father–Daughter Relationship*. Boston:Shambhala Publications, 1982.

Schimmel, S. *Wounds not Healed by Time*. New York: Oxford University Press, 2002.

Secunda, V. *Women and Their Fathers: The Sexual and Romantic Impact of the First Man in Your Life*. New York: Dell, 1992.

Senyard, W.H. & C. Pepper, *The Kiss of God*, Charleston, S.C.: Createspace. 2011.

Shakespeare, William. *The Tragedy of Hamlet* trans., Louis B. Wright. New York: Washington Square Press. 1964.

Shriver, Jr., D. *An Ethic for Enemies: Forgiveness in Politics*. New York: Oxford University Press. 1995.

Shults, F. L. & S.J. Sandage, *The Faces of Forgiveness: Searching for Wholeness and Salvation*. Grand Rapids: Baker Academic, 2003.

Smedes, L. "Stations on the Journey From Forgiveness to Hope." In *Dimensions of Forgiveness*, edited by E. Worthington, 341-354. Philadelphia, Pa: Templeton Foundation Press, 1998.

Snaith, N. H. *The Jewish New Year Festival: Its Origins and Development*. London: Society for Promoting Christian Knowledge, 1947.

Spiegel, M. "Forgiveness and the Jewish High Holy Days." *Journal of Religion & Abuse*, 4(4), (2003, November): 25-27.

Sutherland, R. *Putting God on Trial: The Biblical Book of Job*. Trafford Publishing. 2003.

Tada, J. E. *Pearls of Great Price: 366 Daily Devotional Readings*. Grand Rapids, Mi: Zondervan. 2006.

Tan, A. *The Joy Luck Club*. New York: Ivy Books. 1989.

Tavuchis, N. *Mea Culpa: A Sociology of Apology and Reconciliation*. Stanford, Ca.: Stanford University Press, 1991.

Telushkin, J. *A Code of Jewish Ethics- Vol. 1, You Shall Be Holy*. New York: Bell Tower, 2006.

Thorensen, C., A. Harris, and F. Luskin. "Forgiveness and Health: An Unanswered Question," in *Forgiveness: Theory, Research and Practice,* edited by McCullough, M., K. Pergament, and C. E. Thoresen, 254-280. New York: Guilford, 2000.

Thorensen, C., F. Luskin, and A. Harris. "Science and Forgiveness Interventions: Reflections and Recommendations." In *Dimensions of Forgiveness*, edited by E Worthington, 163-190. Philadelphia, Pa: Templeton Foundation Press, 1998.

Tolkien, J. R. R., *Tree and Leaf, Smith of Wooten Major, the Homecoming of Beorhthoth*. London: George Allen & Unwin Publishers, 1979.

Volf, M. "Forgiveness, Reconciliation & Justice: A Christian Contribution to a More Peaceful Social Environment." In *Forgiveness and Reconciliation: Religion, Public Policy, & Conflict Transformation*, edited by R. Helmick and R. Petersen. Philadelphia: Templeton Foundation Press, 2001.

Volf, M. *Exclusion and Embrace*. Nashville, Tn.: Abingdon Press, 1996.

Wade, N., D. Bailey, and P. Shaffer, P. "Helping Clients Heal: Does Forgiveness Make a Difference?" *Professional Psychology: Research and Practice, 36*(6) (2005, December): 634-641.

Wade, N., and E. Worthington. "In Search of a Common Core: A Content Analysis of Interventions to Promote Forgiveness." *Psychotherapy: Theory, Research, Practice, Training, 42*(2) (2005 June): 160-177.

Wade, N., E. Worthington, and J. Meyer, J. "But Do They Work? A Meta-Analysis of Group Interventions to Promote Forgiveness." In *Handbook of Forgiveness*, edited by E. Worthington, Jr., 423-439. New York: Routledge, 2005.

Walker, D. F., and R.L. Gorsuch. "Dimensions Underlying Sixteen Models of Forgiveness and Reconciliation." *Journal of Psychology and Theology, 32*(1) (2004): 12-25.

Walker, L., A. Lind, and J. Thibaut. The Relation Between Procedural and Distributive Justice. *Virginia Law Review, 65*(8) (1979): 1401-1420.

Warren, R. "Public Trust and Procedural Justice." *Court Review*. (2000): 12-16.

Wiesenthal, S. *The Sunflower: On the Possibilities and Limits of Forgiveness*. New York: Schocken Books, 1997.

Witvliet, C., S. R. Hinze, and E. Worthington.(2008). "Unresolved Injustice: Christian Religious Commitment, Forgiveness, Revenge, and Cardiovascular Responding." *Journal of Psychology and Christianity, 27*(2) (2008): 110-119.

Wohl, M., D. Kuiken, and K. Noels. "Three ways to forgive: A numerically aided phenomenological study." *British Journal of Social Psychology, 45*(3), (2006, September): 547-561.

Worthington, E. Jr. *A Just Forgiveness: Responsible Healing Without Excusing Injustice.* Downers Grove, Il: InterVarsity Press, 2009.

Worthigton, E. Jr. *Five Steps to Forgiveness: The Art and Science of Forgiving*, New York: Crown Publishers, 2001.

Worthington, E., Jr. "An Empathy-Humility-Commitment Model of Forgiveness Applied Within Family Dyads." *Journal of Family Therapy, 20*, (1998, February): 59-76.

Worthington, E. Jr. *Forgiveness and Reconciliation: Theory and Application*. New York: Routledge, 2006.

Worthington, E., *Forgiving and Reconciling: Bridges to Wholeness and Hope*. Downers Grove, Il: InterVarsity Press, 2003.

Worthington, E. Jr., S. Sandage, and J. Berry. "Group Interventions to Promote Forgiveness: What Researchers and Clinicians Ought to Know." In *Forgiveness: Theory, Research and Practice*, edited by M. McCullough, K. I. Pergament and C. E. Thoresen, 228-253. New York: Guilford, 2000.

Worthington, E. Jr. *Dimensions of Forgiveness*. Philadelphia, Pa.: Templeton Foundation Press, 1998.

Worthington, E. Jr. *Handbook of Forgiveness*. New York: Routledge, 2005.

Worthington, E. Jr., and F. DiBlasio. "Promoting Mutual Forgiveness Within the Fractured Relationship." *Psychotherapy: Theory, Research, Practice, Training, 27*(2) (1990): 219-223.

Yandell, K. "The Metaphysics and Morality of Forgiveness." *Exploring forgiveness*. edited by R. Enright and J. North, 35-45. Madison: University of Wisconsin Press, 2003.

Zechmeister, J. S., and C. Romero. "Victim and Offender Accounts of Interpersonal Conflict: Autobiographical Narratives of Forgiveness and Unforgiveness." *Journal of Personality and Social Psychology, 82*(4), (2002): 675-686.

Zehr, Howard. *Changing Lenses: A New Focus for Crime and Justice*. Scottsdale:Herald Press, 1995.

Made in the USA
Lexington, KY
19 February 2016